Pivotal Tuesdays

Pivotal Tuesdays

* ✳ *

Four Elections That Shaped the Twentieth Century

Margaret O'Mara

PENN

UNIVERSITY OF PENNSYLVANIA PRESS

PHILADELPHIA

Published by
University of Pennsylvania Press
Philadelphia, Pennsylvania 19104-4112
www.upenn.edu/pennpress

Printed in the United States of America
on acid-free paper

1 3 5 7 9 10 8 6 4 2

Library of Congress Cataloging-in-Publication Data

O'Mara, Margaret Pugh, author.
  Pivotal Tuesdays : four elections that shaped the
twentieth century / Margaret O'Mara.
    pages   cm
  Includes bibliographical references and index
  ISBN 978-0-8122-4746-6 (alk. paper)
    1. Presidents—United States—Election—History—
20th century. 2. Political campaigns—United States—
History—20th century. 3. United States—Politics and
government—20th century. I. O'Mara, Margaret Pugh.
II. Title
JK528.O43   2015   2015009532

For Molly and Abigail, future voters

CONTENTS

✳

PART IV: 1992

AUTHOR'S NOTE

*

A presidential election changed my life. On 9 July 1992, I stood on the lawn of the Arkansas Governor's Mansion on a stickily hot Southern summer day. Along with the crowd packed tightly around me, I was waiting to see Bill Clinton emerge from inside with his newly announced running mate, Tennessee Senator Al Gore.

I'd graduated from college earlier that summer without having secured a job, and so returned reluctantly to my hometown of Little Rock to live at home, save some money, and wait until rosier opportunities emerged in seemingly more glamorous and distant cities. Yet within a week of arriving, I had discovered that something very exciting was happening in my sleepy little town: our governor was about to become the Democratic presidential nominee, and his campaign headquarters was a mere mile from my house. I knew Bill Clinton—*everyone* in this small Southern state knew Bill Clinton—but working for his campaign had never really occurred to me.

Until 9 July. Three days before that, I had rather timidly trekked downtown to Clinton campaign headquarters and offered my services as a part-time volunteer. Immediately, I found myself in the center of a whirl of activity and excitement. Young people from Washington, New York, and Chicago scurried around the building, working from early in the day to late at night. My first day in this hive of activity was spent standing at a copy machine, churning through contribution slips from small donors, watching the currents of campaign energy stream around me. I came back for a second day, and a third. This was turning out to be rather exciting. Then the announcement of the vice presidential nominee prompted all of us, even the lowliest of copy room volunteers, to make the trip to the Governor's Mansion to see Gore introduced in person.

Standing on the lawn, the July sun beating down on my head, we watched the Clintons and Gores and their children wave to the crowd and the television cameras crowd all around us. My post-graduation funk started to evaporate. This is a cause worth joining, I thought. This is thrilling, and bigger, and important. When offered an official campaign job the next day—moving up from the copy room to the mailroom—I didn't hesitate.

Twenty years later, after five years as a staff person in the White House and elsewhere in the executive branch, five in graduate school, and ten as a teacher and writer of American history, I was asked to give a series of public talks about presidential elections, 1992 included. In putting together these lectures, I discovered things I had forgotten about the history I had lived through, and realized how elections through modern history connect to and feed back on one another.

My time on the campaign trail and in Washington had spurred me to become a scholar of American politics and policy. With this project, things have come full circle.

As I witnessed the scene on the lawn of the Governor's Mansion that July day, I had little understanding of the broader forces that propelled its possibility and its ultimate trajectory. This was a political moment made possible by cultural and political changes that had been decades in the making: economic and geographic realignments, the rise of a new generation of Democratic centrists and Reagan Revolutionaries, the restructuring of the media and the rise of cable television, the ascendance of professional political consultants. It built on the experiences and triumphs and failures of the 50 elections that had come before it. It was a reflection of history, and history in the making. There are many of these moments, in every campaign. They are pivotal to the election at hand, yet possible because of broader historical shifts.

The purpose of this book is to make these connections.

*

Introduction

The process of election affords a moral certainty, that the
office of President will never fall to the lot of any man who
is not in an eminent degree endowed with the requisite
qualifications. Talents for low intrigue, and the little arts of
popularity, may alone suffice to elevate a man to the first
honors in a single State; but it will require other talents, and
a different kind of merit, to establish him in the esteem and
confidence of the whole Union.

—Alexander Hamilton, *Federalist No. 68*, 1788

The newspapers were merciless. One candidate for president was a "libertine"
with a "lust for power." He and his followers were "discontented hotheads"
who had "long endeavored to destroy the Federal Constitution." If he was
elected, warned one political adversary, "murder, robbery, rape, adultery
and incest will all be openly taught and practiced, the air will be rent with
the cries of distress, the soil will be soaked with blood."[1] Similarly sharp
language zinged back toward his opponent, the embattled incumbent. The
sitting president was a man of "limited talents" who was not a defender of
democracy, but the head of a "monarchic, aristocratic, tory faction" that
only cared about the rich and powerful elite.[2]

As the election got tighter, the allegations became more personal.
Drawing-room whispers about the challenger's affairs with his female slaves
became printed denunciations of his "Congo Harem." His earlier expressions of religious tolerance stoked allegations that he was a "howling athe-
ist" who would confiscate the Bibles of God-fearing people. Perhaps the
lowest blows of the campaign fell on the incumbent, whom one scribe

accused of having a "hideous hermaphroditical character, which has neither the force and firmness of a man, nor the gentleness and sensibility of a woman."[3]

Although modern conventional wisdom has it that American presidential elections are nastier and more polarizing than ever, few recent elections can compare with the down-and-dirty partisan warfare on display in the election of 1800. The targets of all this mudslinging: Federalist president John Adams and his Democratic-Republican challenger Thomas Jefferson, two now-beloved architects of the American Revolution.

Once great friends, the men had become bitter political enemies with profoundly different views about how the young nation might reach its destiny. On the one hand, Adams and his Federalist allies believed that the future of the young nation was in its cities and in commerce, and it needed a strong central government to do things like acquire new territories and regulate foreign trade. On the other, Jefferson and the Democratic-Republicans believed that the heart and soul of the United States was in the agricultural countryside, and that all should be done to protect the independent interests of the yeoman farmer. Geography divided them as well. The Federalists had strongholds in the towns and cities of the North; the Democratic-Republicans drew support from the slave-owning South and the hardscrabble Western frontier.

The stakes in 1800 seemed extraordinarily high. In the first years of the new republic, the two-party system as we know it today did not exist, and there was a reason for that absence. Many of the Founding Fathers believed partisan elections did more harm than good. "The common and continual mischiefs of the spirit of party," George Washington had remarked as he left office in 1796, "are sufficient to make it the interest and duty of a wise people to discourage and restrain it."[4] The election of 1800 was only the nation's second partisan election, and the first that resulted in a turnover of the presidency from one party to another. The toxic campaigning and divided polity resulted in a deadlocked election that had to be decided by the House of Representatives barely two weeks before Inauguration Day. Jefferson won, and called his victory over the incumbent "the Revolution of 1800."[5] While subsequent observers have argued over the degree to which the moment truly was a "revolution," the election precipitated the passage of the 12th Amendment to the Constitution, which took the responsibility of breaking a deadlock away from the politics of the House and established a separate, ostensibly nonpartisan Electoral College.

In the two centuries since, many presidential election contests have provided ample evidence that partisan politicking can bring out the worst in human nature. Personal attacks, apocalyptic pronouncements, and intricate political machinations have been hallmarks of nearly every competitive presidential race. The growth of modern media has further amplified the less appealing qualities of the American electoral process. By the time it was completed, the 2012 presidential contest between Barack Obama and Mitt Romney had lasted more than two years, involved campaign expenditures of close to $2 billion, unleashed thousands of television hours of vitriolic campaign advertising and political punditry, and lit up the Internet with heated commentary and name-calling.

Yet the Obama-Romney race also demonstrated that—just as in 1800—the American democratic system could withstand the blows of partisan warfare. In referring to the election that made him president as "the revolution of 1800," Jefferson believed that the basic freedoms for which the American Revolution had been fought were imperiled by the rise of the Federalist Party and its leaders like Adams and Alexander Hamilton, who had advocated for a stronger central government, trading relationships with Great Britain, and more limited democracy. Jefferson saw his election as bringing about a restoration of the founding principles of limited government and individual liberties. Power moved from one party to another without a drop of blood being shed. It was, in his mind, the true culmination of the revolution of 1776.

Historians have since argued over the degree to which 1800 was as significant a turning point as Jefferson liked to portray it, and debates continue to rage over whether his small-government vision was, in fact, truly the Founders' intent. What is indisputable, however, is that a fiercely contested election did not shatter the fragile new republic, as some observers worried. Candidates fought, political operatives schemed, but the system survived and thrived.[6]

More than that, elections from the age of George Washington to the age of Barack Obama have showed the power of presidential contests to provoke and inspire mass engagement of ordinary citizens in the political system. Elections are expressions of national identity, and mirrors of individual desires and priorities. No matter how frustrated or disinterested voters might be about politics and government, every four years the attention of the nation—and the world—focuses on the candidates, the contest, and the issues. As elections have become tighter, and the money spent on them greater, attention and enthusiasm about them has increased rather than decreased. George Washington may not have approved, but the partisan election process has been a way for a messy, jumbled, raucous nation to come together as a slightly-more-perfect union. As they cast their ballots, ordinary people make history.

This book looks back at four presidential races of the past hundred years to show how this history was made. It begins with the rowdy four-way contest in 1912 between Teddy Roosevelt, William Howard Taft, Eugene Debs, and Woodrow Wilson that resulted in Wilson's victory. It continues with Franklin Roosevelt's New Deal campaign and his win over Herbert Hoover in 1932. The third case profiles the eventful and tragic campaign of 1968 and the election of Richard Nixon, and the final story follows the three-way race that led to Bill Clinton's victory in 1992.

Why these four elections? Why not 1948, when Harry S Truman beat Thomas Dewey in perhaps the greatest election upset in American history? Or 1980, when Ronald Reagan's election ushered in a new age of conservative resurgence? Part of the reason is personal: having worked on the 1992 Clinton campaign, I could bring an eyewitness perspective to an election, and an era, that historians are now beginning to explore. Yet there are larger reasons as well. I wanted to use elections as a way to explore bigger changes in American society, from industrialization and urbanization, to the crisis of the Great Depression and response of the New Deal, to the rise of the Sunbelt and the advent of the high-tech economy. These four elections thus help tell us about more than who got elected and why; they illuminate the trajectory of the nation's experience through what publisher Henry Luce proclaimed "The American Century."[7]

While I was writing this book, it became clear that everyone has an opinion about the most important presidential elections in history; indeed, debating the merits of one's list is part of the fun of being a political junkie. But there is more to it than personal preference. Many a former political science major will be familiar with the theory of "realigning" elections, which argues that certain years have been watersheds in terms of both partisan affiliations and policy innovations. Historians, too, once embraced the idea that political history was cyclical, and that the nation's mood swung back and forth from left to right in successive eras.[8] As the criticisms of these theories have showed, however, abstract formulations can ignore the contingencies, the messiness, and the unpredictability of history. Relying heavily on data about voter turnout and preferences, such approaches tend to isolate the process of politicking and voting as something separate from the broader tapestry of economic, social, and cultural change. This obscures the intricate and fascinating interrelationship between formal politics and lived experience, between governments and markets, between the rhetoric of the leaders and the actions of the voters.[9]

The four electoral contests profiled here reveal these rich connections, and underscore the important dynamics of political change that occur in nearly every presidential election cycle. Each of them opens a revealing window not just into their moment in history but into particular aspects of the American political process: its interdependence with economic and social realignment, its distinctive partisan organization, its changing modes of mass communication, and its periodic disruption by particular interests, factions, and third parties.

To be sure, there are many other elections of the past century that served as both hinges of history and windows into a wider landscape of social change. The story of the era's "pivotal Tuesdays" could cover twenty-five elections just as easily as only four. My point here is not to pick favorites. In fact, I deliberately avoided profiling some of the most familiar races and personalities, for to focus on them alone can keep us in the conventional wisdom comfort zone.

Alone, each of these four races is a terrific story. But by putting them together in one book, we can also see the connective tissue between them and better understand the patterns and continuities of history, as well as the remarkable disruptions and pivot points. They reveal the messiness of the past, the foibles of our leaders, and the fractious, frustrating, two-steps-forward, one-step-back nature of politics and policy. Taken together, the cases also challenge modern notions of what is "left-wing" or "right-wing." Candidate and party ideologies in this pluralistic, bumptious political system are rarely black or white, but often made up of many shades of gray. The reality is that elections are evolutionary, not revolutionary; they provide clues to bigger changes that have happened, that are underway, that are soon to come.

It's hardly surprising that presidential contests have received so much attention from scholars and writers, not to mention pundits, policy wonks, Hollywood screenwriters, and pop-culture commentators. Filled with over-sized personalities, overheated rhetoric, and unpredictable twists and turns, American presidential campaigns can make for some of the most entertaining kind of history. Yet they are more than just ripping yarns. They are moments that both reflect their times and shape what comes next. They remind us that leadership matters, and that certain individuals have had an outsized effect on the course of national and international affairs. That's not all. The stories of presidential campaigns remind us that political leaders are one part of a vastly larger picture, and that presidents and would-be presidents are products of their times. Their electoral success and failure depend on a whole host of factors, including ones far out of the candidates' control.

Elections hinge on whether the nation is in economic boom times or recessions, as well as reflect the shifting social and economic priorities of a country as it moved from being predominantly rural and agricultural to urban and industrial, and then suburban and postindustrial. They hinge on who can vote, who is motivated to vote, and the technologies of communication that influence choices at the ballot box. The advisors, campaign managers, and party organization that surround a candidate can make or break an election. Demographics, economics, culture: all these things make the difference between winning and losing. In turn, the elections and their outcomes can have a profound effect on nearly every other aspect of society.

While these connections were present in the eighteenth and nineteenth centuries, it was in the twentieth century that they truly took center stage. After decades of largely unmemorable chief executives who took a back seat to power brokers in Congress, the twentieth century's first elected president, Theodore Roosevelt, enlarged the prominence of the office and embarked on a steady expansion of executive branch powers. Roosevelt's oversized personality helped create a new template for the modern presidency, a role that demanded a leader to be both policy-savvy and paternal, commanding and charismatic, powerful and populist. While the framers of the Constitution had originally envisioned the legislative branch as the instrument of the people's will, the corruption and ineffectiveness of Gilded Age Congresses made the moment right for the presidency to assume the mantle. The growth of the federal government over the course of the century reinforced the centrality of the White House and its occupants. America's dominant role in world affairs further propelled the president to the center of popular consciousness. Innovations in communication technology—from radio to television to Internet—continually upped the demand for a president, or presidential candidate, to be persuasive and likeable.[10]

In the twentieth century, it mattered tremendously *who* was president, and thus the process of getting presidents elected took on a significance unparalleled in earlier eras. Elections themselves became windows into broader changes. They revealed the remarkable evolution of the two major parties, the campaign process, and the modern presidency. They also revealed shifting currents in the American economy and society, in how people lived, worked, dreamed, and voted.

In the election of 1912, Teddy Roosevelt returned from the political sidelines to run a fiery third-party campaign against Democrat Woodrow Wilson and Roosevelt's old friend and political disciple William Howard Taft. No third-party candidate before or since has won such a large portion of the vote. Propelled by modern campaign machinery like barnstorming tours and savvy use of the media, the candidates of 1912 sidestepped traditional party organization and brought their appeals directly to voters. The election also laid bare the great tensions and debates generated by the rapid industrialization, urbanization, and immigration of the Gilded Age. The laissez faire approaches of earlier presidencies seemed to be a thing of the past. Now, all parties agreed that something had to be done by the government to regulate and alleviate the inequities of the industrial economy.

The 1932 election unfolded amid the depths of the Great Depression, in a nation where industrial production had plummeted and nearly 25 percent of Americans were out of work. The two major candidates offered voters different solutions to the crisis. President Herbert Hoover argued that government's role was to encourage business to fix itself, while his challenger Franklin Roosevelt declared that bold government action was the only way to restore prosperity. Voters sided with boldness, and Roosevelt—and his vision of a "New Deal" with the American people— won, fundamentally changing the relationship between citizens and the state. As with nearly every twentieth-century president, Roosevelt won not just because of the substance of his message, but because of the style of his delivery. He used the new medium of radio to deliver powerful, personal messages into voters' living rooms. His campaign staff used stagecraft as well as tough-minded political strategy to edge out the other Democratic challengers and, ultimately, Hoover himself.

Full of political plot twists, electrifying moments, and unbearable tragedies, the election of 1968 redefined both liberal and conservative politics. It also set the stage for the next four decades of presidential campaigning. An incumbent president chose not to run again, hobbled politically by an escalating and increasingly unwinnable overseas war. Inner-city neighborhoods were in flames, protests rocked college campuses, and assassins' bullets felled iconic leaders. Television brought all this strife and cultural transformation into American living rooms. The tensions between the political establishment and the youthful counterculture erupted violently at the Democratic convention, helping set up a Republican victory in November by a candidate whose political career seemed finished only a few years before, and laying the foundations for today's red- and blue-state America.

Ultimately, the story of 1968 doesn't just explain 1968. It explains what comes afterward. The Democratic Party was a much bigger tent, and much more open to new voices, but it had lost the establishment power it had enjoyed from the New Deal through the Johnson years. Meanwhile, the Republican Party had found a new way to talk to voters, and had made inroads into critical parts of the old Democratic base. Twelve years later, Ronald Reagan's landslide victory over Democratic incumbent Jimmy Carter was a triumphal execution of the political messages and strategies employed by Richard Nixon in his first White House win.

For all its drama and hype, the 1992 election can be overlooked because it seems to pale in comparison to the earth-shaking contest of Reagan versus Carter, and the cliff-hanging and hotly disputed 2000 race between Al Gore and George W. Bush. Without diminishing those other two critical political moments, the 1992 election rises in significance because of the profound global transformations surrounding it. It was the first presidential race after the end of the Cold War, and the first to feature a candidate born after World War II. It happened at the cusp of the high-technology revolution, and was the first campaign driven by—and perhaps decided by—the all-consuming media environment of cable television.

Riding high after the success of the Gulf War, incumbent George H. W. Bush seemed at first to be a sure bet for reelection, but a souring economy changed the electoral math. After a series of failed Democratic campaigns for the White House in which "liberal" became a dirty word, Arkansas Governor Bill Clinton ran as a centrist "New Democrat," espousing policies like welfare reform and government efficiency. But the election, and Clinton's ultimate victory, hinged on the insurgent third-party candidacy of businessman H. Ross Perot, whose campaign reflected the growing power of the independent voter and of communication in the Information Age.

Elections connect to one another. The progressive themes of 1912 echoed on in the campaigns following it, creating a rhetorical and substantive foundation for the debates of 1932. The contest of 1968 revolved around debates and constituencies set in place by Roosevelt's New Deal, and reflected both the great hopes and crushing disappointments that emerged from the struggles of the 1960s, from civil rights to Vietnam. It also signaled the rise of a powerful new sort of conservatism, born of frustration with social unrest and anxiety about the new racial and economic order, and fueled by the movement of people and jobs from North to South, East to West. The connective tissue stretches across election cycles. While 1968 laid the groundwork for Reagan's victory in 1980, the Reagan Revolution helped make possible the political rise and electoral triumph of Bill Clinton in 1992.

Three major themes run throughout the chapters that follow. The first is the extraordinary dynamism of the American political spectrum over time. These cases show us that the United States is neither a conservative nor a liberal nation, but one in which political categories and identities are far more messy, multilayered, and difficult to categorize. Politics has a symbiotic relationship to the broader society. The balance between the two ends of the political spectrum and the composition of the debates and temperaments along it change as the economy changes, as culture changes, and as the makeup of the electorate changes. Rather than thinking of American political history as a pendulum swinging between left and right, we should focus on the *center*, which shifted more incrementally in either a liberal or a conservative direction as times changed. In the late 1960s and early 1970s, the center of American politics was several steps to the left of where it landed two decades later, in the eras of Reagan, Bush, and Clinton. Definitions of "liberal" and "conservative" changed over the course of the century, and something considered dangerously radical (or alarmingly conservative) in one generation became centrist in the next.

Successful candidates adapted and responded to these electoral recalibrations. The winners were those who adapted the best to changing times, not necessarily those candidates who first gained traction because they epitomized the new political mood. Teddy Roosevelt brought progressive political ideas to the national stage in 1912, and Woodrow Wilson won partly because he took on some of these ideas as his own. Law-and-order populism propelled the southern segregationist and Democratic candidate George Wallace into the national spotlight in 1968, but Nixon won in part by delivering the same message in less strident and more slickly packaged ways. Reagan led the conservative revolution after 1980; Clinton adapted some of these ideas and words into the platform that brought him victory in 1992.

The second major strand is the continual redefinition of the two major parties through pivotal presidential contests, and the role of third parties in this redefinition. The bedrock constituencies of the Republican and Democratic parties changed profoundly over the course of the twentieth century, as did the issues the two parties championed. At the start of the century, the GOP was the more progressive of the two parties, based in the urban Northeast and advocating a bold government action and promoting the growth of a public bureaucracy. The Democrats were the party of the rural South, of more minimal central government and less federal regulation.

Independent parties and voters also made a difference. In three of these four elections, third-party candidates played a disruptive, even decisive role in the ultimate outcome of the election. Teddy Roosevelt's run siphoned so many votes from the Republicans that the Democrats won back the White House for the first time in years. George Wallace garnered far fewer votes, but he fractured the Democratic base and introduced populist rhetoric that Republicans later employed to win national victories after decades of Democratic dominance. While H. Ross Perot did not manage to win a single electoral vote, he won the largest share of the popular vote of any third-party candidate since TR, and he forced the other candidates to take new issues seriously. Even when third parties don't win, they have an indelible effect on how elections play out—and on the two major parties.

The third theme of the book concerns political communication. Over the century, changes in media and communications changed not only the way campaigns were run, but also the relationship between presidential candidates and individual voters. Breaking with the nineteenth-century pattern where candidates gave few speeches and relied on surrogates to hit the road on their behalf, the 1912 election ushered in a new era of candidate-centered campaigning. The rise of national media further fueled a new emphasis on the personalities and charisma of the men who ran for president. By 1932, most American homes had a radio, and this created an opportunity for an even more personal relationship to develop between president and voter. Television was another earthquake on the campaign landscape by 1968, beaming news from around the world into American living rooms and demanding candidates who were telegenic and able to spout snappy sound bites rather than long-winded speeches. By 1992, the 24-hour news cycle propelled by the rise of cable television news not only created a demand for perpetual feeding of the media "beast" but allowed campaigns ample air time to take their messages, and their campaign "spin," directly to the voters.

All these themes are intertwined and interdependent. Changing modes of political communication contributed to the decline in partisan attachments and helped third-party candidates gain traction. New technologies gave politicians fresh ways to communicate to voters, and an ability to talk to citizens directly without the mediating influence of party organization. At the same time, innovations in the way American elections worked encouraged the widespread adaptation of new media. Late nineteenth-century reforms like the adoption of the secret ballot made more direct means of political communication and persuasion necessary, sowing the seeds of entirely new fields of campaign communications and political advertising. The rise of organized political interest groups in the early decades of the twentieth century helped propel the growth of print media and radio as means of political communication, as different lobbies appealed to voters' hearts and heads through ever more sophisticated appeals. Successive waves of communication innovation, from radio to television to the Internet, allowed third-party candidates to spread their message and win voter support. More broadly, the rapid expansion of the electorate due to population growth, immigration, and women's suffrage meant communication needed to be carried out on a scale that was simultaneously mass in its reach and targeted in its messages.[11]

Ultimately, presidential elections are places where the ordinary and the extraordinary meet. While it is wrong to assert that certain elections "changed everything," they are nonetheless singular and significant events in the historical landscape, with effects that resonate far beyond the first Tuesday in November. Elections are driven by giant personalities and increasingly complex and expensive campaign organizations, but for all their bluster and spin and hanging chads, they are instruments of democracy. Once every four years on the first Tuesday in November, American voters make their choices, mark their ballots, and determine who wins and who loses. The heat and light of a presidential campaign leaves an indelible mark on all who decide to run, and especially those who win. Even the fiercest political rivals ultimately bond together because of the shared experience of being president.

Once friends, Jefferson and Adams became bitterly divided by the election of 1800. With the passage of time and the mellowing of old age, however, their enmity began to thaw. In 1812, Adams finally reached out to

Jefferson, writing a letter to which Jefferson quickly and warmly responded. Adams's letter, he wrote "carries me back to the times when . . . we were laborers in the same cause, struggling for what is most valuable to man, his right of self-government."[12] Thus began a lively and affectionate correspondence between the two old rivals that continued until the end of their lives. On hearing of the election of Adams's son John Quincy to the presidency, Jefferson wrote: "I sincerely congratulate you on the high gratification which the issue of the late election must have afforded you. . . . So deeply are the principles of order, and of obedience to law impressed on the minds of our citizens generally that I am persuaded there will be as immediate an acquiescence in the will of the majority as if Mr. Adams had been the choice of every man."[13] Elections come and go, Jefferson seemed to say, but the values of democracy endured.

Remarkably, Jefferson and Adams died on the same day: 4 July 1826, the fiftieth anniversary of the Declaration of Independence. Politics had consumed most of their lives and torn apart their friendship, but they ultimately found common cause in the democratic ideas that had made them revolutionaries. In the decades that followed, many other giant personalities occupied the office of the presidency. It was not until the turn of a new century, however, that the great debate that had consumed the early republic—big government or small government? a nation of farms or a nation of factories?—took center stage once more in presidential politics.

PART I

* ✳ *

1912

CHAPTER 1

The Great Transformation

In the early morning of 18 June 1910, the ocean liner *Kaiserin Augusta Victoria* steamed into a fog-shrouded New York Harbor. The mist and intermittent drizzle of the morning had not kept a large flotilla of boats—from battleships to pleasure cruisers—from crowding the harbor, nor had it dissuaded the thousands of people who lined the streets in anticipation of the day to come. For the liner *Kaiserin* was bringing home former president Theodore Roosevelt, who was returning to the United States after more than a year overseas. Roosevelt was not only New York City's favorite son, but a beloved national figure. On African safari for eleven months, and then on a tour of Europe for another four, he had been gone but hardly forgotten. Instead, his celebrity seemed to have increased over his prolonged absence.

The celebration that followed on that June day showed what a major public presence the ex-president continued to be, fifteen months after he turned over the White House to his handpicked successor, William Howard Taft. American flags waved as the day turned sunny. Roosevelt paraded down Manhattan streets, tipping his top hat to the jostling spectators, as policemen held back the eager crowds. A band played "Roosevelt's Grand Triumphal March," specially commissioned for the occasion.

On an outdoor stage festooned with bunting, he gave a classic, rousing speech to the assembled throng. Immediately below, reporters scribbled furiously in their notebooks, composing hyperbolic accounts that appeared on the front pages of newspapers from coast to coast. "Well, He's 'Back from Elba,'" proclaimed a banner headline in the *Tacoma Times* in far-off Washington State, calling it the "greatest welcome in the nation's history."[1]

Figure 1. Theodore Roosevelt's triumphal return to the New York City after many
months abroad made front-page news across the country. *Tacoma Times*,
18 June 1910, 1.

Political leaders also showered Roosevelt with praise. In the pages of a leading national magazine, President Taft gave the returning leader a flattering welcome. "After the heavy cares of the presidential office for eight strenuous years, he sought rest by contrast in the depths of the African forest and in great physical exertion in the hunting of large game," Taft wrote. "His path since the time he landed in Europe until he sailed has been a royal progress," a rapturous reception that "shows the deep impress his character, his aims, and his methods as a civil and social reformer have made on the world at large."[2]

In a letter Roosevelt wrote Taft two days later, he could hardly contain his glee at the rapturous reception, even as he professed a desire to stay away from public life. "I am having a perfect fight to avoid being made to give lectures, and even of the invitations I have accepted there are at least half of them I wish I had not."[3]

If bets were being made in June 1910 about the man most likely to win the presidency in 1912, the good money was on Theodore Roosevelt. The odds weighed in his favor not only because of his fame and biography, but also because of the weakness of any other possible contender. Chief among the weak was the incumbent in the White House. TR would have been a hard act for any politician to follow, but it was doubly difficult for Taft—amiable, intelligent, but lacking the political instincts and personality of his predecessor. His political missteps on bedrock Republican issues like the protective tariff had shaken the faith of both the GOP leadership and key constituencies. His more cautious and incremental approach to progressive issues like corporate regulation and conservation had alienated those who desired reform.

On the other side of the aisle, discord and frustration consumed the Democrats. The party had run the same man—William Jennings Bryan—as their nominee in three of the previous four presidential elections. He had lost every time. Grover Cleveland had been the only Democrat elected president since the Civil War. Although Bryan's fiery populism had roused mass support among discontented farmers and working people, it failed as a national political strategy. The inroads that Democrats had made into some traditionally Republican states of the Northeast and Midwest during the Cleveland years had dissipated, and the Party now struggled to rebuild a coalition that could win the White House.[4]

Making the landscape even rockier for the two major parties were independent political movements bubbling up on the leftward end of the political spectrum. The Socialist Party was the most powerful among them, having brought together a range of left-leaning groups and ideologies into a political organization with a powerful and persuasive message about the inequities of industrial capitalism. The Socialist leader, Eugene V. Debs, had run for president in 1904 and 1908 with impressive, if not election-altering results.

Yet seasoned political observers know not to predict election outcomes too far in advance. The odds-makers of July 1910 might have been amazed to learn that the 1912 race would go to a man who, on the day of TR's triumphant homecoming, had not yet been elected to political office.

Woodrow Wilson was a scholarly type who, although politically savvy, disliked the sorts of political spectacles Roosevelt relished. A Southerner of moderate-to-conservative views, the highest office he had obtained prior to 1910 was the presidency of Princeton University, from which he had rather unceremoniously stepped down after attempting dramatic reforms of campus traditions and institutions. Despite this setback, Wilson had already started to build a national political reputation as a leading voice for a new kind of Democratic ideology—an alternative to the populism of Bryan, but one that still supported public action to curb the power of corporations and protect individual rights. To a national Democratic Party looking rather desperately for a fresh face, Wilson provided it.[5]

Two months after Roosevelt's "return from Elba," Wilson won the Democratic nomination for governor of New Jersey. In a spectacular fall campaign, he turned on the machine politicians who had been responsible for securing his nomination and ran as a modern reformer. In November, Wilson secured the governorship, part of a Democratic wave in the midterm elections that signaled deep trouble for the national Republican Party.[6]

In the two years that followed, the political fortunes of the four men who became the significant candidates of 1912—Roosevelt, Taft, Wilson, and Debs—shifted dramatically, as did those of the other men who tried, and failed, to win the presidency. Friendships frayed. Alliances imploded. And as their prospects rose and fell, as new people entered the battle and others faded out of it, these politicians engaged in a debate about the nature of citizenship, corporate power, and government responsibility that had not been seen before in American politics. The men and women who supported their campaigns joined in the conversation, helping turn the nation's focus away from the political issues that had consumed the nineteenth century and toward the ideas that defined the twentieth.

This extraordinary election brought ideas into the political mainstream that had been considered radical only a few years earlier. It realigned both the Democratic and Republican Parties in subtle but significant ways, and showed the power of third-party insurgencies to disrupt—but not overturn—the two-party system. It demonstrated how far the system had come from the styles and methods of politicking that had characterized national races since the days of Jefferson and Adams, and institutionalized an entirely new breed of campaign rituals and strategies that had emerged at the end of the nineteenth century and became business as usual in the twentieth.

America Transformed

Like all presidential contests, the 1912 election only can be fully understood in the context of the changes the United States had experienced in the years leading up to it. And for this election, we must go back farther than 1910, or even 1890 or 1870, but all the way to the eve of the Civil War to comprehend the men who ran and the people who protested, organized, agitated, and voted for them.

A good place to begin is 5 November 1855, when future Socialist presidential candidate Eugene Victor Debs was born into a family of French immigrant grocers in Terre Haute, Indiana. The America baby Gene came into was a place where three of four people lived in the countryside or small towns. Most of them were farmers. No city in the U.S. had more than a million people.[7] While new technologies like the mechanized loom and the cotton gin were transforming markets, and new transportation networks of canal and rail were enabling new flows of goods, people, and communication, most Americans lived according to preindustrial rhythms. People wore watches and consulted clocks, but local time was not standardized and remained governed by the rising and setting of the sun. Families like the Debses immigrated across oceans while native-born white Americans continually migrated westward across the continent, but travel was slow and news moved just as slowly.[8]

Preindustrial rhythms of life held strongest sway in the pre-Civil War American South, where well over 90 percent of the population were rural, the manufacturing economy was minuscule, and roads and railroads were far scarcer than in the North.[9] This was the world into which Thomas

Woodrow Wilson was born in December 1858, the son of a clergyman in Staunton, Virginia. Moving as a baby to Georgia, and then to South Carolina, Wilson had a childhood surrounded by war's terror and its devastating aftermath.[10]

The human suffering and physical destruction wrought by the war propelled a turning point in America's understanding of itself. Before the Civil War, the country had operated as a sometimes tenuously connected "union" of self-governing states with markedly different economies, demographics, and cultural sensibilities. Afterward, the country increasingly came to be understood as, and function as, a "nation" whose federal government wielded increasing power and whose citizens shared common values and culture. As historian James McPherson writes, "the war marked the transition of the United States to a singular noun."[11]

The end of war also escalated remarkable changes already underway in the American economy. In the span of a few decades, the United States became an industrial colossus, home to some of the largest corporations and richest people on the planet. Rapid industrialization triggered foreign immigration and urbanization of unprecedented scale and speed. As the population swelled, a growing nation became a giant consumer market for products made in American factories.

Some of this change became evident well before the Civil War in New York City, where Theodore Roosevelt was born to affluent parents in October 1858. Always a polyglot, multiethnic metropolis, New York had become intensely more so since the 1820s, as waves of immigrants from Ireland and continental Europe arrived at its docks and stayed for good, squeezing into overcrowded tenements and urban slums. Many of these immigrants—and the millions who would follow them in the decades to come—went to work in the new factories that were growing up in New York and cities like it. Men, women, and children alike worked long hours, six days a week, in factory jobs that ranged from moderately to extremely dangerous. They worked for low pay, few benefits, and no safety net if they got injured on the job.[12]

One year before and a thousand miles to the southwest, William Howard Taft had been born into prosperity in the Midwestern river city of Cincinnati. While his family were not quite as rich as Roosevelt's, they were nonetheless quite comfortable and politically influential. Taft's father, Alphonso, was a powerful Republican who served in President Ulysses S. Grant's cabinet as attorney general and as secretary of war. Both a political power broker and an attentive father, the elder Taft had high expectations of his son Billy. The younger Taft rose to them. Although he struggled with obesity throughout his life, he was a natural athlete and became a star baseball player in high school, only giving it up when his parents cautioned him not to neglect his academic studies. He excelled in those as well, winning high grades and following his father and half-brother to Yale in 1874.

By this time, teenage "Teedie" Roosevelt was spending hours in the boxing gym and on the wrestling mat in an attempt to bulk up his skinny physique. Gene Debs had dropped out of school to support his family and was working on the railroad, first as a painter and cleaner, and then as a locomotive fireman. Tommy Wilson was preparing to leave the Reconstruction-era South and head North to college.

By the mid-1880s, Taft was an assistant county prosecutor in Ohio. After graduating from Harvard, Roosevelt had dropped out of law school but still managed to get himself elected to the New York State Assembly. Wilson received one of the very first Ph.D.s in history and was a junior faculty member trying to write his first book. Debs had become a full-time labor organizer for his fellow railroad workers.

In these two decades of change in the four men's lives, the United States was undergoing an extraordinary transformation. In 1869, the transcontinental railroad had linked the West and East coasts. In 1876, Alexander Graham Bell had filed his patent for the telephone, and in 1879 Thomas Edison had developed his first incandescent light bulb. Beginning in the 1880s, the predominantly Northern European character of the nation began to change with the arrival of new waves of immigrants from Southern and Eastern Europe. As new arrivals had done before and since, they took on the dirtiest and hardest jobs, from urban factories to Western mines and oilfields. An increasingly diverse United States became home to millions who brought with them new languages, cultural traditions, and political ideologies.

Everything grew bigger. Farm production doubled. The U.S. population tripled. The value of manufacturing became six times larger. Cities grew up and out; between 1860 and 1910, the number of people living in American cities grew from 6 million to 44 million.

America lacked the institutions and governmental organizations to cope with such massive growth. It was the apex of the era of machine politics in the cities, kickbacks and bribery in the U.S. Congress and the state legislatures, and chaos nearly everywhere else. As muckraking journalist Lincoln

Figure 2. Joseph Keppler, "The Bosses of the Senate," 23 January 1889. Political corruption accompanied the explosive growth of the American industrial economy after the Civil War, and many in the U.S. Congress fell under the sway of big railroads and big oil. Library of Congress.

Steffens put it in his 1904 expose of urban political machines, the debilitating effects of this "boodle"—aka, political corruption—were "so complex, various, and far-reaching, that one mind could hardly grasp them."[13]

Meanwhile, the firms that ran the railroads, owned the mines and oilfields, and controlled the factories grew into enormous corporations and conglomerates of extraordinary power and reach. Their power overshadowed that of the government. In 1891, the Pennsylvania Railroad had 110,000 employees. The entire U.S army was less than a third that size. Federal government spending per capita was about $129, less than 10 percent of gross domestic product.

The speed and scale of change, and the failure of American social institutions to manage it, spurred Americans of all classes, regions, and political ideologies to question the status quo and agitate for alternative approaches. While grassroots protest and reform movements had been part of American civil society since before the Revolution, fast and ubiquitous national and transnational communications networks allowed reform ideas to gather force more rapidly and widely than before. News of strikes and protests crackled across telegraph wires in moments, students returned from abroad with radical new ideas, newspapers printed fiery speeches, and magazine editors filled pages with long-form investigative reporting on the excesses of the era. Cheaper printing, far-reaching networks of road and rail, and higher literacy rates expanded publishing and readership.

Farmers and laborers in the Midwest and West cursed the far-off bankers and corporate titans whose stranglehold on markets drove down crop prices and drove up shipping costs. They mobilized locally in the 1880s through organizations like the Grange, and nationally in the 1890s through the Populist Party, using modern media and charismatic leaders to voice their discontent with the modern order. A new wave of Democratic leaders seized the opportunity to broaden the Party's regional constituencies and pushed for the adoption of key Populist Party principles into its 1896 party platform as well as nominating Bryan, populist firebrand and powerful orator, three times running.

Yet with a Congress under the sway of corporate "boodle" and a series of White House occupants more beholden to party bosses than to changing the status quo, much of the reform energy prior to 1900 emanated from outside national political institutions. Critiques of the industrial order ranged from moderate to radical. Some began to advocate for some regulation of the monopolistic companies that controlled disproportionate chunks of the national economy. Others thought the only solution was to break up the corporate giants altogether. The most ardent anti-monopolists advocated property reform and mandatory wealth redistribution.

Working-class people went on strike and mobilized into labor unions. Their middle-class allies joined them in crusading for workplace safety, workers compensation, and child labor laws. Socialists, communists, and anarchists argued that the entire capitalist system needed to be replaced. Some resorted to violence to express their fury at the system, resulting in a number of acts of domestic terrorism, including the 1901 assassination of William McKinley—the act that propelled Theodore Roosevelt into the President's Office. Women, who didn't get the right to vote in most states until the passage of the Nineteenth Amendment in 1920, played prominent roles in many of these movements, from the anarchist fringe to the "respectable" middle.

The four candidates of 1912 resided at different places in this spectrum of reform. Roosevelt entered politics in 1882 when elected to the New York

State Assembly, believing that more men of his class—educated, enlightened—needed to become involved in what he called "the raw coarseness and the eager struggle of political life."[14] Wilson, in contrast, spent the first three decades of his career in academia. While conservative when it came to social issues like race relations, his long tenure outside formal politics perhaps made him bolder when it came to bucking the party bosses; by the time he ran for president, he would argue for breaking up business monopolies. William Howard Taft was a good Republican Party man, winning a series of plum judicial and administrative appointments as a reward for his competence and amiability. Although sympathetic to Progressive causes, he was a quiet, unshowy sort of reformer.

The rise of Eugene Debs, on the other hand, attested to the great anguish and political discontent among the working people who suffered the most in the new industrial economy. By the early 1890s, Debs had given up working on the railroad and instead was working to represent the interests of railroad workers, becoming head of the powerful American Railway Union in 1893. The following year, workers at the Pullman Company went on strike to secure better wages and working conditions. Pullman was America's leading manufacturer of railway sleeping cars, a critical cog in the railway machine. Debs organized a nationwide railway boycott of the Pullman cars in support. Workers in railway yards across the country refused to couple the Pullman cars to trains. Engineers refused to drive them. The entire national rail system ground to a complete halt.[15]

The railroad was so important to the functioning of the national economy that the federal government intervened. Democratic President Grover Cleveland sided with Pullman, not its workers, and dispatched U.S. soldiers to Chicago to restore the peace. Although Debs already had exhorted his members to keep the main trains running and mitigate the worst effects of the strike, the Cleveland administration still sent him to prison for blocking interstate commerce. He emerged a national celebrity and a hero of the workingman. A lifelong Democrat, he was so disgusted at Cleveland's actions that he switched to the Socialist Party, first running for president on its ticket in 1904.

By this time, the many currents of protest and calls for reform had started to have significant policy implications. While many reform movements (particularly those led by native-born, middle-class women and men) had their origins in religious and voluntary organizations, it was clear that meaningful reform needed more than churches and charities, settlement houses and

Figure 3. Eugene V. Debs, 1912. Debs's leadership of the American Railway Union during the Pullman Strike of 1894 made him a working-class hero and decisively shifted his political allegiance from the Democrats to the Socialist Party. His 1912 Socialist candidacy was his third bid for the White House. Harris & Ewing Collection, Library of Congress.

orphanages. Only larger, public entities could tackle the multiple challenges created by industrialization. Government needed to do more.

The initial push for a larger public role came in big cities, where such problems were most acute and painfully visible. Progressive reformers pushed to clean up corrupt local governments and establish professional civil service systems. Theodore Roosevelt burnished his reform credentials after being appointed to lead New York City Police Board in 1895, where he proceeded to clean up the corrupt institution and pass regulations dear to many reformers' hearts, such as banning Sunday liquor sales. While the federal government remained largely on the sidelines, reformers within and outside state and local governments in the 1890s and 1900s enacted a range of measures from town planning to workers' compensation to stricter child labor laws. Cities built infrastructure from bridges to parks, schools, housing, and water and sewer systems.[16]

The various efforts of middle-class reformers blended particular ideas about morality and correct behavior with a faith in large-scale organization and specialized "expertise." American reform did not exist in isolation; similar movements and politics arose at the same time throughout the industrialized world, and in many instances American reformers took their cues and inspiration from European models. Often referred to as "Progressivism," the reform impulse was not an organized political party nor was it a single ideology.[17]

With the ascension of Theodore Roosevelt to the Oval Office, Progressivism became more central to the national political conversation. After a long succession of rather colorless chief executives who toed the party line, Roosevelt impressed those longing for reform with his forceful personality and willingness to buck the authority of the Republican Party's conservative leadership. While some of his actions as president were bold—particularly when it came to conservation of natural resources—others left Progressives wishing for more. He did not hesitate use his bully pulpit to call Wall Street bankers and corporate titans on the carpet, but he believed in corporate regulation, not breaking up monopolies altogether.

Roosevelt picked Taft to succeed him because he found him a fitting person to carry on his legacy. The same amiability and loyalty that had earned Taft so many good appointments encouraged Roosevelt to believe that Taft would do little to alter Roosevelt's reformist agenda. TR had declined to run for a third term, but in Taft he envisioned a third term by proxy.

Within a few months, the new president proved him wrong. Perhaps the most grievous blow was Taft's firing of Roosevelt's close advisor Gifford Pinchot, who had been instrumental in creating the U.S. Forest Service and crafting a new federal approach to the management of lands and natural resources. When it came to corporate reform, Taft was actually a little more reform-minded than Roosevelt had been. But his political bumbling and reluctance to break with the GOP stalwarts on ossified approaches to trade and commerce gave many people—Roosevelt included—the impression that he was hardly the Progressive hero they wanted and needed.

In a world of increasingly advanced technology and complex organizations, it no longer made sense to have a U.S. government whose biggest agency was the Post Office. As Progressive era author Herbert Croly put it in 1909, "an American statesman could not longer represent the national interest without becoming a reformer."[18]

It was in this atmosphere that the campaign of 1912 began. The United States had had a long and venerable tradition of small government and limited executive power. It was a testament to the incredible changes that had occurred over the four candidates' lifetimes that they all agreed that more government action and regulation was necessary, and inevitable.

They just disagreed on how to get there.

The End of a Friendship

William Howard Taft seemed like an uninteresting president to many of his contemporaries. It might have been because he was uninterested in being president.

Taft's greatest dream was to serve on the U.S. Supreme Court. After obtaining his law degree, his quick ascent in the world of Republican politics came not through winning elections but through a series of judicial and administrative appointments. He once wrote that his professional rise was due to having his "plate right side up when offices were falling."[19] Yet this self-deprecating characterization belied his true accomplishments. First appointed a judge in 1887, by the mid-1890s Taft had distinguished himself as one of the most prominent and well-regarded jurists in the country, often mentioned as a likely appointee to the Supreme Court. Only his youth—he was less than forty at the time—put him out of serious contention.[20]

By this time, Taft and Roosevelt had become good friends. Their age, class, and political outlook gave them much in common. Their radically different personalities, extrovert and introvert, complimented one another. In Taft, Roosevelt had an attentive listener and advocate; in Roosevelt, Taft had both entertainment and intellectual stimulation. In the beginning, Taft was the senior of the two, having been appointed by Benjamin Harrison to be the nation's number-three lawyer, solicitor general, in 1890. Roosevelt had a relatively less important appointment, civil service commissioner. When William McKinley became president in 1897, Taft urged him to appoint Roosevelt assistant secretary of the navy.

That appointment became TR's springboard to national political celebrity, as he famously quit his job the following year to lead a brigade of roughneck cowboys and mercenaries into battle in Cuba. Despite his middle age and the general unpreparedness of U.S. troops, Roosevelt and his

Rough Riders won the Battle of San Juan Hill and catapulted into legend. Riding the wave of postwar celebrity, he became governor of New York. Yet Roosevelt's thirst for reform made him a thorn in the side of Republican Party bosses in New York, and by 1900 this contributed to his being dislodged from a job he enjoyed into one that had far less influence: the vice presidency of the United States. One commentator observed that the preternaturally vigorous Roosevelt had little desire to be "laid upon the shelf at his time of life."[21] He ended up spending little time on that shelf, however. On 14 September 1901, an assassin's bullet felled McKinley, and Theodore Roosevelt moved into the President's Office.

The Spanish American War had resulted in Taft getting a new job as well: governor general of the Philippines, one of the remnants of the Spanish empire left in U.S. hands after the guns had been silenced. From 1900 to 1903, Taft took on this high-stakes, high-risk job and—from the perspective of his bosses in Washington—excelled at it. He walked into a political tinderbox. Most Filipinos had little desire to exchange one colonial ruler for another, and had launched a fiercely fought nationalist rebellion that was, in turn, being quite violently repressed by the U.S. military. By the time he left, the Filipino independence movement had been quashed and U.S.-led social and political institutions were in place that maintained civic stability and protected American economic interests. The regime Taft established helped perpetuate U.S. control over the nation and its people for another forty-one years.[22]

By 1904, Roosevelt had pulled his old friend back home to become his Secretary of War, one of the most powerful positions in Washington. The job further strengthened the relationship between Roosevelt and Taft. After some public dithering about whether to run again in 1908 (he had only been elected once, and the two-term limit then was a tradition rather than a statutory limitation), Roosevelt decided to step aside. Taft—supremely competent, unfailingly loyal, a strategic problem-solver—seemed like an eminently sensible choice to carry on the TR legacy.

It was not easy to convince Taft to run; he still had the Supreme Court highest in his mind. "The President and the Congress," he once said, "are all very well in their way . . . but it rests with the Supreme Court to decide what they really thought." He had repeatedly denied, publicly and privately, that he would ever agree to be put in the running for the presidency.[23] However, Roosevelt had an ally in Taft's ambitious wife Nellie, who had been aspiring to the First Ladyship since her husband's earliest days in politics. Faced with the combined persuasive powers of Teddy and Nellie, Taft agreed to do it. He later called the 1908 campaign "the most uncomfortable four months of my life."[24] He won, quite decisively vanquishing William Jennings Bryan, who would never run for president again.

The next day, Roosevelt sat down to write Taft a congratulatory letter that, while effusive, reflected the complicated nature of the two men's friendship. Taft was the winner, but Roosevelt saw the victory as a validation of his own good judgment. "Dear Will," TR wrote. "The returns of the election make it evident to me that you are the only man who we could have nominated that could have been elected. You have won a great personal victory as well as a great victory for the party, and all those who love you, who admire and believe in you, and are proud of your great and fine qualities, must feel a thrill of exultation over the way in which the American people have shown their insight into character, their adherence to high principle."[25]

Within days, however, Taft began to disappoint Roosevelt's high expectations. The note of thanks the president-elect wrote his predecessor in response expressed great gratitude for all Roosevelt had done to help the campaign, but it also gave some credit to Taft's brother Charles, a Republican Party moneyman and political fixer. Roosevelt fumed. To him, Charlie Taft was a hack; Roosevelt was a statesman. Would Billy Taft be in the White House without Roosevelt's endorsement and encouragement? Was this any way to repay a friend?

Rumors of rift started buzzing in the early months of 1909, as Roosevelt prepared to hand over the reins to his successor. And Roosevelt did little to stop them. "He means well and he'll do his best," he told a sympathetic journalist on the last day of his presidency. "But he's weak."[26] With that, the ex-president steamed away on safari. He and Taft did not correspond for a year.

The real problem was bigger than a breach in etiquette. Theodore Roosevelt had a hard time not being president any more. He was fifty years old, healthy and energetic, and unemployed. He was hugely popular. He also was spending a lot of time thinking and absorbing new ideas as he traveled abroad. Touring Europe in the first months of 1910, he was presented by a range of political ideas and policy solutions more audacious and far-reaching than American reforms. The sweeping social insurance programs of Germany, the support for mothers and children in France, the worker housing programs of Great Britain: all these impressed Roosevelt in their scope and ambition. They presented a new potential for national government to intervene in the workings of markets, to remedy inequity, to promote economic security.

The speeches he gave on this European tour intensified in their bold proclamation of reformist ideas. In Paris, he talked of human rights being more important than property rights. In Oxford, he spoke about income inequality and the need for an "acceptance of responsibility, one for each and one for all." While he refrained from prescribing solutions, he began to develop a more audacious, more compelling language around the need for reform. Coming from a leader of such charisma and passion, the progressive message that TR returned home with in the summer of 1910 was poised to win over American hearts and minds.[27]

In the meantime, the new president had been stepping into one public relations fiasco after another. He flip-flopped on critical issues like the tariff in ways that left pretty much everyone unhappy with him.[28] And as his old boss moved to the left, Taft appeared to move to the right, joining in closer alliances with old guard Republicans in Congress. In reality, Taft and Roosevelt were not that far apart on many issues, but political flubs and media missteps tended to magnify their differences. One aide remarked that Taft "does not understand the art of giving out news" in the way his predecessor had done so masterfully.[29]

Adding to Taft's public relations woes was the mounting gossip about the sour turn that the Roosevelt and Taft friendship had taken. In an effort to quell them, Roosevelt orchestrated an elaborate photo opportunity by paying a visit to Taft at his summer home in Massachusetts on his return to the United States in the summer of 1910—accompanied by 200 scribbling reporters. The *New York Times* reported the meeting as "a warm embrace" involving much laughter and backslapping.[30] Yet this was merely a photo op. The restless Roosevelt continued to complain privately to friends about Taft's job performance.

The Taft-Roosevelt rift was personal and sometimes petty, but it became politically significant because it mirrored a broader identity crisis in the Republican Party as the issues that drove politics in the nineteenth century gave way to the debates that would shape politics and policymaking in the twentieth. Mainstream Republicans of 1912 were the party of industry and enterprise, and they were supporters of tariffs on foreign imports to protect domestic manufacturing. Having controlled both Congress and the White House for most of the late nineteenth century, the mainstream GOP was less a party of reform than one of status quo. Yet this relative conservatism was hardly a laissez faire, small-government philosophy. The Republicans were, after all, the party of Reconstruction, of major public infrastructure projects like the transcontinental railroad and the land grant colleges, and of major welfare programs like the veterans' pension system. In 1912, the advocates of small government and states' rights hailed from the Democratic Party, not the Republican.

Republican constituencies in 1912 also were far different than what they would become over the course of the twentieth century. In 1912, the GOP was still the party of Lincoln. African Americans usually voted Republican, when they could vote, but racially motivated maneuvers like poll taxes and literacy tests in the Jim Crow South had largely disenfranchised the Southern black population. The key to the Republican Party's dominance of national politics in the post-Civil War years was its strong presence in the urban Northeast and Midwest, where the majority of Americans lived at the time. Yet by the beginning of the twentieth century, the growing size of the Republican base in Western states was beginning to shift this regional hegemony. The manufacturing-heavy Northeast and Midwest was the bastion of pro-tariff, pro-business Republicanism. The agrarian Far West represented a vastly different set of interests, ones that blended anti-monopolist politics with crusading middle-class moralism.

While Republicans had held majorities in a political system that was staggering in its level of corruption and favoritism, the GOP was not simply a party of cronies. It was the party of Progressives. Many of the middle-class, native-born reformers came from the base of the Republican electorate, and had very different ideas about the party's destiny. Many of these new Progressive voices came from West of the Mississippi. The GOP, they argued, no longer should be the party of modest market regulation. It should be the party of action. The defining issues of modern politics, the progressive faction argued, was cleaning up an electoral process that favored party insiders, and replacing patronage with efficient, professionalized government bureaucracies. The government was the only possible counterweight to the power of the huge industrial corporations, and government needed to pass and enforce more aggressive laws protecting workers, conserving natural resources, and alleviating poverty. They generated momentum for reform at all levels of government that began to shift the Republican Party from the one of the status quo to the one of hope and change.

The Republicans were not the only political party with an identity crisis on its hands. The Democratic Party had multiple constituencies with quite different visions of the American future. By 1912, the Democrats' big tent encompassed the populists of the Great Plains and West who were demanding national government action on monetary reform and regulation of Wall Street. It included Southern whites with a huge economic and social stake in keeping Jim Crow intact and who were suspicious of a powerful central government that might trample on states' rights to maintain segregation. Foreign-born immigrants also voted Democratic, in part because of the powerful influence of Democratic machines in large cities. And, like the Republicans, the Democrats included some Progressive reformers. These reformers argued that the Democratic Party, not the GOP, could be the standard-bearer for a more activist central government, for better lives for working people, and for breaking up the monopolies and ushering in a fairer capitalist order.

After his return from abroad in 1910, Teddy Roosevelt had seized on the cresting Progressive wave and went on a nationwide speaking tour, sounding more progressive with every stop. More must be done to keep corporations out of politics, Roosevelt told mesmerized crowds of five, ten, and twenty thousand. Corporate directors whose companies broke the law should be subject to prosecution. The national government must do much, much more. In Osawatomie, Kansas, on 31 August, Roosevelt gave the definitive speech that gave this new philosophy a name—the "New Nationalism"—and declared it would not only fix the problems of industrial capitalism, but also allow the nation to transcend its vexing issues of sectionalism, corruption, and class divides.[31]

Yet while barnstorming the country like a presidential contender and drawing massive and enthusiastic crowds, Roosevelt continued to swat away all suggestions of running for president. "There is nothing I want less," he told newspaper editor, leading progressive, and close ally William Allen White as 1910 drew to a close.[32]

Reluctance to challenge his old protégé Taft seemed the least of the reasons Roosevelt was refraining from a run. Like presidents before and after him, he worried that he might not win. New winds were blowing, but Roosevelt didn't think the Republican Party was quite ready to swing to the progressive side. He figured he would have better luck remaking his party in 1916. Given the opposition within the party to progressive ideas, Roosevelt worried that, even if he won in 1912, he might ultimately risk his legacy. "I

Figure 4. William H. Taft and Theodore Roosevelt, 1909. Taft was Roosevelt's hand-picked successor for the White House, but by the early months of Taft's presidency the two men's political alliance—and personal friendship—was in tatters. Brown Brothers, Library of Congress.

do not see how I could go out of the presidency again with the credit I had when I left it," he confessed to White. But, as all savvy politicians do, he left the door open. If his supporters and friends felt he was the only hope for the progressive cause, "it would be unpatriotic of me" not to stand for election.[33]

Whether motivated by duty, ego, or a combination of both, Roosevelt found it increasingly hard to resist the lure of the campaign trail as 1912 neared. As the next chapter will show, this had huge consequences.

CHAPTER 2

*

The Progressive Campaign

Roosevelt continued prevaricating for months, staying in the spotlight, publicly saying he would not run, and privately indicating that his arm *might* be twisted if circumstance allowed. Yet the circumstances started to become less favorable for a Roosevelt candidacy by the middle of 1911.

Wisconsin Senator Robert La Follette, perhaps the most prominent Republican progressive after Roosevelt, declared that he would run against Taft. "Fightin' Bob" La Follette had harbored White House ambitions ever since being elected to the Senate in 1906. He was making the bet that Roosevelt refused to do, running on the belief that the progressive wing was strong enough to triumph over the "stand-patters" in the fight for the 1912 Republican nomination. Some of Roosevelt's closest supporters became donors to the La Follette campaign, and by October the Wisconsin senator had won the endorsement of the National Progressive Republican Conference (an organization he had helped create one year earlier).[1]

Even as Roosevelt continued to dither, the sustained attention paid to both him and La Follette—and the rise of these new sorts of organizations that endorsed candidates but stood apart from the regular party machinery—signaled fundamental changes in the American political system. The nineteenth-century United States was long characterized as "a state of courts and parties," in which a seemingly small federal bureaucracy and individual political leaders were subsumed in importance by the actions of the judiciary and the power of the two major political parties.[2]

Nineteenth-century politics was intensely local, and intensely personal. It also was a major source of entertainment. The parties orchestrated torchlight parades, festive rallies, and neighborhood parties. They delivered jobs, political favors, and Thanksgiving turkeys to those who were loyal to them.

This system led to extraordinarily high voter turnout. In the 1896 presidential election, close to 80 percent of eligible voters went to the polls—and, by and large, voted straight party line tickets.

Yet that same year also introduced new methods of presidential campaigning that upended the old order and created a new partisan apparatus that made campaigning in the twentieth century far different from the nineteenth. Party dominance of all levels of government, from urban political machines to Congressional committees, had begun to decline as progressive reform gained traction in big cities and reform-minded leaders came into power in politics and in the media. Reconfigured party power created an opening for "candidate-centered politics," in which individual candidates became the axes around which elections revolved. Although the 1896 Republican nominee, William McKinley, and his Democratic rival, William Jennings Bryan, had radically different political philosophies and campaign styles, both of their campaigns helped define the nature of the new style of modern campaigning. Bryan barnstormed the country with his Jeffersonian message of agrarian populism. Already well known for his oratorical gifts and charismatic self-presentation, he drew large and enthusiastic crowds. McKinley, in contrast, had the crowds come to him. From the front porch of his Canton, Ohio, home, McKinley gave an audience to any who desired one, and gave speeches while standing on a box or chair. This "front-porch campaign" drew thousands of supporters to Canton over the final weeks of the campaign, and won the attention of thousands more through newspaper coverage of this novel campaign strategy.[3]

Changes in the media landscape of course also contributed to the rise of the candidate-centered campaign. A proliferation of newspapers and magazines competed for readers' eyeballs by reporting on impassioned speeches and colorful political personalities. At the same time, a press that once was fiercely partisan began to adopt a journalistic ethos of impartiality and objectivity. With all these changes, the candidate, not the party, became the center of attention.[4]

In this new environment, a candidate's missteps mattered. In 1912, Robert La Follette made many of them. La Follette thought of himself as a game-changer and rabble-rouser, but he was reluctant to leave the comforts of Washington and regular Senate business to go on the stump. He gave speeches and statements that were guarded in their declarations of progressive values. His campaign sputtered through the summer and fall. In February 1912, it received its death knell when La Follette gave a meandering, vitriolic speech in Philadelphia to a group of newspaper publishers that began at midnight and lasted until nearly 2 a.m. His daughter had been ill, the campaign had proved exhausting, and La Follette perhaps had a little too much to drink earlier in the evening. All these triggered a speech that proved a "rambling, disconnected attack on his audience and the sinister influence of the press." In its wake, the senator, reported to be "on the verge of a physical breakdown," canceled all his campaign events.[5] If progressive Republicans wanted a candidate who might win it all, Roosevelt soon seemed to be the best bet.

Back in Washington, reluctant campaigner Taft was baffled and distressed by this politics of personality. "It seems to me that intelligent men have lost their heads and are leaning toward fool, radical views in a way I never thought possible. . . . The day of the demagogue, the liar, and the silly is on."[6]

By this time, all the uncertainty and speculation about whether Roosevelt would run destroyed what was left of the Roosevelt-Taft friendship. The stress manifested itself in Taft's waistline, as he ballooned to 332 pounds. Roosevelt's opinion of his judicious, loyal lieutenant had plummeted; by August 1911 he was characterizing Taft as "a flubdub with a streak of the second-rate and common in him."[7] Roosevelt's ego colored his assessment. The rapturous crowds that greeted TR at every turn, and the reporters who trailed his every step, gave the ex-president increased confidence in his chances. His confidantes urged him on, and his letters back to them became more encouraging. By January 1912 he wrote progressive journalist Henry Beach Needham that if a nomination "comes to me as a genuine public movement of course I will accept."[8]

After La Follette's Philadelphia meltdown, Roosevelt finally stopped being coy, and announced he would contest Taft for the Republican nomination. On 21 February he traveled to Ohio to deliver a major address designed to kick off his campaign. The speech he delivered rehashed the New Nationalism themes he had been trumpeting for eighteen months, and staked a new, quite radical position supporting the recall of judges whose decisions went against the will of the voters. While Roosevelt indicated he was "pleased over the stir he made," the address was a thunderbolt for the Republican conservative wing, and ultimately turned out to be quite damaging to Roosevelt's chances.[9]

Funnily enough, Roosevelt's decision to run against his former protégé was probably the one thing that fueled Taft to do what he always hated doing: campaign for office. Taft may not have wanted to be president, but he really, really did not want Roosevelt to win. "Sometimes a man in a corner fights," Taft thundered to an audience in Boston. "I am going to fight." As Roosevelt had once observed in the happier days of their friendship, Taft was "one of the best haters he had ever known."[10]

Personal politics lit a fire under Taft, but he also had the great advantage of having spent more than a year working the party machinery to win key blocs of support. While Roosevelt was barnstorming, Taft and his aides were doing the quiet, deliberate work of locking up Republican delegates. Individual charisma and media attention had chipped away at the parties' influence, but the nineteenth-century way of politics still very much held sway in 1912. Moreover, Taft was the sitting president. Having once enjoyed the benefits of incumbency, Roosevelt recognized Taft's advantages and was quick to characterize them as corrupt. "He has not a chance of being nominated if he relies merely on the people," TR wrote Andrew Carnegie as the primary season heated up. "His sole chance, and excellent one, lies in having the wish of the people thwarted by the activity of the Federal office holders under him."[11]

Roosevelt's popularity shone through as he won big states like Illinois and sizeable delegate chunks in Pennsylvania. Vote for vote, Roosevelt won the primaries by a big margin; the combination of votes for Teddy and his Progressive competitor La Follette were nearly twice those for conservative Taft. The president was disappointed. "We had hoped by May 1 to have votes enough to nominate," he wrote his brother Horace. Although things were uncertain, "I shall not withdraw under any condition." The stakes were too high: "it seems to me that I am the only hope against radicalism and demagogy."[12]

The New Politics

On the other side of the political aisle, twentieth-century modern campaigning and nineteenth-century partisan traditions were coming into conflict as well. While Roosevelt threw rhetorical bombs and Taft stealthily worked the party machinery, the Democrats also wrestled with the growing divide between old-schoolers and reformers.

After his victory in the New Jersey governor's race, Woodrow Wilson became a national figure and fresh face for a Democratic Party in need of a new image. Woodrow Wilson Clubs sprang up across the nation, driving support for the New Jersey governor to move to the national stage. A high-minded introvert, Wilson was less a true believer than appearances suggested; "his political convictions," noted his biographer, "were never as fixed as his ambition."[13] In 1911, Wilson sensed that the progressive mood was one he could take all the way to the White House, and he set out on a national tour to build support for his nomination.

Although Woodrow Wilson's rectitude was a far cry from the red-meat populism of William Jennings Bryan, he was progressive in his advocacy of government action to break up corporate monopolies, reform the tariff and banking systems, and reduce the influence of special interests. While not delivering many policy specifics, Wilson gave stirringly progressive speeches and had a winning manner on the stump, where he liked to open an event by reciting a limerick composed for the occasion. He also had the great advantage of strong support in the New York-based national press, where he had cultivated strong relationships with editors during his years in neighboring New Jersey.

Wilson's meteoric political career as a national politician was only possible because of the fundamental shifts in the structure and nature of electoral politics put in motion by progressive reform itself. By 1912, the effort to clean up corruption at all levels of government had successfully replaced many patronage jobs with nonpartisan, professional civil service systems. To end the influence of special interests like big railroads and big oil over state legislatures, reformers pushed through innovations like the initiative and referendum, putting ordinary voters in charge of decisions once left to elected officials. Western states like California, Washington, and Oregon became early movers in this system of direct democracy, and in 1911 California elected a new governor, Hiram Johnson, a former Republican who ran on the ticket of the newly formed Progressive Party.[14]

A second significant reform was the direct primary. In the nineteenth century, both Democrats and Republicans nominated most of their candidates for office through caucuses or party conventions. Unsurprisingly, these mechanisms gave party insiders the advantage, and made it extremely difficult for reform-minded newcomers to obtain electoral office. Secrecy and insider deal-making also allowed corporations—railroads, steel, oil—to maintain a stranglehold on state and national politics by making sure politicians beholden to their interests were nominated and elected, again and again. In the years leading up to 1912, reformers in many states agitated

Figure 5. Woodrow Wilson a few hours after nomination, 2 July 1912. While many
changes had come to presidential politics by 1912, some old traditions remained,
including the practice of candidates not attending nominating conventions.
Here, Woodrow Wilson greets reporters from his seaside home in New Jersey
after receiving news that he would become the Democrats' nominee.
Bain News Service, Library of Congress.

for replacing these systems with direct primary voting—more public, more
professionalized, more democratic. An accompanying reform was adoption
of the secret ballot. By 1910, two-thirds of the states had adopted the direct
primary.[15]

The diminished party power and the rise of candidate-centered electoral
politics set in motion some profound changes in the way people ran for
president. In the old system, candidates could stay out of the fray. Political
operatives and party leaders did the speeches, led the parades, and mobilized voters. In an era of rough-and-tumble, mudslinging politics, presidential candidates did not need to sully themselves with the daily routines of
the stump, much less attend the rowdy and argumentative national political
conventions. In stark contrast to modern conventions that serve as multi-
day infomercials for party and nominee, early twentieth-century candidates

didn't attend these party gatherings. They left the nominating process to the professionals, and then they gave an acceptance speech at a later date. Incumbency conferred even more insulation from the campaign trail, as most sitting presidents ran "Rose Garden campaigns," rarely leaving the White House.

In the new system, advantages started to accrue to candidates like Wilson and Roosevelt who hit the road, giving speech after speech. The bigger the crowd, the better. Yet candidates and campaigns needed to be strategic in the places they visited and when they visited them. The rise of the direct primary and decline of party influence shifted the electoral math. Wooing party insiders in key states remained critically important—as Taft's campaign was showing by mid-1912—but popular momentum built by personal visits by the candidate had a growing effect on electoral outcomes.

The rise of the New York-based national media added fuel to the fire. Technology allowed fast-breaking news—from elections to baseball scores—to be reported across the country. The rise of national newspaper chains meant that the same stories appeared in papers from East to West. The rise in the media also meant other things started grabbing Americans' attention away from politics and toward sports, or show business, or sensational true-crime stories. This forced candidates and their campaign managers to be more dogged and creative in getting press attention. They could do this either by being charismatic and entertaining, or by making bold, headline-worthy policy proclamations—or both.

Living only a short train ride from the center of the media universe, Wilson not only benefited from the rise of a new journalistic elite but also mastered the art of making headlines. He staked a claim as a leader for a new era, but he was a different breed of Progressive than Roosevelt. Still a Southerner in allegiance and temperament, Wilson was a strong defender of states' rights and a believer in maintaining the southern racial order. He fell in with many others in his party by having little patience with Roosevelt's New Nationalism, which appeared to put a dangerous amount of power in the hands of the federal government.

Wilsonian progressivism was one that reached more boldly into the corporate capitalist order by arguing that the great trusts should not just be regulated, as Roosevelt advocated, but broken up altogether. He coupled this antitrust stance with support of strong regulation at the state level. Wilson simultaneously carried the conservative banner of limited federal control while articulating a progressive message of a government that fought for the interests of ordinary citizens. While derided in Republican-leaning editorial pages as "the New Jersey school master," Wilson represented an exciting new hope for a Democratic Party desperate to win the White House. He was a traditionalist of the nineteenth century and technocrat of the twentieth: a potent combination in an election year that blended past and present.[16]

The Conventional and Unconventional

For both Democrats and Republicans, the 1912 national conventions became where the tensions between the new politics and the old order burst out into the open. Although conventions during this era were often rowdy affairs, the 1912 editions were remarkable in their furious back-room dealmaking, cliffhanger votes, and dramatic public displays of raw emotion and personal animosity. Yet personal feuds were not the sole engine of discord, but merely reflections of bigger, fundamentally divisive policy differences in each party. Both Democratic and Republican unity foundered on divisions of class, region, and political philosophy.

Personal resentments and internal tensions had brewed through the Republican primary season. Taft and Roosevelt's attacks on each other had gotten fiercer as the spring wore on. Despite the wild popularity of Roosevelt and the uninspiring campaign of Taft, the race was very close. This was mostly the fault of TR, who was so swept up in his celebrity that he mistook popular adoration for real political support, and who spent so much of his time in a Progressive echo chamber of supportive friends that he underestimated the strong support that remained within the GOP for "old-fashioned" issues like the protective tariff. He dismissed the old guard as corrupt and patronage-addled, and came out swinging against some core issues of the Republican platform.

Taft, in contrast, reached out to state delegations and placed allies in critical party positions where they would have control of when, where, and who voted during the Republican Convention. Despite the rise of the direct primary, 15 of the 48 states still adhered to the old system. Even the primaries that were direct were not binding. Convention delegates did not have to follow the will of the people; a state that went one way in the primary did not necessarily have to back the same candidate at the convention.[17]

Figure 6. Udo J. Keppler, "Salvation Is Free, But It Doesn't Appeal to Him," 7 August 1912. After Taft beat Roosevelt for the Republican nomination, and TR bolted to run as a third-party candidate, the battle for the GOP's soul began. In this August 1912 cartoon, Puck's Joseph Keppler satirizes the evangelical fervor of Roosevelt and the conservative recalcitrance of Taft and his allies. In reality, the two men were not all that far apart in matters of policy. Library of Congress.

The stickiness of the math became apparent as the Republican Convention opened in Chicago in early June. Roosevelt and Taft were the leading candidates, but La Follette was still in the race, as were others. There were so many contested delegates that no candidate had the number needed to win the nomination. Letters flew between Roosevelt and his allies darkly predicting that the Taft forces would stop at nothing to obtain the nomination, and framing the contest in stark good-and-evil terms. "My concern for this country has been the attitude of so many educated persons," wrote Roosevelt on 4 June, while Taft championed "the cause of the political bosses and of special privilege in the business world."[18]

Roosevelt's greatest fears started to come to fruition as the Republican National Committee came together in Chicago a week before the convention's start, and started to rule on the 254 delegates not yet committed to a candidate. By the time they were finished, 235 of these votes had been awarded to Taft. By the time the convention formally opened, the president's forces were in control.

Roosevelt decided it was time for some bold moves. Two days before the opening night of the full convention, in a headline-making break with tradition, he came to Chicago in person. Predictably, he got an overwhelming reception. Amid a summer heat wave, the streets of the city were packed with crowds shouting "we want Teddy!" and brass bands playing rousing marches. Speaking to a packed house of supporters in the same building where the convention would take place, he proclaimed that his fears of vote-stealing had come to pass: "we are fighting for honesty against naked robbery." In a subsequent letter to the Republican party leaders, he called on them to reverse the actions of the National Committee members, which, Roosevelt asserted, had stolen "eighty or ninety delegates" and "substitute[d] a dishonest for an honest majority."[19]

Things went from bad to worse once the Convention got underway on 17 June. Inside a sweltering convention hall, fistfights broke out. When Taft's supporters tried to take the floor, Roosevelt's people whistled and tooted, shouting "steamroller!" When the vote finally was taken, Roosevelt delegates sat on their hands in protest. Roosevelt's evangelistic outcry had little effect, however, and in fact may have further slimmed his chances of overcoming the old guard. Taft's supporters dug in their heels. La Follette, who might have been a potent ally in the fight against the stand-patters, refused to join forces with his old rival or displace the Taft men who were running the convention machinery.[20]

When the vote was taken, 558 went for Taft and 501 for his rivals. While new politics may have dominated the primaries, the GOP convention was old politics at its finest. Taft, the reluctant politician, won.

The Democratic Battle

The smoke was still clearing from the Republican showdown in Chicago when the Democrats gathered in Baltimore at the end of June 1912. When it opened, Woodrow Wilson did not even have close to the majority of delegates, much less the two-thirds majority needed under Democratic Party rules. There were a number of rivals to Wilson, and the leader in the delegate count was Champ Clark, speaker of the House, a plain-talking

Missourian and an old-style party politician. Clark was fond of saying things like "I sprang from the loins of the common people, God bless them! And I am one of them." His campaign theme song had a chorus that went "you gotta quit kickin' my dawg aroun'."[21]

Even though he had the delegate lead, the conventional wisdom was that Clark was not up to the job of being president. The other leading contenders—including powerful Alabama Representative Oscar Underwood—seemed old-fashioned, regional candidates. At the same time, an alarming number of delegates were "pledged to favorite sons" or "uncertain," which in this era meant their votes were controlled by powerful Democratic machines like New York's Tammany Hall. In the days leading up to the convention, Wilson was not particularly bullish that he could overcome the forces of tradition and inertia. "Just between you and me," he wrote his close friend Mary Hulbert, "I have not the least idea of being nominated, because the make of the convention is such . . . that the outcome is in the hands of professional, case-hardened politicians who serve only their own interests."[22]

Yet Wilson had some important advantages. He had a national network of wealthy supporters and endorsement from important newspapers across the continent, including the most powerful Democratic newspaper in the country, the *New York World*. Wilson stuck with tradition and didn't set foot in Baltimore, but he had state-of-the-art communications hooked to his seaside home in Sea Girt, New Jersey, that would keep him apprised of news soon after it happened.

The outcome of the Republican Convention altered the political calculus of the Democratic one. With Taft the winner, and Roosevelt likely to bolt and run as a third-party candidate, the drumbeat became stronger for the Democrats to nominate Wilson over conservatives like Clark and Underwood. Only a progressive could defeat TR. Funnily enough, the man who made sure this would come to pass was none other than the man whose defeats had hobbled the Democratic Party's national power: William Jennings Bryan. Despite the past electoral debacles, Bryan remained a powerful force in the party, and his passionate "Wall Street versus Main Street" populism retained a broad base of support in the Democratic base. Seeing how perilously close the Democrats were coming to nominating a conservative, Bryan launched a media campaign to turn things around. In a 21 June dispatch distributed to papers nationwide, he wrote: "with two reactionaries running for president, [Roosevelt] might win and thus entrench himself in power."[23]

Bryan then proceeded to drive the cause of reform on the floor of the Baltimore convention—seeding the same evangelistic fervor Roosevelt had done with his appearance in Chicago. Still a legendary orator, Bryan egged on progressive supporters in the convention hall and encouraged voters all over the country to telegram their support to the delegates. "The fight is on," shouted one delegate, "and Bryan is on one side and Wall Street is on the other."[24] The progressive forces took control of the proceedings. Nominating speeches began at midnight on Thursday evening and continued until the next morning. At 7 a.m. the first ballot was taken. Clark won—but not a two-thirds majority. Another vote. Still no clear winner. The behind-the-scenes deal-making was furious. Through Friday and Saturday, vote after vote, Wilson started to chip away at Clark's lead. The delegates took Sunday off for church and rest—and more negotiations in hotel rooms and barrooms. Over the course of multiple rounds of balloting, day after day of the convention, Wilson steadily increased his support. On Tuesday 2 July—on the 46th round of voting—Wilson secured 990 votes, enough to win the nomination.[25]

Wilson's nomination victory had to do with smart politics, good press, the weaknesses of his opponents, the power of his allies, and incredible luck. One Washington pundit later said of Wilson: if he "was to fall out of a sixteen story building . . . he would hit on a feather bed." Wilson saw a higher power at work. Later, after his election, he would say quite simply: "God ordained me to be the next president of the United States."[26]

Bolting from the Parties

Once William Howard Taft beat Theodore Roosevelt to win the Republican nomination, the ex-president did what most people had suspected for a while: he bolted. He broke with the party that had been his home since the beginning, taking a large cohort of earnest reformers with him. Driven by personal animus and a healthy dose of messianic zeal, Roosevelt became the presidential candidate of the newly formed Progressive Party. His crusade as a third-party candidate was seen by some (then and now) as quixotic and egotistical, yet the ideas he advanced during what came to be known as the "Bull Moose" campaign crystallized ideas about the role of government, and the need for a countervailing force against the power of capitalist markets, that had been percolating for some time. Although running a flawed and ultimately unsuccessful campaign, Roosevelt nonetheless won a greater percentage of votes than any other third-party candidate before or since, and his progressive campaign put radical ideas into the political mainstream in ways that shaped the Wilson presidency, the New Deal, and the character of the American state into the early twenty-first century.

The kickoff for this new political era came in August, when Roosevelt returned to Chicago—the site of the Republican Convention two months before—for the inaugural nominating convention of the Progressive Party. Instead of bejeweled millionaires' wives sitting in the front row, there were ranks of young women, reformers and settlement workers, in simple white cotton shirtwaists. Reporters repeatedly compared it to a religious revival. "It was more like a Methodist consecration meeting than a political gathering," commented one scribe.[27] Roosevelt himself contributed to the tone by naming his keynote address, "A Confession of Faith."

As Roosevelt stepped up to deliver it, he first basked in nearly a full hour of cheers, applause, the singing of hymns and patriotic songs. Once the hall finally quieted, he delivered a speech that was part sermon and part stem-winder, putting forth ideas that would have been considered radical only a few years before. "The old parties are husks with no real soul within either, divided on artificial lines, boss-ridden and privilege-controlled," Roosevelt trumpeted. "There must be a new party of nation-wide and non-sectional principles [representing] the cause of human rights and of governmental efficiency."[28]

After his speech, everyone in the hall was so moved that all had to join in a singing of "The Battle Hymn of the Republic" to pull themselves together. Then came the more routine business of the formal nomination. In her speech seconding the nomination of Roosevelt, settlement house pioneer and Progressive Party leader Jane Addams moved away from religious rhetoric and underscored the global implications of this new political organization: "the American exponent of a world-wide movement towards juster social conditions" and a "modern movement" whose time had come.[29] The finishing touch was the nomination of Hiram Johnson of California as Roosevelt's vice presidential running mate, uniting East and West under one national progressive banner.

Through the course of that fall, riding a wave of celebrity and unbound from party doctrine, Roosevelt traveled back and forth across the country

Figure 7. National Progressive Convention, Chicago, 6 August 1912. Taking place in
the same hall the Republicans had occupied earlier in the summer, the Progressive
Party convention presented a very different sort of political spectacle. Reporters
likened it to a religious revival, and played up the contrast between the bejeweled
millionaires' wives of the GOP convention and the young women who filled the
same seats at the Progressive gathering, wearing simple cotton shirtwaists and fervently
singing hymns and patriotic songs. Moffett Studio and Kaufmann,
Weimer & Fabry Co., Library of Congress.

spreading the Progressive gospel. He introduced policy ideas that foreshadowed the New Deal his cousin Franklin would usher in more than twenty
years later. He called for regulation to ensure on-the-job safety. He talked
about development of the impoverished and flood-prone Mississippi River
Valley. He proposed a minimum wage for women and restrictions on child
labor.[30]

The Progressive Party wasn't just Teddy Roosevelt. It ran many candidates in state and local races across the country in 1912. But it was dominated by Roosevelt's celebrity and outsized personality, so much that it
quickly became known by Roosevelt's own nickname, forever remembered

as "The Bull Moose Party." And if the Democrats and Republicans of 1912 were leaning toward modernity, the Progressives were thundering toward it, shaking off old political machinery, strategically using the press, and bringing new constituencies, especially women, into its tent. However, in becoming so closely associated with one leader, the Progressive Party—like other third-party efforts afterward—lost much of its steam when that leader was no longer at its helm.

In the fall of 1912, however, the Bull Moose was going strong. And his full-throated message of reform was irritating the heck out of Eugene V. Debs.

While Republicans imploded and Democrats battled, the Socialist Party had been steadily building support among working-class constituencies across the country. In the years since Debs had launched his first insurgent presidential campaign in 1904, the Socialists had moved from being seen as ultraradical to nearly respectable. In both 1904 and 1908 Debs had won close to half a million votes. By 1912, both Milwaukee and Syracuse had elected Socialist mayors. The Party had denounced the violent tactics of labor radicals and distanced itself from the anarchist fringe. One socialist paper proclaimed, "the American Socialist is no longer a creature of hoofs and horns."[31] While Socialism still operated on the margins of mainstream politics, and Eugene Debs had no illusions he would actually win the presidency, he sensed that 1912 could be the year his party could become a significant electoral force.[32]

When he formally kicked off his campaign in June with what a Socialist paper termed a "monster picnic" in Chicago, Debs expressed increasing confidence in the Socialists' chances as the standard-bearing agent of true reform. "There is no longer even the pretense of difference between the so-called Republican and Democratic parties," he told the crowd, "they are substantially one in what they stand for." The infighting of the primary season showed that "both of these old capitalist class machines are going to pieces" and their destruction was imminent, and inevitable.[33]

Roosevelt's breakaway from the Republicans challenged this formulation, but in Debs's estimation TR was just as much a capitalist tool as ever. So Debs fumed when Roosevelt started saying things leftists had been saying for years. He steamed as Roosevelt brazenly stole the Socialist brand by making a red kerchief a symbol of his Bull Moose campaign. As the fall campaign neared, Debs dismissed the Progressive's claims of true reform and reminded his working-class audiences that only the Socialists would

fight for their interests. "The Republican, Democratic and Progressive conventions were composed in the main and controlled entirely by professional
politicians in the service of the ruling class," he raged in August. "Wage-
slaves would not have been tolerated in their company."[34]

The problem was that Debs was good at taking others down, and not so
good at saying what he would do differently. His speeches were energetic,
but skimpy on the policy details. Discontented voters might have turned to
Socialism as a third-party alternative, but now the rise of the Progressive
Party created another outlet for this voter frustration. Progressives had taken
up some radical ideas, and in doing so they had left the true radicals behind.

Woodrow Wilson also saw TR as his chief rival as the fall campaign
began. "The contest is between him and me," he wrote Mary Hulbert, "not
Taft and me." Wilson worried about how he'd stack up. Roosevelt "appeals
to their imagination; I do not," he admitted. "He is a real, vivid person . . .
I am a vague, conjectural personality." With these concerns in mind, Wilson fired up the progressive rhetoric and the political theatrics as he hit the
campaign trail.[35]

Wilson's first major address of the fall campaign was on Labor Day in
Buffalo to a large, largely working-class crowd. Denouncing corporate greed
and worker injustices, he sounded similar themes to TR but drew stark
contrasts between how he and his Progressive opponent would address
these problems. Regulating business, as Roosevelt proposed to do, was not
enough. Creating a large government bureaucracy to manage markets and
institute things like the minimum wage would be even worse for the working class than the current order, Wilson argued. "Do you want to be taken
care of by a combination of the government and the monopolies?" he asked
his audience (a listener shouted out, "No!").[36]

This message won Wilson key endorsements, most notably Samuel
Gompers, head of the American Federation of Labor, as well as many of the
populist Westerners who had once supported Bryan. This well-mannered,
professorial candidate was taking on the issues and interests that most
appealed to them and speaking eloquently about their individual rights and
freedoms.

The notion of individual rights—and the idea that a large, central government threatened personal autonomy and opportunity—was a critical
distinction between what Wilson called his "New Freedom" and Roosevelt's "New Nationalism." For Roosevelt, a strong and more muscular government in Washington could regulate a runaway capitalist system and

ensure rights through expert and efficient public administration. Wilson had a states'-rights centered philosophy that argued that the only way to ensure the rights of all was to break up the large corporations and resist the creation of a large central bureaucracies. States and localities should be the loci of government activism. Washington should stay out of the way. This was the debate that had animated partisan politics since the days of Jefferson and Hamilton, updated for the modern industrial era.

At the end of the day, both men had the same goals—and thought political action was the way to achieve them. But they had different visions of how Washington should go about it. This distinction would have an important legacy on politics through the rest of the twentieth century.

The Home Stretch

By October, the election was all about Roosevelt and Wilson. Eugene Debs was off preaching to the Socialist faithful, but not winning many converts. His campaign schedule was highly unstrategic, planned according to where Debs had the largest numbers of supporters—not according to where the largest numbers of electoral votes were in play. As has happened other times in leftist politics, it was difficult to mobilize a disciplined, well-organized campaign led by people and groups whose political ideology was firmly anti-establishment and anti-hierarchical, and who strongly disdained central organization.

After his victory at the Republican Convention, nearly nothing could go right for William Howard Taft. Even by late July, he was already complaining, "there is no news from me except that I played golf." By late September, he glumly wrote a friend, "I am already reconciled to defeat." To add insult to injury, Taft's vice president James Sherman died about a week before Election Day, forcing him to rustle up a last-minute replacement.[37]

By that point, no one seemed to notice or care. The Republican Party establishment had concluded that Taft was not going to win, yet the party bosses hated Roosevelt for his betrayal. Instead, they actively campaigned for Wilson. The GOP had imploded on itself, and Wilson was the beneficiary. Roosevelt's weaknesses, too, were starting to lessen the momentum of the campaign over the fall months. His positions on regulation (rather than breaking up monopolies) as well as his failure to range too far from

Figure 8. "The Statesman's Playtime—Hon. William H. Taft on the Golf Links, at Hot
Springs, Virginia," 1908. President Taft found it difficult to draw the attention of
voters and reporters away from the electrifying race between Wilson and Roosevelt.
Ignored by the media and isolated from old allies, the incumbent president
complained as early as July that "there is no news from me except that I played golf."
Keystone View Company, Library of Congress.

Republican orthodoxy on the tariff created weak spots Wilson exploited in
his increasingly effervescent appearances on the stump.

There was still another twist yet to come in this pivotal campaign, however. By 14 October, Roosevelt had visited 32 states since his nomination.
He had given over 150 speeches. His voice was hoarse, and despite his
incredible strength and endurance, his energy was flagging. Although he'd
canceled two speeches in the days before, Roosevelt insisted on speaking in
Milwaukee—a Socialist stronghold and a great place to stake his claim as
an alternative to Debs and to counter some of Wilson's attacks.

Just like everywhere on the campaign trail, crowds of admirers surrounded Roosevelt as he climbed into an open-air car to travel from his

hotel to the lecture hall. He stood up to wave and shake more hands. As he did so, a man broke from the group, drew a gun, and shot the candidate at close range.

Amazingly, the bullet's path stopped short of Roosevelt's heart—blocked by an eyeglass case and the 50-page speech manuscript in Roosevelt's breast pocket. This saved his life. Bleeding from the chest, Roosevelt insisted on delivering the speech before accepting medical help. He told his audience, "It takes more than that to kill a bull moose." The shooting and Roosevelt's extraordinary speech after it dominated the news for the rest of the campaign, bringing voters' attention back from the World Series and other news of the day. Oddsmakers were rating TR's chances as 1 in 4 before the assassination attempt. After, his chances improved to almost 1 in 2.

Yet it was not enough to change the course of the race. After suspending his campaign to allow Roosevelt to recover, Wilson went back on the stump for a furious last round of speeches and events.

Election day was 5 November. And it was an electoral landslide for Wilson. He won 40 states. Roosevelt won 6. Taft won 2. The popular vote was less clear-cut. Wilson only won a plurality, not a majority of the popular vote. Roosevelt came in second, with 27 percent. Taft was third, with 23 percent. The Socialists won nearly a million votes, but their total fell far short of what Debs and his colleagues dreamed of at the start of 1912.

Turnout in the election of 1912 demonstrated how much the political system had changed in this age of reform. Overall, less than 60 percent of eligible voters went to the polls. In 1896, before the widespread adoption of the direct primary and other progressive reforms, turnout had been 80 percent. The system had been modernized and the parties' power curbed, but at the cost of broad-based popular participation. The 1912 turnout set a precedent followed by most presidential elections of the twentieth century and the early twenty-first.

The Legacy

In the aftermath of election, the four candidates went in different directions. Some stayed in the spotlight, and others receded. William Howard Taft got to depart the job he hated and, nine years later, he got the job he always dreamed about, when Warren Harding appointed him chief justice of the Supreme Court.

Eugene Debs would go on to run again for president—including campaigning from prison while awaiting a verdict on charges of sedition—but 1912 would be his finest hour. He and the Socialists would never poll quite as strongly again, and their political legitimacy came under attack in the days during and after World War I, when the Bolshevik Revolution and an increasingly isolationist American public ushered in increasingly anti-immigrant sentiment and marginalized the voices arguing for alternatives to capitalism. By the early 1920s, Socialist leaders like Debs as well as other leftist radicals were being harassed, arrested, and deported. The American Left would not have a major impact on national politics until the Great Depression validated some of their arguments about the failures and inequities of capitalism.

Teddy Roosevelt had lost, and he hated it. Victory had seemed close at certain points, and defeat was made worse by the fact that a progressive candidate won—and that candidate was not Roosevelt. So Roosevelt went hunting again, setting off on a sixteen-month voyage down the Amazon. Along the way, he contracted malaria and a serious leg infection. He came back and stayed active in national affairs, but he never ran for president again. The Progressive Party tried to recruit him as a candidate in 1916, but he declined their offer. Illnesses from the Amazon left him weakened for the rest of his life. The hyperkinetic, ebullient Roosevelt died at the surprisingly young age of sixty in 1919. Taft came to the funeral and stayed longer than anyone else. After the crowds of mourners had dissipated, Taft stood, weeping, by Roosevelt's grave.

Not only did Wilson win the White House but the Democrats won control of both houses of Congress. This meant passage of quite a number of reformist policies that owed a big debt to Teddy Roosevelt's insurgent progressive campaign. Ironically, although he campaigned against big government, President Wilson presided over a steady increase in central government authority over his two terms. During his term in office, the United States established the Federal Reserve System to reform and regulate banking. A federal income tax imposed limits on the great fortunes of America's wealthy. Support of labor unions, aid for education and agriculture, and other progressive initiatives brought the country closer to other industrialized nations in its social policy programs. The size and influence of the central government jumped even further after the formal U.S. entry into

World War I in 1917, which created a wartime economy driven by military spending and regulated by federal price controls. By the time Wilson left office, the Democratic Party in many ways had moved away from its nineteenth-century agrarian and regionalist past and toward a modern, technocratic future. Despite the continued prominence of segregationist and agrarian Southern interests, the Democratic Party had begun to exhibit recognizable contours of modern liberalism that William Jennings Bryan had laid out in 1896 and to which Wilson had given added political legitimacy with his win sixteen years later. In 1912, it was unclear which party would become the party of progressive reform. By 1920, it was becoming clear that the Democrats would be that party.[38]

The election of 1912 was the moment the American political system had its first major reckoning with the challenges of industrial capitalism, and we can draw three important lessons from this. First, the reckoning changed the two major parties—but it didn't destroy them. This was a moment when either the Democrats or the Republicans could have become *the* Progressive party, and the title went to the Democrats while the conservatives consolidated their power in the GOP. Although Wilson campaigned on small government, it was the Republicans who went forth in the twentieth century as the party of small government, of unfettered markets, of fiscal conservatism.

There are some lessons about third parties here. The pattern we see in 1912 has repeated itself since. Independent parties introduce new ideas into the political system, turning the radical into the mainstream. But they often lack the organization to sustain the momentum after their celebrity candidates leave the spotlight. Instead, the two major parties open their tent flaps, and bring the new parties and their voters in. As historian Richard Hofstadter famously observed some decades later, "Third parties are like bees. They sting, and then they die."[39]

Second, 1912 showcased a new style of politics that had its roots in the 1896 election but had gained important momentum by economic, technological, social, and political changes in the intervening years. Political reform and the new media made elections about candidates, not about parties. Charisma and celebrity mattered, as Teddy Roosevelt's journey showed. Barnstorming tours and good relationships with the media mattered, as Woodrow Wilson exemplified. Staying put in the White House and relying on party machinery to win elections no longer worked. Taft learned this lesson the hard way.

Third, this election redefined the role of government in industrial America after fifty years of incredible change. It introduced ideas that were under debate a century later. The 1912 election was one where a consensus emerged that a government should do more than deliver the mail and have a standing army. It should protect workers, regulate markets, and ensure basic freedoms. Politicians then, and politicians now, generally agree on this basic principle but differ on the way to get there. Is the United States a nation that has an activist central government? Where markets are strongly regulated? Should government spend big? Should it raise taxes? Or should America be a nation that has less interference in individual lives? Should it deregulate business, and cut taxes?

Now, it wasn't as if everything changed and stayed that way after 1912. The political road is rarely that straight. Change takes time. While Wilson and a Democrat-led Congress ushered in a remarkable amount of reform, the progressive and activist momentum slowed in the 1920s. A world war, anti-immigrant sentiment, and rising prosperity for many Americans tamped down the urge for change. Even women winning the right to vote did not—to the surprise of many—alter the general political temperament of the American public. Parties adapted to the modern styles of campaigning, and to the reformed, media-driven political system. They regained some of their power. So, in some respects, things seemed to go quiet in the '20s. As the 30s would show, however, the Progressive impulse was dormant—not dead.

The next chapter explores what happened when those Progressive ideas came back, and continues to examine the legacies of the age of reform on modern presidential politics.

PART II

* * *

1932

CHAPTER 3

*

The Road to the New Deal

If 1912 was a good year to be a Democrat, 1928 most certainly was not. It was, wrote Democratic operative James A. Farley, "a disaster as overwhelming as anything that ever happened in [the Party's] century of existence." Although the decade began with the scandal-marred Republican presidency of Warren Harding, the era of his successor Calvin Coolidge had been one of buoyant prosperity and economic optimism, of rising incomes and rising consumption. Coolidge's secretary of commerce Herbert Hoover embraced this sunny outlook when he became Republican presidential nominee in 1928, proclaiming that "we in America today are nearer to the final triumph over poverty than ever before in the history of any land." The majority of American voters appeared to agree, giving Hoover a landslide victory. Despondent Democrats, wrote Farley, felt that "breaking the power of the Republican Party seemed impossible." Perhaps the Democratic Party itself had "outlived its usefulness."[1]

Even when the stock market crashed in late October 1929—a "Black Tuesday" that came after nearly two months of roller-coaster volatility—many observers regarded it as a blip on the broader economic picture. With only 2 percent of Americans holding any investments in the market, the crash seemed like a crisis for Wall Street, not for Main Street. If history served as a guide, the market would right itself eventually just as it had in other crises and panics, which had occurred with some regularity since the beginning of the industrial age. Stock market crashes were an inevitable side effect of industrial capitalism, so the reasoning went, and the market corrected itself over time.[2]

One person who did not buy into the conventional wisdom was President Herbert Hoover, who looked at Wall Street with some worry. Things were different from what they had been in previous market dips. In the wake of World War I, the U.S. economy was tied far more tightly than before to Europe, and European economies had been stumbling for close to two years. In war-ravaged Germany, which had been further hobbled by punitive sanctions and reparations obligations to the Allies, business failures were up and stock prices were falling by the summer of 1928. Stocks started plummeting in Great Britain, the Netherlands, and Sweden as well. In other industrialized nations like Canada and Japan, industrial output dropped and wholesale commodities prices rose. By the time what Hoover termed the "orgy of stock speculation" crested in the United States in the summer of 1929, driven by rising consumption and the ebullient public attitude that had helped get him elected, the ties that bound global commerce were pulling the United States in Europe's direction. As Hoover put it, "some readjustments were due."[3]

The global nature of the recession prompted Hoover to try to persuade American political and business leaders to take a more interventionist approach. Reassuring nervous markets was key, he recognized, but "it is action that counts."[4] A month after the Crash, he summoned the nation's business leaders to the White House for two weeks of intense discussion, emerging with some unprecedented measures to stabilize the economy, including an agreement that industries would not cut workers' pay. In an economy that had become driven by consumer spending, Hoover felt this concession by the industrialists was critical to economic stabilization.[5]

Hoover then turned to the nation's governors and mayors, urging them to do their part by fast-tracking infrastructure and construction projects that would put people to work and get the economy humming. He asked Congress for an additional $140 million to build new federal office buildings and facilities. The requests for new expenditures in a time of recession sat uncomfortably with some political leaders, including New York governor Franklin Delano Roosevelt. Spending should not exceed available revenues, Roosevelt warned, and with tax receipts down there was a limited amount his state should do. In a private letter to a friend, he looked on Hoover's energetic interventions with a jaundiced eye. "I am very much opposed to the extension of Federal action in most economy social problems," he wrote.[6]

How ironic, then, that four years after Hoover's landslide victory and three years after the Crash that he had worked so energetically to mitigate, he lost the presidency to Roosevelt. The governor who had expressed skepticism about the usefulness of federal intervention had campaigned on a bold message of government help and hope, attacking his opponent as hopelessly old-fashioned and out-of-touch. Hoover, a thoroughly modern workaholic who considered himself innovative in his thinking and effective in his leadership, could not believe what had befallen him. As he plaintively wrote in his memoirs, after recounting all that he had done to respond to the Depression, "it is not given even to Presidents to see the future."[7]

Yet the 1932 election set in motion that future: one in which the federal government had a much larger presence in Americans' lives than ever before, one where the personal connection of the president with the people mattered more than in the past, one shaped by media and political strategy and stagecraft. The broad contours of the defeat of Hoover and victory of Roosevelt have become familiar to readers of history textbooks and followers of presidential politics. As often happens, popular characterizations about the election and its legacy can diverge sharply, depending on who is making them. To some on the left, the election of 1932 is one in which the enlightened, bold White Knight triumphs over the old-fashioned and hard-hearted bumbler. Conservatives see it differently, as the triumph of a reckless ideologue over a prudent and effective statesman, and a disastrous start down a road of government bloat and high spending antithetical to the nation's founding principles and individual freedoms.[8]

The reality was not so linear, and much more interesting. For most of their lives, Hoover and Roosevelt traveled in the same circles and shared many ideas about the role of government. They were ideological heirs to TR and Wilson; they were progressive-minded technocrats rather than old-school partisans. For both men, these philosophies were tested and transformed by the economic disaster that unfolded after October 1929, and they emerged with distinctly different ideas about what the government should do and how it should do it. Over the course of a sharply fought and combative campaign, their relationship went from one of warm and respectful collegiality to one of mutual loathing. Out of the aftermath of the election, the two rivals went dramatically different ways, one presiding over an unprecedented expansion of the federal state and the other loudly urging that such expansions endangered the rights and liberties on which the country was founded. These political battle lines remain over eight decades later, and have shaped every election in between.

The Not-So-Roaring 1920s

As the story of the 1912 election showed, the massive changes of industrial-ization precipitated a flurry of Progressive debate and action between 1900 and 1920. The thirst for reform seemed to ebb with the end of the Wilson presidency, however. The national state had grown in size and activism during the Wilson years, thanks in no small measure to Democrats control-ling both houses of Congress as well as the White House, enabling them to push through long-debated measures like creation of the Federal Reserve System and establishment of a national income tax soon after Wilson took office. As Republicans retrenched, Democrats became the home base for many reformers, especially those fighting for the rights of working people to form trade unions, to have safe workplaces, and to ensure support in case of disability or death. After Roosevelt's Bull Moose run, the Progressive Party became a far less viable national political force, although insurgent third-party runs continued into the 1920s, siphoning reformist energy away from the two major parties.

The political landscape after the end of World War I also became a challenging one for reform and government activism. The over 100,000 U.S. war dead paled in comparison with the millions of European soldiers killed in the conflict, but many Americans nonetheless believed the price of foreign engagement had been far too high. While ordinary people had scrimped and saved, and sent their boys off to war, the financiers of Wall Street seemed to have made off like bandits, growing their already immense wealth by lending money to Great Britain and the other allies, and financing the great expansion of military production both before and after the United States formally entered the conflict. Adding to the wrenching human costs of the dead and wounded, and the resentment against those who had gotten rich in the process, was the glum economy that had resulted from wartime demobilization. Military spending had been a powerful stimulus to the economy, putting thousands to work and propelling millions of Americans to start migration from rural farms to bustling cities. This movement, par-ticularly that of African Americans escaping the injustices of the Jim Crow South, would continue for another six decades and fundamentally reshape the American political and economic landscape.[9]

The postwar economic slowdown pitted worker against worker in a competition for scarce jobs. This, coupled with rising anxiety about the threat of Communism in the wake of Russia's 1917 Bolshevik Revolution, drove virulent protests against blacks, immigrants, and political leftists and radicals. Against this backdrop of resentment and growing isolationism, Woodrow Wilson embarked on his crusade to convince the United States to join the League of Nations. Wilson's internationalist vision fell short of winning the support it needed. The enfeebled League went on without the United States in it. Already exhausted by barnstorming the country in support of the League's ratification, Wilson became debilitated by a series of strokes, and he died shortly after leaving office.

His Republican successors—Warren Harding and Calvin Coolidge—presided over a very different kind of White House. However, while the Harding and Coolidge eras may have appeared more laissez faire than the two decades of reform that preceded them, even these "conservative" years of the 1920s demonstrated how the definitions of national government responsibility had fundamentally changed. Although it was a consistent opponent of efforts to regulate markets and curb corporate power, the Republican-dominated executive branch of the 1920s presided over bold government interventions like Prohibition, unprecedented immigration restriction and deportation, and government revenue increases through raised tariffs on foreign imports. Moreover, a great deal of progressive social reform continued at the municipal and state levels, as citizen-activists and politicians of both parties pushed through further measures to protect workers, provide aid to mothers and children, and regulate commerce. American industrial society was no longer the free-for-all it had been in the Gilded Age. The era of reform left its mark. Yet the political mood was distinctly different from a decade earlier.[10]

The American people turned inward in the 1920s. Increasingly stringent quotas cut off new foreign immigration, especially for people from Southern and Eastern Europe and Russia; grassroots violence against foreigners and people of color escalated. The Ku Klux Klan reached its highest membership levels ever in the 1920s, and it was a national phenomenon, with some of its biggest chapters emerging north of the Mason-Dixon Line.[11]

America turned its back on the world because it could afford to do so. After the postwar economic slowdown, the U.S. industrial economy roared back within a few years, led by the boom in automobile industry. Innovations in manufacturing, distribution, and selling made consumer products better, cheaper, and more abundant. To reduce turnover and increase productivity, Henry Ford famously introduced "the five-dollar day" that doubled his workers' salary and benefits, and conveniently gave them enough in their pockets to purchase one of the Model T cars that rolled off Ford's assembly line. Decisions by Ford and others who ran giant companies employing hundreds of thousands reverberated across the American economy. To accommodate the needs of both Jews and Christians who desired a day off on the Sabbath, employers like Ford instituted the two-day weekend. Other industries followed suit. By 1929, Detroit was making 4.4 million cars per year. Most American households had a car—almost none had in 1900. The auto industry employed close to half a million people.

With more leisure time and with cars that allowed them to explore, American workers went to the movies and bought radios, home appliances, clothing, and other consumer products by the millions. Credit flowed easily, allowing families to make big purchases with only a little cash down. Homeownership went up, and speculative real estate bubbles grew. The biggest bubble was in swampy and subtropical Florida, where con men and respectable brokers alike sold small investors on the promise of making a quick dollar on second homes, apartments, and hotels. The popping of the real estate bubble in Florida and around the country in 1926 gave its victims a taste of the financial disasters that lay around the corner.

Easy credit, spiking consumer spending, and dependence on a few large employers meant that the prosperity of the Roaring Twenties was not built to last. But one would not have known it from the prognostications of the politicians in Washington, who continued to trumpet the message that the United States had entered a "new era" where old economic rules no longer applied. Irrational exuberance extended to the business world as well. Banker Paul Mazur (who, ironically, later became a key advisor to FDR's vaunted "Brains Trust") proclaimed in 1928, "there is every probability of a continued virility in the strength of American business."[12] Had they looked more closely at the particulars of this prosperity, however, political and business leaders might have been less bullish.

In truth, the Roaring Twenties were not roaring for everyone. The nation was really two Americas, divided and unequal. While average income levels rose overall between 1921 and 1929, the top 10 percent of earners saw their incomes rise much more steeply than those of everyone else, and by 1928 they had a 46 percent share of the national income. Average income statistics masked the large numbers of Americans who were barely getting by in the 1920s. At a time when the minimum income deemed necessary for a decent standard of living was $2,500, 71 percent of American families made less than that.[13]

Another dimension of the American divide was geographic. The 1920s were perhaps the high-water mark for the great American city. For the first time, more than half the nation's population lived in urban areas, and the great industrial metropolises became the centers of the decade's prosperity. Good manufacturing jobs paid well enough for families to buy cars, and gave enough time off to go to the movies and baseball games. Soaring new skyscrapers rose upward from city streets, downtown shopping districts bustled, and old slums gave way to new parks and parkways. Women cut their hair. Jazz music reigned. Prohibition was openly flouted.

The ascendance of urban culture masked the persistence of rural landscapes, where over 40 percent of Americans still lived in 1930. There, more than 80 percent of the population did not have indoor plumbing and 98 percent of farmhouses did not have electricity. Threatened by the "decadence" of the cities they read about in newspapers and watched at the weekly picture show, rural people even more strongly clung to traditional values. They supported the continuation of Prohibition. Some joined organizations like the KKK, many more—in countryside and city—joined churches, and evangelical movements and charismatic religious leaders drew many thousands of followers.[14]

More significantly, on the American farm, hard times had begun well in advance of Black Thursday. Just as new technologies had helped pump up manufacturing productivity, powerful and sophisticated new harvesters, combines, and tractors had opened millions of acres to cultivation in the 1920s. In doing so, they had not only sharply reduced the need for farm labor, but had helped spur a wave of overproduction that drove down commodity prices and depleted soils. The economic effects rippled over the countryside, from farmers to merchants to small-town banks. Again and again throughout the 1920s, Congress introduced bills creating price supports for beleaguered farmers, only to be vetoed by the Coolidge White House.[15]

Despite the triumphal messages he delivered on the stump in 1928, Herbert Hoover had watched all these things with some worry over the course of the 1920s. On New Year's Day 1926, as commerce secretary, he had warned, "psychology plays a large part in business movements, and overoptimism can only land us on the shores of overdepression."[16] Compounding the problem of this magical thinking was a dearth of reliable statistical information on the American economy. There were not monthly or weekly measurements of employment or output. Reliable poll data were nonexistent; economic statistics were far less dependable or predictive.

Figure 9. Unemployed men queuing outside a depression soup kitchen opened in
Chicago by Al Capone, 1931. The scope and depth of the Great Depression left few
Americans untouched, and left traditional sources of authority and welfare unable
to cope with the effects of mass unemployment. National Archives.

The instability and deep inequality that had characterized the not-so-
Roaring Twenties meant that the there was little to stop the American economy from sliding into a deeper economic hole in the wake of the 1929
crash. And by 1931 that hole had opened up. An independent-minded Federal Reserve had declined to infuse new capital into shaky markets, as central banks often did during economic crisis. Wall Street's crisis spread to
Main Street by 1930, as small community banks started failing, one by one,
adding up to over 9,000 closures over the next three years.

Then, in 1931, the enfeebled economies of Europe started to go off the
edge. The previous year, Hoover had signed into law a protective tariff that,
ironically, had its roots in a desire to help beleaguered American farmers
by fending off foreign competition. This highly restrictive measure, while
adhering to Republican economic orthodoxy, proved devastating. Of all the

policy actions Hoover took in response to the Depression, the tariff had the biggest effect—one that was negative, rather than positive. Deeply indebted to American banks since the end of the war, and lacking any means to pay off their debts, European economies went into a tailspin as the drying up of Stateside credit cut off the stream of capital to debtor nations and the tariff restricted their ability to sell to American consumers. The tightly interdependent global economy was a house of cards, and its collapse had devastating economic consequences.[17]

From the perspective of today's monetary economists, the government's choices in the crisis seem stunning. They go against all that is now known about economic stimulus and monetary policy on both left and right. From the perspective of the early 1930s, it makes more sense. Federal expenditures were only 3 percent of Gross Domestic Product (by 2010, they were 40 percent). State and local governments spent about five times more in total than the entire federal budget. The Federal Reserve was independent from the executive branch. Making matters worse were the results of the 1930 midterm elections, which left the House of Representatives evenly split between Democrats and Republicans. Under rules then in force, the Congress could not be seated until the deadlock was broken. Eventually, the Democrats squeezed out a one-seat margin, but not until the House had been out of session for thirteen months. Thus, for more than a year of spiraling crisis, the business of legislation ground to a halt.

Hoover was a firm believer in the usefulness of government action, but even his relatively modest forays into interventionism were met with fierce resistance from financiers and politicians who believed these sorts of upheavals were necessary to release unproductive labor and capital from the marketplace. Hoover approved the tariff because his fellow Republicans overwhelmingly supported it, and he had reelection on the horizon. In light of the flurry of New Deal reforms that came afterward, Hoover seems conservative and myopic. In that moment, as he so assiduously argued later, he did all he thought he could do.[18]

The scope of the nation's economic problems challenged conventional wisdom and demanded a redefinition of the politically possible. People who had been economically secure their whole lives now faced unemployment, homelessness, and dire poverty. Keeping in mind the effect of psychology on business outlook, President Hoover sought to rebrand the downturn as a "depression" rather than a crisis or a panic, as the latter terms were so deeply associated with economic traumas of the nineteenth century. The name stuck, and soon the depression became Great. Unemployment kept getting higher, more businesses and banks kept failing, hunger and poverty kept rising. By early 1933, about 1 in 4 Americans had lost their jobs.

Amid this crisis, voters did not care much about *how* political leaders did something. They just wanted them to *do* something to fix it. In 1932, both parties had to reckon not only with the magnitude of this crisis but also with a divided America that had divergent ideas about culture, society, and the economy. Their presidential candidates put forth two very different answers to the problem.

The Individualist

In the lists of "worst presidents" that emerge from time to time, Herbert Hoover invariably makes an appearance. So many of the most dire aspects of the Great Depression have become associated with his name, most notably the vast shantytowns of the unemployed called "Hoovervilles" that sprang up throughout urban America. He failed to relieve joblessness and poverty, and some actions he took actually made the Depression worse. Over the years, an image emerged that was more caricature than character study: a bumbling, out-of-touch, hard-hearted fellow who left a giant mess behind him. It has obscured the remarkable career Hoover had before the Depression and the fact that he once was one of the most admired men in America.[19]

Hoover was the sort of person who appears frequently in American mythology but rarely in real life: the truly self-made man. Born the son of a blacksmith in West Branch, Iowa, in 1874, Hoover was orphaned at an early age and sent to live with an uncle in Oregon's Willamette Valley. By the time he was a teenager, he resolved "to be able to earn my own living without the help of anybody, anywhere."[20] He went to Stanford, which had been founded just that year and was a tuition-free university—perfect for a penniless kid from Oregon. He graduated, still broke, and went to work as a day laborer in the California gold mines.

Ferociously smart and intensely hard-working, Hoover was promoted quickly: from miner to writer of mining reports to a position as mine manager. His rise after that was even faster. In 1897 he took a job with a British mining conglomerate and moved to Australia and China as an engineer. Within three years, he had impressed his employers so much they made him a partner. He relocated to London and spent the next several years roaming the globe to oversee existing mining operations and scout out new ones. He retired at thirty-two, a multimillionaire, but continued to travel widely as a "doctor of sick mines." When not on the road, he enjoyed the good life of Edwardian London, attending sparkling dinner parties and mingling with the rich and aristocratic.[21]

When war broke out in 1914, Hoover and his wife Lou Henry found themselves stranded. President Wilson quickly recognized that this smart, wealthy American could be valuable eyes and ears on the ground in the foreign capital, and that someone with his logistical expertise was exactly what the United States needed in this chaotic moment. Hoover seized the moment. He already had been thinking about how to become involved in "the big game back home," and this presented a ripe opportunity. His first government job was to find a way to get marooned American expatriates home. His second was even bigger: providing relief to the 10 million civilians in Belgium and northern France who were stuck between the German and Allied lines. It was a massive logistical operation, and he excelled at it.[22]

Hoover later called the job the most unpleasant thing he ever had to do. Witnessing the breadlines of hungry war refugees brought him to tears. Yet he was proving himself invaluable, and he admired Wilson. When the United States entered the war, the president recruited Hoover to run the U.S Food Administration—a giant operation controlling food production and consumption on the home front as well as getting food to wartorn European Allies and neutral nations.

The appointment was not without controversy. Hoover had been out of the country for years and no one knew whether he was a Democrat or a Republican. Some members of Congress questioned why Wilson had put so much power in the hands of "a gentleman from England." Some questioned whether Hoover was actually a citizen. Yet to the Progressives on both sides of the aisle, Hoover was the perfect example of an effective technocrat who put commitment to public service over allegiance to a particular party. For Hoover's part, he kept silent on where his party preference lay.[23]

Hoover's work during the war showcased his management talents as well as his marketing savvy. His agency used slogans and mass-marketing to persuade citizens to join in the cause. War relief posters proclaimed, "food will win the war." In stark contrast to later derogatory associations, Hoover became so famous that his name became a verb, as families "Hooverized" by rationing food.[24]

Figure 10. "Food Will Win the War," U.S. Food Administration, Education Division, c. 1917. President Wilson recruited successful businessman Herbert Hoover to run the U.S. Food Administration during World War I. Presiding over a campaign unprecedented in its logistical accomplishments and marketing savvy, Hoover became a household name. National Archives.

The U.S. Food Administration experience revealed some other characteristics as well. Hoover was extremely good at running complicated and high-stakes logistical operations, but he was a micromanager who liked to be in charge of nearly every decision. He was masterful at crafting persuasive messages and compelling propaganda, but he felt strongly that persuasion should not slide into coercion. Calling up "the spirit of self-sacrifice," and encouraging Americans to consume less was preferable to forcing them to do so by rationing.[25]

After the end of the war, Hoover for President clubs sprang up spontaneously around the country, even though voters still did not know what party he belonged to. There was a huge amount of pressure on Hoover to run in 1920. Rich, accomplished, and looking for another challenge, he reluctantly put his hat in the ring for the California primary election—as a Republican. He lost the primary, in a big way, to iconic progressive (and Theodore Roosevelt's 1912 running mate) California governor Hiram Johnson, who had by then left the enfeebled Progressive Party and returned to the Republican fold.

So Hoover picked up the pieces, endorsed Warren Harding, and got repaid for his loyalty by being appointed secretary of commerce after Harding won. Commerce wasn't that big a job, but Hoover made it bigger. Focused, visionary, and eager to shake things up in Washington, he negotiated leadership on a broad portfolio of issues, from housing to infrastructure to business relations. The newspapers called him secretary of commerce and "assistant secretary of everything else."[26]

Two years into his tenure, Hoover published a book that gave a window into the way he approached the world. He titled it *American Individualism*. In it, Hoover revealed himself as a moderate-to-conservative thinker with a political philosophy that focused on individual ability rather than collective responsibility. Hoover thought laissez faire approaches allowed inequality and inefficiency. Centralized state planning, however, dissuaded useful social collaboration and stifled individual autonomy. Instead, he argued that the true American system was one that mixed individual freedoms with measures that steered and encouraged the nation in a direction that ensured the greatest opportunity. He believed in fairness, and he believed in meritocracy. Hoover was an orphan who had become a millionaire. He felt this was a true American success story—and that anyone had the potential to do the same.[27]

Hoover's individualism was not rugged but collaborative. Translated into policy terms, this meant voluntary coordination between business, labor, and government. The best outcomes came when leaders got together and decided on the wisest course of action, informed by data, above petty politics, and acting cooperatively. Hoover believed in strategic deployment of government resources, but he did not think the government needed to do the work of charity. His response to another crisis before his presidency illustrates that vividly, and helps explain how the triumphal "Great Engineer" became a "forgettable" president.

In 1927, the Mississippi River flooded its banks. About 27,000 square miles of land in Arkansas, Louisiana, and Mississippi was underwater. Close to a million people had to leave their homes. The official death toll was 246, but unofficial accounts placed the deaths in the thousands. Already desperately poor and in the throes of the 1920s farm depression, the flooded region could not cope with the devastation.

Hoover coordinated the government response. Just as in wartime, he reassured the public, coordinated private relief efforts, and deployed government resources to build new infrastructure. Individual economic assistance, however, was not part of his relief effort. That, in Hoover's eyes, should be the job of private charity. Thus, the Red Cross became the organization that distributed food and tents to the flood victims. The federal government stuck to directing emergency evacuations and building levees along the Mississippi's banks so that a disaster of this magnitude would not happen again.

The 1927 flood vindicated Hoover's belief that private aid, not government help, was the way to handle individual needs. Many people in the Mississippi Delta felt differently. The Red Cross did not have the resources to help people over the long term. Once the food and tents ran out, residents still needed homes and jobs. Private charity did not have the capacity to provide that, and the recovery in the Delta was long, hard, and incomplete. In times of deep distress, Hoover's approach wasn't enough. The Great Depression proved it.[28]

The Natural

On 5 November 1930, as the economy hurtled downward and the credibility of the Republican in the White House sank along with it, reporters lounged in the headquarters of the New York State Democratic Party, gossiping about the day's big political story: the landslide reelection victory of

Governor Franklin Delano Roosevelt. Roosevelt already was a darling of the liberal wing of the Democratic Party, so much that he complained privately that the chatter about his possible 1932 candidacy had "become a positive nightmare."[29] The margin of victory had been huge, twice as large as the predictions of the Democratic Party itself, and reporters wanted to know what this might mean for Roosevelt's future political prospects. Jim Farley gave it to them. "I fully expect," the state Democratic chair read in a prepared statement, "that the call will come to Governor Roosevelt when the first presidential primary is held, which will be late next year. . . . I do not see how Mr. Roosevelt can escape becoming the next presidential nominee of his party, even if no one should raise a finger to bring it about."[30]

For Franklin Roosevelt, this was an extraordinary political ascent. He had been elected governor only two years before, in one of the few Democratic bright spots in the debacle of 1928. He brought charm and ease to the office and the campaign trail, making a big job seem effortless, disarming reporters and voters with his wit and joviality. He seemed a natural at politics. Yet part of his mastery was how well he hid the great deal of effort he put into this effortless political persona, and how much sharp-eyed political maneuvering he did to ensure that he would become the nominee, and win the presidency.

At the heart of Roosevelt's disguise were the elaborate measures he took to overcome the crippling disability he had developed less than a decade earlier, and to hide the fact that he could not walk unassisted. Only insiders like Farley fully understood the daunting odds Roosevelt had overcome to get this far in politics in the first place, and how close he had come to being written off as a possible contender for *anything* only a few short years before.

In contrast to Hoover, Franklin Roosevelt was a child of privilege. He was born in 1882 into a wealthy New York family, and he was so much younger than his older half-siblings that he was raised, effectively, as an only child by an adoring and overprotective mother. Theodore Roosevelt was a distant and much-admired cousin, but his branch of the family was quite different. When they got together on vacation, TR's children derided their cousin Franklin because he liked sailing. Teddy had insisted his children row their boats—because it was more "strenuous." The young FDR was witty and friendly, but didn't seem to impress anyone with his intellect. Cosseted and protected in his early home life, he struggled to fit in socially at prep school and Harvard, where he was crushed by his failure to be invited into its most elite secret society, the Porcellian, of which both Roosevelt's father and his illustrious cousin Theodore had been members.[31]

Yet soon after graduating, the young aristocrat started to chase more serious pursuits, driven to do something more than live a life of leisure. Roosevelt was a lifelong Democrat. His only vote on the Republican side was in 1904, when his cousin Theodore was running for reelection. He entered Democratic politics formally in 1910, when he ran for and won a New York State Senate seat. His home district of Dutchess County was mostly countryside, and the experience gave him an understanding of rural life, and credibility with rural voters. This proved valuable in his political career ahead. Yet even as he embarked on a career in politics, he brought with him an aristocratic demeanor that failed to impress potential allies and voters. His colleagues in the New York state legislature, in a play on his first two initials, took to referring to him with the dismissive nickname "Feather Duster."[32]

However, by the time he won reelection in 1912, Roosevelt was a man to watch. He had tamped down his upper-class mannerisms after enlisting the help of a gruff and intensely pragmatic campaign advisor, Louis M. Howe, who helped him cultivate key political alliances and build a more down-to-earth public persona. Before Roosevelt could dig into his second term, however, he was recruited by the newly elected Woodrow Wilson to join his administration in Washington, and take up the job that had been his cousin TR's first appointment as well: assistant secretary of the navy.

During his time in the Wilson administration, Roosevelt and Hoover became friendly with each other. They attended the same dinner parties, were colleagues, and had rather similar political views—centrist, yet also progressive and reformist. Roosevelt still projected more style than substance. Hoover was still the organizational master and the consummate technocrat. Roosevelt admired him greatly. "I wish we could make him President of the United States," he enthused in 1918. "There could not be a better one."[33]

However, by 1920 their political lives had diverged. While Hoover ran as a Republican for president, Roosevelt became vice presidential nominee on the Democratic ticket. Now on opposite sides of the aisle and consumed with other things, they rarely saw each other. Thus, their Wilson-era impressions proved important to the 1932 campaign. Each believed that the man he was running against was essentially the same person—in temperament and political beliefs—as the person he had known during the wartime years in Washington. But the 1920s changed both men in impor-tant ways. Especially Franklin Roosevelt.

During the summer of 1921, after visiting a Boy Scout camp, Roosevelt contracted polio. The devastating disease, also known as infantile paralysis, was a child's illness. The sheltered and pampered childhood of Roosevelt had kept him largely isolated from other children, and their germs. So, as a vigorous, athletic adult, he contracted the viral illness that ate away at his spinal cord and left his lower body withered and nearly useless.

Polio upended Roosevelt's life. He had to drop out of the public eye, enduring months and years of rehabilitation. His wife Eleanor later observed that the experience of polio made him far more patient. For once, the restless and energetic Roosevelt had to sit still. The disease forced this strong-minded son of privilege into a deeply uncomfortable new state of extraordinary vul-nerability, reliant on the help of others for his recovery. His response was to try to take charge of his life, and his health, as much as he possibly could—even if it meant pushing away those who loved him most. His mother Sara pleaded with him to abandon his political aspirations; he would hear none of it. He distanced himself from his wife Eleanor, both emotionally and geo-graphically, spending months in Florida and Georgia in search of remedies to eradicate his disease. Yet even amid his self-absorbed quest to regain his former life, Roosevelt now had personal experience that people could not do it alone. They needed to belong to something bigger.[34]

The relentless optimism that would characterize the public Roosevelt for much of his presidency came through in his letters to friends and family in the early months of his recovery. If he could not beat the disease, he at least could try to convince everyone otherwise. He was "in better health than I have been for years," he assured one friend in 1922. Yet his physical fitness did not match his sunny prognostications, and he was a no-show at two years of political events, fueling speculation in the political world that he was too disabled to carry through on his once-considerable political ambitions.[35]

FDR's return to the political spotlight came in 1924, at the Democratic National Convention to give a speech in support of his political mentor and fellow New Yorker, Governor Al Smith, who was running for president. It was a dramatic moment. Everyone knew of Roosevelt's illness. Everyone knew how disabling polio could be. Roosevelt had prepared for this moment for months and years, reviving himself not through the power of medicine but through sheer grit and tenacity over hours of physical rehabilitation. The audience may have expected a man in a wheelchair, but

Roosevelt came to the stage on crutches. He stood as he addressed the throng, gripping the podium with every ounce of upper-body strength he possessed in order to stay upright. He had gone from a thin, average shaped man to a person with a broad chest and powerful arms—on top of spindly and useless legs.

Roosevelt altered his speaking style to take people's attention away from his disability. He leaned forward over lecterns and used a powerful voice and intonation to get his audience to focus only on the waist up. Revealing his genius for delivering a political catchphrase and making it stick, he extolled Smith as the "Happy Warrior," fighting for the common man. While the convention (and the election) turned out to be a disaster for the Democrats, FDR's 1924 nominating speech was triumphal, and it resurrected his political career. Continuing to improve his physical strength, he went back to work behind the political scenes, building important networks and alliances within the Democratic Party. And this became another unintended advantage that the horror of polio bestowed on Franklin Roosevelt. It kept him out of the spotlight—and away from running for office—during a decade when Democrats were losing election after election.

In 1928, he got back in the game. Al Smith decided to run again for president, and with Smith's blessing Roosevelt ran for governor. On the stump, he tested ideas and rhetorical tactics he would use to great effect four years later. As a New York City Catholic whose core political constituency was urban working people, Al Smith had governed New York State on a platform of an activist labor and welfare program. Recognizing the crucial importance of this bloc, Roosevelt pledged to continue Smith's approach. Along with the growing Democratic base in the cities, he made direct appeals to the economically struggling rural voters like those who had populated his home district when he was a state senator. "I want our agricultural population . . . to be put on the same level of earning capacity as their fellow Americans who live in cities," he proclaimed in an October 1928 speech. He urged his audience not to "doze upon the Hoover pillow" and be lulled into thinking that prosperity had been equally shared.[36]

With this coalition and this message, Roosevelt won the governorship, despite the Hoover landslide. So by the time Herbert Hoover got to the White House, Franklin Roosevelt was one of the most prominent and powerful leaders of his party. Two years into their respective terms, Hoover was battling the Great Depression and Roosevelt was being talked up as the most likely man to take the White House back for the Democrats.

Figure 11. Franklin and Eleanor Roosevelt, Hyde Park, New York, 1927. As he recovered from polio and reentered political life in the late 1920s, Roosevelt carefully staged his public appearances to mask the evidence of his disability. A few family photographs are the only places the viewer can clearly see the braces that always encircled his ankles. Courtesy of the Franklin D. Roosevelt Library and Museum.

Two men, with different visions. One thought government action should be limited to building things—not government handouts or mandates on business. The other thought the government had a bigger role to play—and that in times of trouble the government needed to do more to help individual people get back on their feet. These differences mattered in 1932, as did the way they were communicated to the voters.

The Selling of the President

The political rises of both Herbert Hoover and Franklin D. Roosevelt attested to changing winds in American electoral politics. In the years since

1912, which had been a presidential election that bobbled unpredictably between party-dominated deal-making and candidate-centered public appeals, the system of electing presidents had shifted markedly toward the latter. Mass media had a great deal to do with this. It was the golden age of newspaper reporting, and the beginning of the golden age of radio. The modern professions of marketing and public relations also emerged during these decades, developing ever more sophisticated techniques to persuade American consumers to buy new products. As the marketplace became more crowded, messages relied on striking visuals and punchy slogans to grab the viewer's attention. Companies began to break their customers into market segments, targeting products and advertising to different groups depending on their gender, age, and purchasing power. Unsurprisingly, the American automobile industry led the way, with Alfred P. Sloan of General Motors famously promising "a car for every purse and purpose."[37]

By the early 1920s, these trends of market segmentation, streamlined messages, and strategic deployment of mass media had reached politics. Journalist Walter Lippmann homed in on this trend in his 1922 *Public Opinion.* Aided by speedy communications technologies and a crowded and chaotic marketplace, Lippmann observed, leaders had started to deploy simplistic, symbolically loaded messages that played on stereotypes and ignored the messy realities of modern society.[38]

Herbert Hoover was the master of this new political style. From wartime food administration to the Department of Commerce, he had been a refined practitioner of the arts of public persuasion through posters ("Food Will Win the War!", "Sow the Seeds of Victory!"), targeted marketing (promoting "Better Homes in America" to young families as commerce secretary), and savvy media outreach. "The world lives by phrases," he commented, "and we are good advertisers." As a candidate, Hoover made himself an accessible figure to the Washington press corps, but he also carefully controlled the terms of that accessibility and kept his remarks as restrained as his starched shirt collars. He sensed that marketing and advertising, not just newspaper reportage, could be powerful tools to win voters' hearts. In 1928, he looked at his base of political support like corporate CEOs looked at their prospective customers, identifying their main interests, and breaking them into market segments.

While still doing his due diligence in traditional party institutions to ensure good Republican turnout, Hoover used new communication technologies to appeal to voters, and matched his message to the media. He

Figure 12. "President Herbert Hoover Posed Outdoors for a Talking Motion Picture,"
c. 1929–1933. As a candidate and as president, Hoover embraced new media like
talking motion pictures, and appeared in films shot on the White House lawn.
As the economy worsened, he lost his smooth handling of public relations, and his
relationship with the press became chilly. National Photo Company Collection,
Library of Congress.

went on the radio, where his flat Midwestern accent was a huge advantage
over the New York honk of Al Smith at a moment when many in Middle
America were already suspicious of cities and Catholics and immigrants. At
a time when 90 million movie tickets were sold per week, Hoover's campaign not only made promotional films but also made *talking* pictures—a
brand-new, innovative technology.[39]

After Hoover's 1928 victory, Republicans controlled the White House,
the Senate, and the House of Representatives. The Democrats were left with
the press as the only public forum where they had about as much power as
the GOP, and they did something unprecedented to wrest an advantage.
The national Democratic Party hired a full-time journalist, Charles Michelson, away from his newspaper job and installed him as the its first full-time

publicity director. Campaigns had had press secretaries in the past, but there had not been a campaign going on. Instead, Michelson's job was to hammer away at the Republicans in charge while they were trying to govern.[40]

Michelson's job got busier as economic indicators spiraled down over the course of 1930 and 1931. Republican fortunes started to slip in the elections of 1930, when Democrats won back control of both houses of Congress, felled not simply by the dour economic outlook but by the growing public opposition to Prohibition, which most Republicans supported. Yet by the time the Democratic House was finally seated in December 1931, House Speaker John Nance Garner sensed that Michelson's value would be in pounding away at Hoover on the economy. "It was Michelson's job," Garner crowed, "to whittle Hoover down to size." The former newspaperman, who loathed Hoover personally, jumped at the task. He wrote speeches that Congressional Democrats gave on the House and Senate floor. He wrote press releases and shot them out to hundreds of newspapers. He came up with pithy sound bites and slogans. The Republicans didn't have a comparable spin machine. Instead, ironies of ironies, they had a president who seemed to be hopeless at spin.[41]

Faced with hard times and few tools to combat them, President Hoover began to lose his footing with the press. The master sloganeer resisted becoming a president of sound bites. Instead, he became a president of lengthy explanations. He also talked in a way that seemed oblivious to the suffering of the Depression, and his firm belief in the power of positive thinking caused him to make statements that later would come back to haunt him. When the economy had a little uptick in March 1930, Hoover declared: "The depression is over." In October 1930, he said: "The income of a large part of our people is not reduced by the depression . . . but is affected by unnecessary fears and pessimism." When he started looking to the 1932 campaign ahead, he and others in the GOP thought that the election would not turn on the economy, but would once again depend on social issues, chiefly Prohibition.[42]

Meanwhile, Democrats were making sure Hoover's actions to combat the Depression came across to a suffering American public as out-of-touch and unfeeling. In remarks bearing the fingerprints of Charlie Michelson, Senator Burton K. Wheeler of Montana declared in early 1932: "The general feeling in the North and Middle West is that the relief program of the administration has not been of benefit to the small business or laboring man. The people out there feel that President Hoover's course has been directed at helping those on top, the railroads, the banks, and the insurance companies."[43] Wheeler's critique was sharply partisan, but it had a core of truth. Hoover had taken a trickle-down approach, aimed at shoring up large businesses and banks on the assumption that their rehabilitation would have positive ripple effects on the broader economy. In a nation where populist sentiment was surging and citizens needed immediate, visible results, Hoover seemed to be choosing the interests of the powerful over the welfare of the ordinary people.

Americans were upset, and Hoover was getting blamed for it. A dysfunctional Congress, the burden of European war reparations, and a passive Federal Reserve contributed to the crisis, but by 1932 the Great Depression had become Hoover's problem. Part of the reason Hoover got so much of the blame for bad times was that he and his fellow Republicans had identified themselves so closely with prosperity in 1928. Along with sunny proclamations on the stump, on the radio, and in the newspapers, the Hoover campaign gave out bread boards reading, "Vote for Hoover, and your board will never lack a loaf." They distributed "lucky pennies" that read "Good for four more years of prosperity."

Another reason Hoover got the blame was that Michelson and the Democratic spin machine made sure he would. When shantytowns began springing up in cities across the country, filled with the unemployed and homeless, it was Michelson who started calling them "Hoovervilles." Yet looming above the rhetoric and clever spin was the basic material failure of Hoover's policies. The efforts of his administration were doing little to alleviate the economic crisis. In fact, things got worse.

With reporters covering all this, every day, the president started to despise the Washington press corps. The candidate-centered politics so important in 1912 had escalated in significance in the two decades since, and Hoover had previously gone along with the new rules of the game. He had held weekly press conferences, and while he held to prior White House protocol in only answering questions reporters had submitted in writing in advance, he had proved himself genial, expansive, and generous in the time he spent with the media.

Now, he clammed up. He started to sound like a person who didn't like his job very much. He referred to the presidency as "a repairman's job" that lurched from one crisis to another. Hoover liked building things: legacy projects like the wartime food administration, or flood relief programs, or monumental infrastructure like the huge Nevada dam that would one day bear his name. Rather than rising through GOP ranks, he came to the Republican Party after he was already a national figure. He had run for office only twice in his life, and the first time was merely a brief foray into the 1920 California primary. He was not a party insider, and he disliked the muck of partisan politics. He particularly resented having to work with Congress, whose traditions and hierarchies he neither understood nor respected. His disdain for its political theater was so strong that he sent the written texts of his State of the Union addresses over to Capitol Hill instead of making the speeches there in person.[44]

Faced with a hostile press and gridlocked Congress, the always workaholic Hoover exhausted himself physically to address the growing economic crisis. His propensity for micromanagement became a huge disadvantage in this struggle. Rather than negotiate with an ossified legislative branch, the Great Engineer tried to run recovery single-handed from the White House. Rather than delegate to staff or cabinet members, he worked around the clock, pulling late-night sessions in his office as he chewed on an unlit cigar and snapped at underlings. His vaunted organizational efficiency began to slip. H. G. Wells had a brief audience with Hoover at the White House in 1931 and found him an "overworked and overwhelmed man, a month behind in all his engagements and hopeless of ever overtaking them."[45]

By the time a Democratic Congress came into session in early 1932, Hoover had been battling the Depression alone and bitterly. He had fractured support within his own party after signing into law the now-hated tariff bill in 1930, which had alienated his old friends and allies in the party's progressive wing. Even conservative Republicans had broken away from Hoover's voluntaristic creed, and had begun to argue for creation of new government institutions to stabilize the banking system. Hoover's efforts to bypass Congress and work directly with business and labor interests had left those on Capitol Hill unwilling to do anything to cooperate with Hoover or run the risk of passing legislation that might give the president credit for economic recovery. It was better, Congressional leaders reasoned, to wait for a new president to come along altogether.

Ironically, the man who had presided over giant government-funded aid efforts in wartime continued to fiercely resist the creation of similar agencies to fight the crisis of the Great Depression, well into the last year of his presidency. But the pressure from both right and left made it impossible to keep up such resistance. In January 1932, Hoover signed a law creating the Reconstruction Finance Corporation (RFC), which would lend money to struggling financial institutions. At the signing ceremony, defensively countering his critics, Hoover remarked that the RFC "is not created for the aid of big industries or big banks."[46] Yet while the aid provided by the law flowed to smaller financial institutions, it remained hard for regular voters to see or understand. Hoover asked Congress to appropriate more money for farm loans as well. But it seemed like too little, too late. The Democrats stoked the populist fire, raging against Hoover as an elitist and an egotist. "The people are not so slow-thinking," chided Arkansas Senator Hattie Caraway, "as not to see how little has been done to better conditions, nor how what has been done with good intent has been construed always for the benefit of the 'interests.'"[47]

From 1928 to 1932, the public image of Herbert Hoover had descended from one of technological wizardry to utter ineptitude. By mid-1932, historian Allan Nevins reflected the confirmed sentiment among the political class when he wrote that Hoover "is an admirable planner, organizer and administrator, but a very poor policy-maker and leader. . . . Leadership and organization require two different sets of qualities . . . and Mr. Hoover has only one."[48]

CHAPTER 4

*

The Promise of Change

While Hoover stumbled through the presidency, Roosevelt governed New York State, testing some ideas he later took to the national stage. Although resistant to Hoover's early requests for stimulus-inducing infrastructure projects, and initially wary of big-spending government relief programs, Roosevelt shifted his position as the crisis worsened. Unlike Hoover, who doubled down on his conservative ideologies while the economy unraveled, Roosevelt, as one biographer put it, "retained a child's openness to new experience, a child's reactive flexibility." Roosevelt initiated new programs for direct relief and jobs for the unemployed. He continued to be adept at connecting to his rural constituencies and building coalitions between the city and the countryside. He also had a human touch, a sense of humor, and an ability to connect with political bosses and voters alike.[1]

Part of Roosevelt's effectiveness as a leader and a candidate came from the people who surrounded him. This is another important development emerging clearly in the 1932 campaign: professional campaign advisors whose full-time job was to get a candidate elected and reelected. Of course, candidates had relied on close advisors in every presidential campaign since the era of Washington, Adams, and Jefferson. Traditionally, however, these men had been elected officials themselves, or had held formal positions in party organizations. The new breed of operative was different. These men often were not politicians, but professional staff with backgrounds in policy, government, or journalism. Most important, they were loyal to the candidate, not just to the party, and—like Charles Michelson—they could work as hard in the off years as during campaign season.

In Roosevelt's case, he had a powerful team of two at his side who could work both old and new politics, both crafting a compelling political message and candidate persona, and doing the necessary retail politics to secure key alliances and constituencies. Neither had been a major player in national Democratic politics before, and both had their chief alliance to Roosevelt. The message came from Louis McHenry Howe, the former political reporter who had been Roosevelt's press operative since he was in the New York State Senate. Temperamental and chain-smoking, the diminutive Howe was as disheveled as his boss was debonair. The politics came from Jim Farley, whom Roosevelt recruited away from the New York State Democratic Party in early 1931 to start laying the groundwork for his campaign. Farley, a New York Irishman with deep roots in the Democratic Party, had been an Al Smith man, but quickly became a passionate FDR loyalist. Roosevelt was "one of the most alive men I had ever met," Farley recollected. "I had an intuition that there was a touch of destiny about the man."[2]

Farley's initial impressions of his fellow campaign manager Howe were less inspiring. He "seemed about the oddest little duck I had ever known," he wrote, but his appreciation of Howe's loyalty grew quickly. "Rebuffs never discouraged him, and he was grim as a little bulldog in hanging onto what he wanted." Roosevelt needed this tenacity. Down in Washington, Democratic Party chair John Raskob had announced his intention to make repeal of Prohibition a plank in the 1932 platform. This was political dynamite for a party base sharply divided on the issue. Rural Democratic constituencies supported staying dry; the growing urban base was strongly for repeal. Roosevelt needed to appeal to both. It also was becoming clear that Raskob was strongly against the Roosevelt bandwagon and determined to prevent his nomination. The list of possible rivals started to grow. While Roosevelt returned to the business of being governor and other Democratic candidates gathered in the wings, the two operatives got to work.[3]

The first step was mass mailing. Still wearing his hat as chief of the New York Democrats, Farley sent a copy of an innocuous little booklet listing the state's elected officials to every party committee leader of any significance, in every state in the country. The mailing said nothing about Roosevelt's candidacy, but it opened lines of correspondence between Farley and the people who held the keys to the 1932 nomination. The ground campaign began to take root.

Yet by the summer of 1931 it was clear that Roosevelt's competition was getting stiff, and Farley and Howe worried they needed to do more outreach—not just by mail, but also in person. A faithful member of the Benevolent and Protective Order of Elks, Farley had a long-scheduled plan to travel to Seattle that summer to attend their annual convention, building a vacation around the visit. With competition intensifying, he threw vacation plans by the wayside and instead decided to make his trip an extensive—and covert—reconnaissance mission for FDR.

On a bright Sunday morning, Howe and Farley made their way seventy-five miles up the Hudson River to Roosevelt's home in Hyde Park. In their luggage were a Rand McNally atlas of the United States, a stack of train timetables, and a list of Democratic committeemen and state chairs. Retreating to Roosevelt's study, the three men spread the materials on the table and plotted Farley's trip out West, making sure his progress touched every possible party official on the way. The next day, Farley was off. His trip ended up 30,000 miles long. "My line seemed to go over pretty well, if I do say it myself," he reflected. "People seemed to think I meant every word I said." When he got back to New York, he dictated letters back to every person he had met on the road.[4]

The team also understood that they needed to lay a good foundation in the press. Task number one was to dispel rumors that Roosevelt was too disabled to do the job. As Roosevelt's national profile rose, the buzz about his health had increased, in both Republican and Democratic circles. With the Democrats split between "wet" and "dry" candidates, Roosevelt's health became a rationale for those who didn't find him a strong enough supporter of Prohibition. The militantly "dry" president of the National Women's Democratic Law Enforcement League put it flatly: "This candidate, while mentally qualified for the presidency, is entirely unfit physically."[5]

Press man Howe stepped to the fore. Reaching out quietly to friendly journalists and physicians, he embarked on the delicate task of getting a national story placed that would quash the innuendo about the governor's health. In July 1931 it appeared as a cover story in the popular illustrated weekly *Liberty Magazine*, titled "Is Franklin D. Roosevelt Physically Fit to be President?" The answer, the "experts" in the article concluded, was an unqualified yes.[6]

By this time, Roosevelt had become highly skilled at masking the fact that he could not walk. He made sure he was not seen in public, much less photographed, in a wheelchair. Portraits taken during his New York years showed Roosevelt standing tall, leaning on one cane. A closer examination of the image showed that he actually had a second cane strategically hidden behind his other leg.

Figure 13. Franklin D. Roosevelt throwing out ball at baseball game, 1932. Roosevelt's aides worked assiduously to project an image of a healthy, vigorous candidate, and Roosevelt worked hard at it as well. Whether giving a speech or throwing out the first pitch, he used a tight grip on whatever was in front of him to keep himself upright. Library of Congress.

Such stagecraft was possible only when he wasn't moving. When he needed to move, his son James accompanied him everywhere, giving him an arm while Roosevelt supported himself with a cane on the other side. As governor, and as a potential candidate, he kept up a punishing schedule of travel and back-to-back events, signaling with his constant activity that he was just as fit as any man—perhaps more so. With his big waves to the crowds and his hearty smile and jaunty expression, Roosevelt projected an image of vigor and health. The lengths to which he had to go to hide his disability made him acutely aware of image and perception, an awareness that served him well in the campaign to come.

As he geared up for his run, Roosevelt was realizing that most members of his party were falling into the same trap as Hoover and the GOP. Like the Republicans, mainstream Democrats thought Prohibition would be the biggest issue of the 1932 election. The political dustups of 1931 were invariably about "wet" versus "dry" and where potential nominees stood on the issue. Like many social issues, Prohibition became a proxy for bigger divergences within the party—rural constituents and temperance groups on one side, urban blocs and technocratic modernizers on the other. The rift played out in widely different views about how to combat the Depression. Fiery populists and liberal lions called for bold measures targeted at the working class and small farmers. But their voices were in the minority. Many more mainstream Democrats took a somewhat conservative, incremental view about how government should respond. And a good number paid little attention to the economic question at all.

Roosevelt saw this as an opportunity. He saw that third parties with more radical messages were getting traction. "The common man," wrote John Dewey in the pages of the progressive *New Republic*, "is convinced that neither the Democratic nor the Republican party represents him or his interests."[7] Roosevelt agreed, sensing that voters were deeply frustrated with the status quo in Washington—and he saw first-hand in New York the powerful impact government action could have on poverty and unemployment. It seemed like the same thing was needed at the national level.

At the very least, the nation had to try.

Roosevelt declared his candidacy in January 1932, a week before his fiftieth birthday. The field proved crowded, and competitive. Powerful Congressional Democrats like House Speaker John Nance Garner were running. Roosevelt's old ally—now his rival—Al Smith was considering it. To Hoover, Roosevelt seemed the most beatable of the bunch. Throughout the primary season and into the summer, the White House tracked the Democratic race closely. Hoover still remembered the Roosevelt of the "Feather Duster" years. He was "a pleasant fellow and well meaning, but without a rudimentary grasp of the issues involved," some aides recollected Hoover saying. He also was far too disabled, Hoover reasoned, ever to be a credible opponent. "He is a sick man," Hoover observed privately on another occasion. "He wouldn't live a year in the White House."[8]

Roosevelt immediately marked his territory by being more liberal, bolder than his competitors. He gathered some of the sharpest liberal policy thinkers of the day in what he called his "privy council" but the press

Figure 14. New York City Deputy Police Commissioner John A. Leach, right, watching agents pour liquor into a sewer following a raid during the height of Prohibition, 1921. Both Republicans and Democrats initially believed Prohibition would be the biggest issue of the 1932 election. Whether to repeal the 18th Amendment had been one of the most animated and divisive political issues of the 1920s, particularly in the Democratic Party, whose core constituencies included urban "wets" and rural "drys." Library of Congress.

quickly labeled the "Brain Trust." As Roosevelt was not an ideologue, but generally open to new ideas, the work of these advisors proved influential in convincing him the answer to the Depression lay in more forceful government intervention into markets. Old hands like Louis Howe watched with alarm as Roosevelt started to tack leftward.[9]

On 7 April, Roosevelt sent out political shock waves with a ten-minute radio address authored by one of his key Brain Trusters, Raymond Moley. Speaking to a national radio audience, he called for bold plans "that build from the bottom up and not from the top down, that put their faith once more in the forgotten man at the bottom of the economic pyramid." For all its emotional resonance and populist audacity, FDR's "forgotten man" speech did not have many specifics about how a plan might be implemented. Instead, he was running on an idea that a beleaguered nation needed to test an array of new approaches and see if they worked. In a May speech in Atlanta he said: "The country needs and, unless I mistake its temper, the country demands bold, persistent experimentation. It is common sense to take a method and try it: If it fails, admit it and try another. But above all try something."[10]

In a modern age of media saturation and dwindling attention spans, it is tempting to presume that campaigns of long ago were weighty, substantive affairs: all about policy details, substance over style. They weren't. Like many before and after him, Franklin Roosevelt could be vague on the stump about what he was going to do once he got to the White House. Like many before and after him, he was bold in his pronouncements, but careful in how he played his politics. The Democratic Party was a cobbled-together bunch of constituencies with very different interests. This is the era when Will Rogers famously remarked, "I am not a member of any organized party—I am a Democrat."[11] Moreover, the Democrats still found themselves compromised in their ability to appeal to African American voters, given the power of white Southerners within the Party.

The "black vote" meant little to national politics for over four decades, as the vast majority of black adults lived below the Mason-Dixon Line where state party systems had maintained near total black disenfranchisement since Reconstruction. Yet as more African Americans moved out of the segregated South and into the urban North, shifts in their loyalties began to appear. Starting with the 1928 candidacy of urban ethnic Al Smith, and propelled more decisively by the economic distress of the early 1930s, African Americans began to move away from the Party of Lincoln. The Democratic Party still had its problems, but it was the lesser of two evils, reasoned some black opinion-makers. "It is my opinion that the Republicans will not be able to master the economic alteration of today with its present nominee as president because he favors the few at the expense of the many," ran one letter to the prominent African American newspaper, the *Chicago Defender*.[12]

Strong commitments to particular positions might alienate these ever-shifting constituencies, and Roosevelt not only declined to take a firm stand but vacillated between left and right throughout the campaign, depending on to whom he was speaking. "He would unite East and West, North and

South," opined the *New York Times*, "in one grand brotherhood of inconclusive phrases and glittering generalities."[13] In Atlanta in May he had spoken of bold experimentation in a way that might have made a socialist like Eugene Debs happy. In San Francisco in September, now the nominee and speaking to a group of business-minded civic leaders at the Commonwealth Club, he sounded far more conservative, saying "government should assume the function of economic regulation only as a last resort, to be tried only when private initiative . . . has finally failed." Implied, but not stated, was that the past three years had proved decisively that the private sector had failed. Roosevelt was too careful with his politics to say it.[14]

Some pundits took this as meaning Roosevelt was "not a man of great intellectual force or supreme moral stamina." The ever-influential Walter Lippmann disdained Roosevelt's political flexibility as a sign the candidate was a lightweight: "a highly impressionable person, without a firm grasp of public affairs and without very strong convictions." Even some of the "forgotten men" became impatient with FDR's lack of specificity. "Instead of giving us clear, hard, cold facts, the Governor is still talking generalities," St. Petersburg, Florida, resident John Harrison wrote in a letter to the *New York Times*. "His reference to what Jefferson, Lincoln, Wilson and Theodore Roosevelt did is very interesting, but he ought to tell us what Franklin D. Roosevelt proposes to do now."[15]

Roosevelt was taking a bet that the Great Depression had altered the rules of the political game. He sensed that the election would hinge on emotional appeals and the power of language that could brighten dark economic times. Americans were seeking answers, and escape. There were many different political constituencies, but the Great Depression was an experience that cut across class, party, and region. It was the power of emotion—not the details of policy—that would pull the different constituencies together into a winning coalition.

This is the crucial thing Hoover missed.

The Head and the Heart

One medium dominated the final months of this pivotal campaign: radio. By 1932, radios were fixtures in American households. Radio broadcasts already had turned events like Charles Lindbergh's first solo flight across the Atlantic into shared dramas, listened to together live by people from coast to coast. Radio brought entertainment into people's living rooms, and it became a critical source for any political news. Three decades later, Marshall McLuhan assessed radio as the quintessential "hot" medium, "the tribal drum," and "the medium for frenzy" that become more effective and persuasive the more intensely dramatic and emotional it became. Radio serials capitalized on this power, using sharp dialogue, raucous sound effects, and cliffhanger plots to drive up their audience share. In 1932, politicians got on the bandwagon.[16]

As they had since 1924, radio networks broadcast gavel-to-gavel coverage of the two party conventions. Both happened in Chicago, in the new Chicago Stadium. The Republicans went first.

Hoover, keeping to tradition, stayed behind in the White House, which was where he had been for most of 1932. Although he had faced a primary challenge, it had not been a significant one. So he didn't hit the road that often. Instead, he relied on the advantages of incumbency by presiding over official events, all of which were filmed by the newsreel companies and projected nice images of Hoover acting presidential. He gave radio addresses from the Lincoln Bedroom of the White House as GOP operatives invoked Lincoln's campaign slogan from 1864: "Don't Change Horses in the Middle of the Stream." It was compelling coming from Lincoln; it proved dispiriting coming from Hoover.[17]

A Rose Garden campaign might have worked in an ordinary year, but this was not an ordinary year. Compounding all this, the Republican Convention was a mess. There were many empty seats. Few members of Congress attended. The proceedings became consumed with platform fights over Prohibition. Hoover refused to come down firmly on one side or the other, leaving both "wets" and "drys" unhappy. As one stalwart Republican clubwoman later noted with displeasure, Hoover's position was "You be dry and I'll be moist."[18]

There was little mention of the economy or what was to be done about it, even though there were breadlines crowding the sidewalks and streets of Chicago as the delegates met. Newspaper reporters in attendance told their readers about the half-empty galleries, the droning speeches, the delegates who fought for Prohibition in the convention hall and drank beer and whiskey outside it. In his dispatches to the *Baltimore Evening Sun*, the ever acerbic H. L. Mencken concluded that "this convention of country postmasters, Federal marshals and receivers in bankruptcy, masquerading as the heirs of Lincoln, is the stupidest and most boresome ever heard of."[19] For the radio listeners at home, the GOP convention reinforced the paucity of new ideas, and new energy, in the Republican Party.

The GOP and the Hoover White House allowed such a lackluster show in Chicago partly because they did not believe that the Democrats would win. Many pundits agreed with them. Despite oceans of newspaper ink and radio time devoted to the race, 1932 remained an age where there was little solid information based on good data. This included reliable political polling. The science of survey research was in its infancy. Hearsay and punditry often informed politicians' understanding of where the voters' loyalties lay. Media outlets used letters to the editor and self-selecting reader surveys as the bases for their predictions. It would be four years before George Gallup took on the business of polling voter preferences in presidential contests, and many more years after that before polling data became a sophisticated barometer of voter behavior.[20]

Breadlines aside, the economy actually *was* getting better in late spring 1932, in part because of the measures the Hoover administration and Congress had taken to shore up banks and loosen credit. Yet Congress went out of session for the summer of 1932. When they did, the Fed tightened credit again. So the economy started trending downward. In the absence of good economic statistical reporting, the Hoover administration—and the men and women at the GOP convention—didn't understand where it was headed.

The Democratic Convention took place in the same Chicago hall, two weeks later, and was anything but boring. It was a true political spectacle and cliffhanger, full of energy and controversy and dramatic made-for-radio moments. Unlike the Republican gathering, where the inevitability of Hoover's nomination loomed large throughout, the Democratic meeting was a horse race. No candidate, including Roosevelt, came into the convention with enough delegates to win. As in 1912, primary results were not binding. Chicago was where the decision would happen.

Going into the convention, Roosevelt's odds of winning seemed steep. Mencken noted that Roosevelt "is anything but popular, either in the convention or outside." Favorite sons of the party like Garner seemed to have the inside track. Al Smith was less a threat, but his hatred of his friend-turned-rival Roosevelt was such that he came determined to prevent a FDR win. Animosity ran both ways. "A majority of the Roosevelt men are really not for Roosevelt at all, but simply against Al Smith," Mencken wrote.

Adding to Roosevelt's challenges was the fact that his operatives were neo-phytes in national politics, while his opponents had some of the most sea-soned convention veterans around.[21]

Nominating speeches began the night of 30 June. There were ten jaw-dropping, mind-deadening hours of them, starting at 5:00 p.m. and lasting until 3:00 a.m. The radio networks kept up coverage through the whole thing, and the Democrats in the hall seized the opportunity to have some airtime. In the wee hours, as speeches finally wound to a close, Roosevelt's people grabbed their own moment, and forced a first vote, at 4:28 a.m.

One ballot. Two ballots. Roosevelt made small gains but not decisive ones. Smith's people howled in outrage at the audacity of the Roosevelt campaign. It was summer. Everyone was sweating. Farley handed out fans with Roosevelt's picture on them. The radio networks kept their coverage going throughout. On the third ballot, at 8:00 a.m., Roosevelt got five more votes. The exhausted delegates slumped back to their hotel rooms for a nap.

In the ten hours that followed, there was furious politicking throughout hotel rooms and hallways, resulting in a true game changer: newspaper magnate William Randolph Hearst threw his support behind Roosevelt. Hearing of the endorsement, Garner released his California and Texas dele-gates, putting FDR over the top with the two-thirds majority he needed to win the nomination. Bitter and angry, Al Smith refused to do the same. He—and many others at that gathering—understood that Roosevelt's win was not the result of a sudden popularity surge, but instead was a rebuke and dismissal of Smith, the man who had failed to win the White House for the Democrats in 1924 and 1928.

Thus, on ballot number four, Roosevelt got the nomination. Radio lis-teners at home did not see the degree of antipathy and Democratic infight-ing that lay behind his victory. They heard drama, a David who had slain Goliath. FDR seized the media moment. He broke with tradition and flew to Chicago to accept the nomination in person. It was another, triumphal moment of Roosevelt stagecraft. Flying from New York to Chicago in 1932 was no small undertaking, and by making this arduous and rather risky trip on the spur of the moment Roosevelt telegraphed his endurance and fitness for office. "Any man who can fly in a storm from Rochester to Chicago to make an acceptance speech, and can carry on as vigorous a campaign as Roosevelt is carrying on," observed one letter to the Baltimore *Afro-American*, "is not likely to die the very minute he is inaugurated."[22]

Standing before the crowded and sweltering convention, Roosevelt left all mention of politicking and Prohibition behind and talked about the issue consuming the people listening at home: the economy. It was significant, he told them, that he had broken traditions and come to accept the nomination right there and then: "may this be the symbol of my intention to be honest and avoid all hypocrisy and sham." In a foreshadowing of the speech he would give at his inauguration the following year, he said "this is no time for fear, for reaction or for timidity." Instead, he promised "a new deal for the American people."[23]

The Republicans hadn't talked about the economy. All Roosevelt did was talk about it. The organist at the Chicago Stadium played the popular ditty "Happy Days are Here Again" at both conventions. At the GOP gathering, it sounded like a dirge, a mockery to the radio audience listening at home. After the Democratic convention, the assembled media picked up on the song as a theme for the Roosevelt campaign. Roosevelt used it for every election afterward. Many years of struggle lay ahead for American families, but Roosevelt's powerful, stirring oratory was able to make them believe happy days might be just around the corner.

Hoover's political battering continued through the summer. At the same moment that the two parties were gathering in Chicago, a wave of unemployed World War I veterans from across the country had started to converge on Washington to demand early payment of their veterans' pensions. The dire economic situation, they argued, made it heartless for the government to wait in giving those who fought for their country what was due to them. They called themselves the Bonus Expeditionary Force, and set up encampments right in the heart of official Washington. This was a particularly visible and politically problematic sort of Hooverville: highly visible, intractable, and filled with people using the language of patriotism and military service to make their case.

By July, the situation had become intolerable. The squatters were preventing half-constructed federal buildings from being finished, halting the infrastructure activities at the heart of Hoover's economic recovery program. The camps were messy and disorderly, and Hoover and his aides strongly suspected they were hotbeds of political radicalism. The racial integration of the camps was a disturbing sign of it, as in 1932 this sort of tolerance was found only in the Communist Party. Communists were indeed there, but not in the numbers Hoover assumed.[24]

After Congress adjourned for the summer and official Washington set-
tled into its torpid summer quiet, Hoover called for the Bonus Marchers to
be removed. The troops sent in to do so, led by General Douglas MacArthur
and an up-and-coming officer named Dwight D. Eisenhower, took their
orders above and beyond Hoover's intention for a quiet, orderly operation.
Soldiers on horseback, kitted in uniforms nearly identical to the ones the
Bonus Marchers had worn two decades before, set upon the marchers
aggressively. The troops took on not only the camps at the center of the
city, but those on the outskirts, along the Anacostia River, where women
and children joined their husbands and fathers. The confrontation turned
violent, tear gas poisoned the air, and the camps went up in flames. The
DC press corps was on hand to write down everything they saw.

The Bonus March debacle became a public relations disaster for the
president, reinforcing a political narrative that he was both hapless and
heartless. Hoover "summoned the United States army to rout and maim a
pitiful and inoffensive crowd of ragged and unarmed bonusers," accused a
spokesman for the Veterans of Foreign Wars. Democratic Representative
Wright Patman of Texas scornfully suggested that the president should have
instead "use[d] the army to drive the international banking lobby from the
capital city." Hoover seethed at the mess MacArthur had created for him,
but he never issued a public reprimand of the general or an apology to the
marchers.[25]

Roosevelt was mystified by Hoover's bungling of the Bonus March. This
was not the Hoover he remembered with such admiration from the Wilson
administration. Why set on the marchers with tear gas and bayonets, he
wondered aloud to an aide? Why not just send them coffee and sandwiches,
and listen to their complaint? FDR started to realize the profound weaknesses of his opponent. He began to think he could win this election. His
fellow Democrats agreed, and Hoover's fellow Republicans became more
worried. As the fall campaign neared, observed one reporter, "partisans on
both sides are busily engaged in polishing up their epithets."[26]

The Election Nears

The fall campaign showed the stark contrast between Roosevelt's appeals to
the heart and Hoover's appeals to the head.

Hoover still was a reluctant campaigner. When on the stump, he could be soft-spoken and hard to hear. He was not a fiery orator, but a great explainer. He scoffed at Roosevelt's use of speechwriters. Instead, he took on the exhausting task of writing all his speeches himself, loading them with facts and statistics. "Mr. Roosevelt not only advanced the thesis that I was responsible for the depression," Hoover later wrote, "but also insisted that I had done nothing about it." To combat this, he gave lengthy, densely detailed speeches that outlined all he had done, and complained about the "hideous misrepresentation" of his record.[27]

The result was campaign oratory that was depressing, dogmatic, and dull. Hoover's over-arching message was that greater disaster would befall his listeners if Roosevelt won.

Hoover also forgot the power of radio. Earlier in his term he had passed up the opportunity to give regular ten-minute radio addresses from the White House—the format of the "fireside chats" Roosevelt later made famous. Hoover did not believe he could relay anything of substance in ten minutes; the master of slogans and phrases seemed to have dialed back in time to the age of nineteenth-century oratory instead of the twentieth-century era of shrinking attention spans. Modern media also rewarded the softer side of political personality, and the Great Engineer had long disliked being the subject of human interest stories geared to make him more likeable and relatable. In 1928, he had fiercely resisted aides' suggestions to film a documentary about his life, saying it would "get votes only from the morons."[28]

In contrast, FDR used radio to his advantage. Even with his aristocratic voice, he delivered his message in a way that made him more of a "man of the people" than Hoover. "It is pleasant and clear, with a pleasing inflection," one radio producer declared of Roosevelt's voice. "But above all, it has a tone of perfect sincerity, a quality that is supremely essential." In contrast, "President Hoover's voice is typical of the engineer, and, generally speaking, this type is seldom an interesting talker on the radio." The media had become the message.[29]

Delivering authoritative and reassuring speeches over the airwaves, Roosevelt used radio as the ultimate distraction from his disability and the ultimate expression of his elegant phrasing and rhetoric. Through the fall, on the radio and on the stump, Roosevelt ran a campaign that tended to be short on policy details and long on emotions. His criticism of Hoover also became fiercer as the fall wore on, and as he got wind of the derogatory things the president had been saying about him, and as he got more and more confident of victory. Roosevelt got a further boost from the most glamorous of places, Hollywood, where studio moguls like Jack Warner and A-list talent like Will Rogers lent their endorsement and star appeal to FDR's candidacy.[30]

Roosevelt's reliance on a multitude of speechwriters, although disparaged by Hoover, allowed him to float above the fray of competing policy visions and appeal to a range of constituencies. His various speechwriters competed for Roosevelt's affection and attention by seeding their own pet ideas in his speeches; Roosevelt was adept at picking the most politically saleable ideas and leaving out the possible land mines. It was clear, by this point, that the idea of a more vigorous state had become Roosevelt's North Star, but the way he characterized this vision was very careful in its spin and stagecraft. He was an old-style progressive turned New Deal liberal, but he remained attentive to the basics of retail politics.

In the final weeks of the fall campaign, he crossed the country in a custom campaign train labeled the "Roosevelt Special." Among its innovative features was a fully furnished press car. The venue was perfect. Roosevelt came out on a platform at the back of the train. He powerfully grasped the railings and the microphone stand, his broad chest and shoulders looming as he gestured with one arm. His voice boomed. The crowd cheered. The reporters hopped out of their comfortable press car, mingled with the crowd, wrote it all down, and hopped back on the train. It was meticulously planned political theater, a routine that varied little from town to town and state to state. Further helping Roosevelt's odds was that Al Smith had finally gotten over his embarrassment in Chicago and endorsed the full Democratic slate, helping cement the support of urban working-class voters who remained passionate about Smith.[31]

On 22 October, Hoover finally hit the road as well, but his whistle-stops were less joyous. It horrified him that Roosevelt—lightweight, rudderless, untested—might win, but this seemed more and more likely. People and groups who had long been dependably Republican deserted Hoover. In Des Moines, Iowa, a farmer marching in an anti-Hoover, pro-Roosevelt parade declared, "If Hoover is re-elected, he will be the last American President." The Down Town Republican Club of Los Angeles canceled a dinner and rally for Hoover after a poll of its members found that 70 percent of them were supporting Roosevelt. The Progressive League launched a campaign "to turn the progressive wing of the Republican party away from President

Figure 15. Franklin D. Roosevelt on campaign train, Seattle, 1932. The "Roosevelt Special" barnstormed the country in the final days of the campaign, helping cement support for his candidacy and for the full Democratic slate. Courtesy of the Museum of History and Industry (MOHAI).

Hoover." The *Chicago Defender*, the influential newspaper of the black community, departed from a past pattern of Republican endorsement and refrained from expressing a strong preference for Hoover. By the end of October, another prominent black paper, the Baltimore *Afro-American*, answered the question "Roosevelt or Hoover" more decisively: "Roosevelt." Hoover's flip-flopping on Prohibition chipped away at his base of support as well. The executive secretary of the Methodist Board of Temperance disdained voting for either major party candidate: "I, personally, am casting my ballot for [Socialist] Norman Thomas."[32]

As his campaign train steamed angrily across the country, Hoover stuck to his guns. He declared that "the forces of depression are in retreat" and that "no defense is needed" of his administration's policies, because they had been the right ones. He ever more staunchly defended the tariff he had signed into law in 1930, which by that time had become despised by Democrats and Republicans alike as a main culprit in the economic crisis. He positioned himself as a true believer, while Roosevelt was "a chameleon on plaid." Roosevelt's campaign train was met with cheers and bouquets of flowers. Hoover's train was met with unemployed men wearing placards saying things like "Hoover—Baloney and Apple Sauce."[33]

The smoothness and professionalism with which Roosevelt ran for president in those final weeks impressed observers, and set a precedent for sophistication in campaign machinery. "If the end crowns the work in his case," editorialized the *New York Times* on the eve of the election, "the example which he has set ought to be full of instruction, as well as of warning, to politicians anxious to learn the secrets of their trade." The election also hinged on the power of personality. "I tell you, lady," said a Washington cab driver to political reporter Anne O'Hare McCormick, "I figure out that if we get rid of Old Gloom and put in a feller that can laugh and act human, the Depression will be half over." Yet ordinary voters' loyalties were not always this unswerving. "Now what I'd like to see is Roosevelt and Hoover elected and Garner and Curtis licked," a milkman told McCormick the same day. "Whatever happens, though, I guess the old flag will still be flutterin' in the hot air over the Capitol and I'll be deliverin' the milk as usual."[34]

Election Day brought a landslide for Roosevelt. He won 472 electoral votes, Hoover 59. Roosevelt won over 57 percent of the popular vote. Coming into the Democrats' corner were the people hardest hit by the Great Depression: urban workers, farmers, and a good number of African Americans. Roosevelt also had decisively grabbed the Progressive vote that had been shared between the Democratic and Republican parties since the days of his cousin Teddy. In his memoirs, Hoover limited his assessment of the loss to one grim sentence: "As we expected, we were defeated in the election." The conservative, pro-business, incrementalist vision of Hoover had lost resoundingly to an activist, reform-minded "new deal."[35]

After November

Most people who run against one another for president end up not liking one another very much. Herbert Hoover and Franklin Roosevelt ended up hating each other. They hated each other so deeply, in fact, that they refused to work together in the four months between election and inauguration (for American presidents still took office in March).

Hoover had to turn from the shambles of the electoral returns to the shambles of a country in crisis. Yet the defeated president did not want to take the full blame for emergency measures, like closing the banks. He asked FDR to work jointly with him during the transition. However, Roosevelt refused to commit; just like Hoover, he did not want to share the blame or credit with his rival. Roosevelt had distinct policy ideas that were markedly different from anything the conservative Hoover might have agreed to do. Why should the President-elect abandon the principles that had won him the election? Driven by ideological distance and personal animosity, their stand-off continued as the economy hurtled further downward.

By the time Inauguration Day rolled around, the enmity had cemented. Hoover and Roosevelt shared a car ride from the Capitol to the White House without a single word to each other. Roosevelt's first hundred days was a legislative flurry that involved enacting into law many things that were already moving through Congress while Hoover was still president. By then, Hoover had retreated to his home in Palo Alto, California, licking his wounds and distaining the political limelight. Roosevelt took up these measures and added to them, resulting in an extraordinary first three months of audacious and unprecedented executive-branch action.

The profound legacy of Roosevelt's New Deal has been dissected, debated, catalogued, and contested by historians, journalists, political leaders, and citizens in the eight decades since.[36] What is uncontestable is that the government action set in motion by Roosevelt in 1933 *did* pull the United States out of the Great Depression, although sometimes haltingly and unevenly. The 1932 election is a window into how and why the New Deal became possible, and how it fits into the broader landscape of American history. The utter failure of capitalism in 1929 and the years that followed opened American leaders and voters to new ideas. The results were not only progressive, they were a radical reframing of the national government's role in American life. As we see from the 1932 campaign, Roosevelt was not a revolutionary but an experimenter. He could at times be frustratingly vague, and he could be cunningly political. He was not an ideologue. He wanted to fix capitalism, not overthrow it.

Yet Roosevelt and the men and women of his administration—as well as their allies in business and labor—did manage to stake out a profoundly

Figure 16. Franklin Delano Roosevelt and Herbert Hoover in convertible automobile on way to U.S. Capitol for Roosevelt's inauguration, 4 March 1933. After a bruising campaign and combative transition, the defeated incumbent and new president rode together down Pennsylvania Avenue on Inauguration Day. Library of Congress.

new role for the government, based on the premise that the state had a responsibility to ensure basic economic security for its citizens. It took ideas that had been floating out there ever since the days of the robber barons and turned them into federal agencies. It was a radical notion in 1932 that became the status quo.

A second significance of 1932 was that it was a campaign that showed the growing importance of stagecraft, strategy, and a new breed of campaign advisors. Roosevelt's political operative Jim Farley wasn't just good at taking 30,000-mile trips across the country to visit the Democratic establishment. He, and his boss, proved effective at bringing new constituencies into the Democratic Party by a careful combination of retail politics and emotionally resonant and widely broadcast personal appeals by the candidate. They appealed to groups that previously had voted Republican, from native-born small farmers to urban Progressives to African Americans. The result was that the Democrats enlarged their electoral base in ways that allowed it to dominate national politics for fifty years.

What was not obvious at the time was that the 1932 election started to mobilize a new conservative movement. One of the chief catalysts for this was Hoover himself. After spending a little time out of the spotlight, recovering from the election-year onslaught, he came back into public life— swinging. He became one of the loudest and fiercest critics of the New Deal, and helped mobilize conservative business leaders against it. His critiques helped seed new interest groups and political tactics that would help the Republicans redefine their base and redefine politics several decades later.[37]

Last, 1932 was a campaign in which the relationship between politician and voter became personal. Herbert Hoover lost because he did not fully internalize that it was all about the economy, or realize that his ideology and approach were inadequate to redress systemic crisis and reassure a traumatized public. Although highly attuned to the importance of national mood to economic indicators, he failed to deploy the tools of psychology and persuasion to convince Americans that they, and the Republic, would endure. Although a past master of new media, Hoover failed to play by the rules of the new media machine. Roosevelt won in part because he mastered both the messaging and its delivery.

All blame cannot lie on Hoover's choices in the campaign. Some of his problem was one of incumbency. He was trying to stay the course, and no one had faith that the course would correct itself. It was not as if his challenger won on policy. In fact, particularly toward the end of the campaign,

Roosevelt and Hoover were voicing policy positions that sounded markedly similar. Yet these ideas were bathed in generalities as they came from Roosevelt, and straitjacketed in morose defensiveness as they came from Hoover.

It is striking, in listening to the voices of ordinary voters during and after the election, how much their choices hinged on how much they liked and trusted the candidate. Hoover understood the power of image, but not how the magnitude of crisis demanded a compassionate and empathetic leader.

The legacies of 1932 remain. Voters make their choices not on just what candidates say, but on how likeable they seem. Campaign strategists and pollsters slice and dice the electorate into every possible interest group and try to squeeze votes out of them. And, regardless where Americans sit on the political spectrum, all have a relationship with the federal government that simply did not exist prior to 1932. The vast enlargement of the government under Roosevelt—and the further expansion that occurred in the terms of both his Democratic and Republican successors—meant that what happened in Washington had ripple effects across the country, and across the world. Whether American voters think the government should act to do more or do a lot less, they see the relationship between citizens and their government—and their president—as a highly personal one.

These legacies endured, intensified, and became disrupted thirty-six years later, in the election year of 1968.

PART III

*　*　*

1968

CHAPTER 5

*

The Fracturing of America

On 31 March 1968, President Lyndon B. Johnson gave a televised address to the nation. His subject was the Vietnam War, which by this time had escalated into a bloody conflict involving over half a million American soldiers. Two months earlier, the North Vietnamese had launched the Tet Offensive, an assault that moved the guerrilla warfare of the countryside into the streets of Vietnam's cities—beginning with a bold and devastating attack on the U.S. embassy in Saigon. The war had come to the heart of the American presence as well as to where all the reporters were, and television news reports beamed nightly images of bloody urban combat into American homes.

Although the United States inflicted heavy casualties and prevented the North Vietnamese from taking control of new territory, the Tet Offensive was a public relations disaster for the U.S. military and its commander in chief. The generals and Johnson had been assuring the American public all along that the end of the war was in sight, that things were going in the right direction. After Tet, these assurances no longer seemed credible. "For the first time," said one Democratic activist, "a large proportion of the country was capable of being convinced that the government had lied to them."[1]

In late February, venerated CBS news anchor Walter Cronkite appended a short, devastating commentary on the war at the end of a regular evening news broadcast. Pulling off his glasses and looking intently through the camera's lens at his audience of millions, Cronkite grimly announced that his recent trip to Southeast Asia had convinced him that "it seems more certain than ever that the bloody experience of Vietnam is to end in a stalemate." Cronkite's words had "seismic" impact—not simply because a

Figure 17. "War Comes to the Living Room," 13 February 1968. Warren K. Leffler, photographer. Unlike earlier conflicts, the Vietnam War became a much more emotionally and visually immediate experience because of the medium of television, which beamed nightly reports of the war's progress into American living rooms. This heightened during the Tet Offensive of early 1968, where the battle came in from the countryside and onto the streets of Saigon. Library of Congress.

paragon of journalistic objectivity had decided to voice his opinion, but because he expressed the same thing so many of his viewers already were thinking.[2]

The strain of all these events visibly weighed on the president that March evening, and he looked tired and old. The glare of the studio lights showed the deep lines etched in his forehead. He listed the steps the nation was taking to wind down the war, bring the troops home, and negotiate with the North Vietnamese—all things that, for years, had seemed inconceivable admissions of failure. At the end, he made an announcement. Because of the importance of resolving the Vietnam conflict, he said: "I do not believe that I should devote an hour or day of my time to any personal partisan causes. Accordingly, I shall not seek, and I will not accept, the nomination of my party for another term as your president."[3]

And that was it. Lyndon Johnson—the master of the Senate, the consummate politician, and the man who had been among the most powerful dealmakers and power brokers in postwar Washington—was not running for reelection in 1968.

Only a few years earlier, this scenario seemed impossible to imagine. In November 1964, Johnson had won a landslide victory over his Republican challenger for the White House, conservative Arizona senator Barry Goldwater. Goldwater was a Cold Warrior and fiscal conservative who believed in a strong defense but in limited government otherwise. He condemned the Democrats for being willing to negotiate with the Soviets, and darkly warned his supporters of Communism's "unrelenting drive to conquer the world." Such a drive could only be stopped, declared Goldwater, through "peace through preparedness": a strong military, robust nuclear defense, and unflinching leadership.[4]

The Republican establishment in 1964 was similarly hawkish, but otherwise diverged from the uncompromising Goldwater in both style and substance. The party had a strong electoral base in the pro-business urban middle class of the Northeast and Midwest. Beyond the hot buttons of Cold War geopolitics (on which the Democrats could be as hardline as many Republicans), the mainstream GOP had changed little since the Hoover era. It remained strongly pro-business and pro-employer, often ideologically and substantively resistant to market regulation, while at the same time presiding over audacious expansions of government authority. Dwight Eisenhower was a case in point: while championing free markets and American style capitalism, he presided over the building of the interstate highway system and big increases in defense spending. The influence of this on the domestic economy was so staggering that Eisenhower himself darkly warned of a growing "military-industrial complex" as he departed the Oval Office in 1961. Social issues rarely came on the radar screen of mainstream Republicanism. When they did, many in the party still retained some of its old progressive spirit and took positions on welfare and urban policy that now would be considered quite liberal. Embodying all these qualities and contradictions was New York Governor Nelson Rockefeller: staggeringly rich, handsome, intelligent, and the GOP establishment's candidate of choice.[5]

Just as in 1912, deep-seated rifts in the seemingly smooth façade of the Republican Party spilled into the open in 1964. The explosive growth of the Sunbelt in the decades after World War II not only moved the Republican base southward and westward, but also contributed to the Republican base as a whole taking on a more conservative cast. These voters were staunchly

Figure 18. Barry Goldwater Supporters with Black Eyes, Montgomery, Alabama,
17 September 1964. "Us Goldwater people would rather fight than switch!" A group
of young female supporters of Barry Goldwater's 1964 presidential bid played on a
popular advertising campaign for Tareyton cigarettes as they attended a rally in
support of the GOP nominee. Although Goldwater lost in a landslide, he drew
enthusiastic participation from regions and constituencies that had not traditionally
voted Republican, and that later became keys to victory for both Nixon and Reagan.
Bettman/Corbis/AP Images.

anti-Communist, suspicious of big government, and resentful of public
intervention into personal choices. Barry Goldwater spoke their language.
Buoyed by passionate grassroots support and an increasingly powerful network of conservative political organizations, Goldwater shocked Rockefeller
Republicans by winning the nomination and carrying his unflinching conservatism to the national stage.[6]

Lyndon Johnson ran on a very different vision, backed by a different set
of interests. The Democratic Party of 1964 was built by the New Deal and
FDR, whose programs had created a strong working-class base for the party
in the industrial cities and in rural farms and small towns. African Americans migrated to the Democratic column during the Roosevelt years, and

Johnson's signing of the Civil Rights Act of 1964 cemented this loyalty, as well as the support of white liberals. But it marked the disintegration of another critical Democratic bloc: racially conservative white Southerners. In the wake of federal action on civil rights, the Solid South that had been the key ingredient of past Democratic presidential victories began to unravel, as did the malodorous set of compromises that had kept both white segregationists and African Americans in the Democratic tent since the 1930s.[7] Without assured support south of the Mason-Dixon line, Democrats had to work harder to keep the other pieces of the New Deal coalition in the fold as the decade progressed.

Rifts emerged in both parties in the 1964 election, but the Democrats did a better job of keeping their competing interests together. The spirit of the times helped. The New Deal ethos had evolved in the early Cold War years into a dominant liberal strain that leaders like Johnson epitomized. These politicians believed in the welfare state and an active federal government. They believed in strong defense and containment of the power of the Soviet Union. It was a sort of neo-Progressivism, believing that government by "enlightened" experts could win out over "backward" small government and states-rights advocates.

This brand of politics matched the temperament of the postwar era, when the United States experienced an extraordinary and unprecedented run of prosperity. It was prosperity built on big organizations and institutions: corporations, labor unions, and the federal government. It drove its energy and ideology from a high-stakes struggle with a big, dangerous enemy, the USSR. It was built on a foundation forged through the shared struggle of the Great Depression and World War II—that Americans should all be "in it together" and every citizen should be treated equally. It presumed that Americans shared a set of values and had a shared destiny. The engagement in Vietnam was itself a manifestation of this grand project, and reflected what Richard Hofstadter once identified as both parties' "belief that we have an almost magical capacity to have our way in the world . . . at a relatively small price."[8]

Johnson's 1964 campaign delivered such a thumping defeat to the Goldwater effort because it embraced this bigness. It preyed on people's fears that Barry Goldwater was playing to small prejudices rather than fighting for big, shared goals. "Extremism in the defense of liberty is no vice," proclaimed Goldwater in his acceptance speech at the Republican convention. Extremism, Johnson reminded the American voters, was a step backward from the ethos of togetherness that had knit the nation together through depression and war and peacetime prosperity. Television advertising became the medium through which these increasingly combative messages flowed, the most notorious of these being Johnson's "Daisy" ad, with its dark implications about Goldwater's irresponsible eagerness to press the nuclear button. The commercial aired only once, yet became legendary for its boldness.

The 1964 election results seemed to prove that the rest of the country agreed Goldwater was not the right person to have his finger on the nuclear button. Johnson won forty-four states. The six that went for Goldwater, however, were bellwethers of things to come: his home state of Arizona, and five Deep South states that had gone for Democrats since the Civil War.

On the one hand, the tale of 1964 versus 1968 is a testament to how quickly things can turn in politics. On the other, the Johnson-Goldwater contest sent out many signals of the coming fracture of American politics— and American culture—that exploded in 1968. Republicans took Goldwater's defeat as a definitive rejection by American voters of the kind of sharply conservative politics espoused by the Arizona senator. They were wrong; Americans may have rejected Goldwater the candidate, but his conservative ideas resonated more deeply and widely than the party elders appreciated. The New Deal coalition Franklin Roosevelt built in 1932 had endured and strengthened, turning the Democrats into the largest and most nationally dominant political party of the postwar years. Yet at the same time, a conservative wing of the Republican Party had been growing steadily stronger, building an alternative economic vision to Keynesian liberalism and arguing that the federal government's growth was imperiling free markets and individual rights.[9]

Lyndon Johnson was too savvy and seasoned a politician to interpret his victory as a mandate. "I was just elected President by the biggest popular margin in the history of the country—16 million votes," he told White House advisors in January 1965. "Just by the way people naturally think and because Barry Goldwater had simply scared hell out of them, I've already lost about three of those sixteen. After a fight with Congress or something else, I'll lose another couple of million. I could be down to eight million in a couple of months."[10] With a fragile base of support and a breathtakingly ambitious legislative agenda, the Johnson administration had to move quickly. In the coming months, Johnson would push through a domestic policy agenda of the scope and scale never seen since FDR's first hundred days in office. Some of these measures did not outlive the 1960s. Others—notably Medicare and Medicaid—continue to have a profound effect on the political landscape and the lives of ordinary citizens. While recognizing the political challenges, Johnson and his Democratic allies had faith that this collective enterprise could keep the New Deal coalition knit together, and assumed that domestic affairs would prove far more politically important than the conflict in Vietnam. They were wrong.

The election of 1968 became pivotal because it marked both the full-throated emergence of modern conservatism and the agonizing disintegration of the New Deal Democratic coalition. That both dramas played out, in color, on the small television screens in living rooms across America and across the world made these two political transformations on right and left so vivid, so visceral, and so profoundly influential.

The Breakdown

The first ripples of political revolution came in California, not surprising for a place that journalist Carey McWilliams forecast in 1949 as "a revolution within the states . . . tipping the scales of the nation's interest and wealth and population to the West."[11] California's Democratic governor, Pat Brown, was one of the most powerful and iconic liberal politicians of his generation. He was popular, and seemingly unbeatable. In 1962, Rich ard Nixon had run against him and lost. Coming on the heels of Nixon's loss to John F. Kennedy in the 1960 presidential election, the defeat seemed to be the end of Nixon's political career. "You won't have Nixon to kick around anymore," the former vice president scowled to reporters afterward.[12]

But in 1964 and 1965, things started to happen. At the University of California flagship campus in Berkeley, students walked out of classes and held mass demonstrations to protest the university's restrictions of on-campus political activities. More students were attending college or university in the United States than ever before in the nation's history, and once they got to these campuses many of these children of American postwar prosperity started to question the status quo and the men who created it. Taking cues from the civil rights movement and its tactics of organized, peaceful protest, the students at Berkeley voiced their displeasure through mass demonstration and continuous occupation. The expansive liberalism of Pat Brown had helped build the California system into the jewel in the crown of American public higher education; now the beneficiaries of this system were turning against it.

The following summer, another big crack appeared in the liberal consensus. Less than a week after Johnson signed the Voting Rights Act into law, the black neighborhood of Watts in Los Angeles exploded into fiery violence. A brief struggle after the arrest of a young black man named Marquette Frye on drunk-driving charges set off six days of violent rebellion. After the fires died down, 34 people were dead, more than a thousand were injured, and the neighborhood lay devastated. The nightly news captured all of it, transmitting raw footage of angry looters and storefronts in flames to viewers sitting in comfortable suburban cul-de-sacs only a few miles away. The tragedy of Watts underscored the incomplete nature of the civil right revolution, which had brought about political rights but had done nothing to ameliorate black poverty.

Enter Ronald Reagan. The movie star had already morphed into a major power player in conservative political circles, and in the late days of the 1964 campaign had burst out onto the public stage with an eloquent televised speech in support of Barry Goldwater. Reagan said many of the same things as Goldwater, but communicated them in a telegenic, compelling, sympathetic way. Messages that seemed scary coming from the 1964 Republican nominee sounded more reasonable when they came from Reagan. Emboldened and encouraged, he ran for California governor in 1966. His campaign was devastatingly effective, painting Brown and his big-government vision as responsible for the chaos on college campuses and Los Angeles streets. Because of soft liberal policies, "this great university has been brought to its knees by a neurotic, dissident minority," Reagan said. And when it came to Watts, the problem lay with "the Governor turning to these government programs as an answer to poverty." Reagan defeated Brown, who had seemed so unassailable four years before. His big win was the first shot in the Reagan Revolution.[13]

Yet another funny thing happened on the way to the 1966 election in California. In the primaries, an antiwar candidate named Robert Scheer won 45 percent of the vote in the Democratic primary for California's Seventh Congressional District. Scheer hailed from left-leaning Berkeley, where the peace movement certainly was the strongest, but his strong challenge to

Folder 19. Reagan Victory Party, Biltmore Hotel, Los Angeles, 1966. Ronald Reagan ran for governor of California in 1966 on a law and order message with great appeal to voters made anxious and angry by civil disorders in Los Angeles and student protests in Berkeley. His victory over liberal incumbent Pat Brown was a critical sign of growing conservative momentum among voters. Courtesy Ronald Reagan Library.

a Democratic incumbent and Johnson stalwart was a warning shot for the intraparty warfare to come.

What was the meaning of California? political pundits asked. Was America becoming more liberal, more conservative, or both? Only one thing was clear: the 1968 presidential race was not going to be as predictable as Democratic liberals and Rockefeller Republicans had hoped it might be.

The Great Society

Lyndon Johnson had used his 1964 electoral victory as leverage to advance an ambitious agenda designed to ensure that American prosperity was equally shared. He had unveiled this vision in a speech in the spring of 1964 at the University of Michigan that came to encapsulate the bold, optimistic thinking of postwar liberalism. "In your time," he told the assembled students, "we have the opportunity to move not only toward the rich society and the powerful society, but upward to the Great Society." Johnson continued:

> This rests on abundance and liberty for all. It demands an end to poverty and racial injustice, to which we are totally committed in our time. . . . The Great Society is a place where every child can find knowledge to enrich his mind and to enlarge his talents. It is a place where leisure is a welcome chance to build and reflect, not a feared cause of boredom and restlessness. It is a place where the city of man serves not only the needs of the body and the demands of commerce but the desire for beauty and the hunger for community.[14]

Government action, Johnson believed, was at the heart of what was needed to bring all these things about. His vision had broad resonance. One Republican legislator mused that Johnson "has not only taken the center, he's taken most of the right and left as well."[15] After reelection, he set about putting the Great Society agenda into place. To appease the critics of ever-spiraling tax rates (the marginal tax on the rich was the highest it would be at any point in the twentieth century), he pushed through a massive tax cut. Confident that an ever-growing economy would provide the necessary revenue for new social programs, he and his legislative allies passed legislation establishing Medicare and Medicaid, the biggest domestic programs since Social Security.

Drawing inspiration from Franklin Roosevelt, he turned his attention to the people that the New Deal ultimately had failed to help: the poorest of the poor, long-term unemployed, and the young people of color trapped in grim urban ghettos. Johnson had begun his career as a schoolteacher in the hardscrabble Texas Hill Country, and the plight of the mostly Mexican immigrant children he taught had never left him. The result of LBJ's efforts was a stunning set of legislative achievements during the 89th Congress of 1965–66, ranging from immigration reform to voting rights, education to housing, urban programs to child nutrition.[16]

The high-spend, low-tax regime of the Great Society did not take into account the spiraling costs of Vietnam. In his 1966 State of the Union address Johnson acknowledged, "because of Vietnam we cannot do all that we should, or all that we would like to do," but continued to argue that the bold domestic agenda must go forward.[17] Some fellow Democrats disagreed. "Despite brave talk about having both 'guns and butter,'" Arkansas senator William Fulbright declared, "the Vietnamese war has already had a destructive effect on the Great Society."[18]

Over the course of 1966, the Vietnam War began to burst into the forefront of national consciousness as more and more young American men were conscripted into the military. Between 1960 and 1964, an average of 100,000 men had been drafted annually. In 1966, it peaked at more than 380,000. To avoid the uncertainties of conscription and increase the odds of securing jobs away from the front lines of combat, about four times that many enlisted voluntarily in the military, so that by 1968 a third of all American twenty-year-old men were in uniform.[19]

These soldiers were members of a new and politically challenging generation. The baby boom after World War II had produced a huge wave of young people who had grown up in an America more affluent, more educated, and more comfortable than any period before in its history. *Time* magazine named the under twenty-five generation (men and women) its "man of the year" in 1967. In flowery newsweekly prose, *Time* reporters wrote, "This is not just a new generation, but a new kind of generation. . . . He is the man who will land on the moon, cure cancer and the common cold, lay out blight-proof, smog-free cities, enrich the underdeveloped world, and no doubt, write *finis* to poverty and war."[20]

However, the young people in the suburbs and on the college campuses were not thinking that they would solve the world's problems on their parents' terms. In fact, they thought society's problems mostly came from things their parents' generation had done in the first place. By the time they became "man of the year," they were not as singularly focused on cancer cures and moon landings as their elders expected them to be. They were growing their hair long, dropping out, marching and striking, and condemning their political leaders for doing far too little to stop the carnage of Vietnam, address racial discrimination, and fix economic inequality.

The looming specter of the draft made the Vietnam crisis deeply personal for the under twenty-five generation. The proportion of eligible Americans who served in Vietnam ultimately was far smaller than in either World War II—when eight of ten eligible men had entered the military—or Korea, but the uncertainty of the draft, and the particular vulnerability of young, unmarried men to being called up, made it an ever-present worry. Anxiety escalated as Johnson called for more and more troops. Poor and minority men proved much more likely to be called up and see active duty.[21] "It seems like every time you hear about a Chicago boy getting killed over there, it turns out to be a Negro," one shopkeeper on Chicago's Westside commented to a reporter. Civil rights leaders like Martin Luther King, Jr., started to raise their voices in sharp criticism of the men Johnson had put in charge of running the war. "The bombs in Vietnam explode at home," King told a Senate subcommittee in late 1966. "They destroy the hopes and possibilities for a decent America."[22]

Many other voices joined the chorus. The nonviolent tactics King and others had used to mobilize broad-based support for civil rights had shown other Americans how these strategies could organize and mobilize other kinds of social protest. College students were among those most energized by these sorts of tactics, and the great spike in college attendance after World War II meant that more and more young people were on campus, talking about Vietnam, and ready to protest against it. In the summer of 1965, over 17,000 peace activists crowded into Madison Square Garden to protest the war; a few months later, more than 30,000 marched on Washington. In early 1966, leaders of the peace movement announced plans to mobilize support for antiwar Congressional candidates. The antiwar movement was growing.[23]

By 1967, it was abundantly clear that Vietnam had painted Johnson into a political corner and was eating away at all the other achievements he had made in his domestic agenda. Liberal Democratic activists started a "Dump Johnson" movement and busily started vetting various antiwar senators as potential primary challengers. Republicans condemned Johnson both for the conduct of the war and for the conduct of the war protesters. Venerable commentator Walter Lippmann concluded that Johnson had "gone off the deep end."[24]

The venomous reaction people had against him personally was made all the more infuriating because Johnson had entered his presidency with many doubts about Vietnam. Speaking to his political mentor, Georgia senator Richard B. Russell, in a phone call in the spring of 1964, he had confessed that he kept asking himself "what the hell are we going to get out of it?" But withdrawing didn't seem an option: "I don't see any other way out," he said, ruefully. Instead, he turned around and told his advisors that he was determined not to "lose Vietnam." Besides, it wasn't even a real war yet; the public had little inkling of the decisions being made and the rationale behind them. The next year, escalation began.[25]

Johnson became Target Number One for an under twenty-five generation anxious about the draft, outraged about racial prejudice and frustrated with society's attempts to right the wrongs of poverty and injustice. The author of the Great Society, who considered himself a fighter for the poorest of the poor, was now vilified as a symbol of a heartless establishment. "I don't understand these young people," Johnson later told a biographer. "Don't they realize I'm really one of them? . . . I'm not some conformist middle-class personality."[26]

The tragedy of Vietnam caused Americans to lose faith in Johnson, and along with it they lost faith in the consensus liberalism and big politics he championed. Government no longer promised solutions; instead, it created problems. Both Democrats and Republicans started to break away from the vast moderate middle that had dominated politics from Roosevelt and Truman through Eisenhower and Kennedy. Other American voters, particularly younger ones, turned away from party politics altogether. They moved toward the left, and toward the right. As they did so, their ideas about the source of society's problems and the necessary solutions started to diverge dramatically. Yet coming into the election season of 1968, there was general agreement on both ends that the Vietnam conflict had been grossly mismanaged, and that the men in the White House were to blame.

Another catalytic political shift was occurring in the civil rights movement. Johnson had magisterially presided over signing the Civil Rights Act into law in 1964, followed by the Voting Rights Act in 1965. Both were landmarks, remedying decades of political and legal injustice, but they had done little to help the deep economic inequality faced by communities of color. The civil rights movement had largely played out in the South, where Jim Crow segregation and overt racial bigotry and violence had horrified a nation and built support for federal intervention. Yet an increasingly large portion of black America lived in the ghettos of northern, urban industrial cities, and civil rights legislation had done nothing to alleviate their plight.

Many African American leaders felt that Johnson's war on poverty agenda did not seem to do much either. Although the president talked a big game, the legislative results merely chipped away at social problems with big, systemic origins. "My major criticism," testified the Urban League's Whitney Young in a Senate hearing, "is that we are, in effect, using a slingshot for a job that calls for nuclear weapons." People in the most affected communities agreed. On Chicago's majority black South Side, "the residents in the community are becoming convinced that the whole program is a farce," community activist Marie Brookter told a reporter.[27]

This frustration spilled out vividly and violently in poor black neighborhoods, beginning with small disturbances and escalating into much larger ones. After the devastating rioting in the Los Angeles Watts neighborhood in the summer of 1965, similar paroxysms of violence tore apart black neighborhoods across the country in the summers of 1966, 1967, and 1968. Whenever the weather heated up, mayhem followed. White liberals, who had marched for civil rights and shared Johnson's Great Society idealism, began to recognize that bigger problems were not being addressed "The social dynamite created by poor, black central cities surrounded by comfortable white suburbs," one man wrote to the *New York Times*, "may present a more serious challenge to our democracy than Communism in Vietnam."[28]

The summer of 1967 saw two civil disorders unmatched in size and devastation—one in Newark, and another in Detroit a week and a half later. Afterward, President Johnson charged a federal commission with investigating the causes of these events, which grimly concluded, "white racism is essentially responsible for the explosive mixture which has been accumulating in our cities since the end of World War II." The people in Watts and Newark and Detroit had known that for years.[29]

Momentum shifted away from some civil rights leaders and toward others. Some in the new generation of African Americans began to be impatient with the nonviolent tactics of Martin Luther King, Jr., and his allies. They were frustrated by alliances with white liberals, who could sympathize with the cause of racial equity but never had to experience discrimination themselves. They saw both Vietnam and the War on Poverty as policies for which people of color paid the highest price. Stokely Carmichael, an activist who had participated in the Freedom Rides alongside white college students in the early 1960s, was one leader of a new Black Power movement that placed economic injustice front and center and took a more militant approach to the civil rights struggle. As Carmichael put it: "You can't form a coalition with people who are economically secure. College students are economically secure; they already got their wealth; we are fighting to get ours. And for us to get it is going to mean tearing down their system, and they are not willing to work for their own destruction."[30]

Carmichael was articulating a new sort of identity politics that was the antithesis of big politics of Cold War consensus liberalism. It wasn't a vision where "we all are in this together," where government insures universal welfare and equal rights. It was a vision of an America that was diverse, often unjust, and where different groups didn't necessarily see eye to eye.

The New Year

The liberal effort to block Johnson from reelection and get an antiwar candidate before the voters bore fruit at the end of 1967. Minnesota senior senator Eugene McCarthy announced he would run for the Democratic nomination. Gene McCarthy was a fifty-year-old former college professor with a love for poetry and an impatience for petty legislative politics. One colleague said McCarthy was "the most intelligent man in Congress"—but he did not intend this to be a compliment. McCarthy had his first moment of national prominence in 1960, when he spoke in support of Adlai Stevenson's candidacy for the Democratic nomination. The eventual nominee, Jack Kennedy, never forgave him for it, and the deep dislike between McCarthy and the Kennedys had grown ever since. Johnson had toyed with nominating McCarthy as his vice president in the 1964 race, but went with the other senator from Minnesota, Hubert Humphrey.[31]

By late 1967, McCarthy was bored with the Senate and deeply frustrated by the Johnson administration's conduct in the Vietnam War. He was bitter that others had risen to higher office while he languished in the legislature. "I'm twice as liberal as Hubert Humphrey . . . and twice as Catholic as Jack Kennedy," McCarthy once said, not entirely joking. The father of college-age children, he ultimately became convinced to throw his hat into the ring by his daughter Mary, a Radcliffe freshman. "The aging politician," noted one election chronicler, "raised the flag for a children's crusade."[32]

However, the smart money was still on Lyndon Johnson. The first primary was in traditionally conservative New Hampshire, and polling data before the election indicated McCarthy was not going to make a serious dent. To seasoned political observers, the McCarthy campaign's heavy reliance on student volunteers made it seem even more like amateur hour. Major national newspapers spent little time covering the candidate; when one supporter of McCarthy wrote the *New York Times* complaining of its inattention, the paper replied that the Minnesota senator was a "one-issue" candidate not deserving any more than cursory coverage.[33]

The polls, professionals, and papers were wrong. When the final tally came in, Johnson won the Democratic primary, but McCarthy came in only 7 percentage points behind. The "student power" McCarthy had employed turned out to be extraordinarily effective: more than ten thousand young people who came to New Hampshire full of passion and willing to do anything to see their candidate succeed. "Not since the civil rights march on Mississippi in the summer of 1964 had so many young Americans committed themselves so fervently to a major national cause," *Time* magazine reported with some amazement. Their devotion extended to shaving off beards and cutting long hair in order to be "Neat and Clean for Gene," as the campaign slogan proclaimed.[34]

New York senator Robert F. Kennedy was watching all this unfold. The loathing between Robert Kennedy and Lyndon Johnson is legendary. In the flurry of back-room dealing that chose a running mate for John Kennedy in 1960, Bobby Kennedy had worked himself into all kinds of political contortions to prevent his brother from choosing Johnson, whom he considered imperious, crass, and racist. Johnson, in turn, considered the younger Kennedy brother an impertinent and amoral attack dog. During the Kennedy presidency, Attorney General Robert Kennedy and Vice President Lyndon Johnson continually butted heads. It got worse after JFK's death. Kennedy once said of Johnson: "In every conversation I have with him, he lies." Johnson, in turn, dismissed Kennedy as a "little snot-nosed son-of-a-bitch."[35]

From the moment Johnson became president, people around Robert Kennedy kept floating the idea that he should run for the White House himself. History seemed to advise against RFK's trying to do it in 1968. No incumbent president had ever failed to become his party's nominee, and the seasoned advisors around Kennedy—as well as the man himself— concluded he should wait until 1972.

Yet as the years passed, Kennedy sensed the change in the country's mood, and his politics were shifting as well. He traveled around the country relentlessly, and his visits to burned-out inner cities made him increasingly focused on the problems of racial injustice and poverty. Although he had been part of his brother's inner circle as it made early, crucial decisions on Vietnam, he watched with horror as the conflict escalated. His experience in his brother's administration had made him suspicious of what military and intelligence leaders said and did. Seeing Johnson sink farther into the Vietnam quagmire, he began to suspect that his old enemy was not merely loathsome, but actually insane.[36]

McCarthy's victory in New Hampshire showed Kennedy that antiwar sentiment was strong enough to topple the president. An obscure senator from Minnesota might not be able to do it. But a Kennedy could. RFK had forcefully denied planning to run as recently as January, but no sooner were the New Hampshire results tallied that he said, "I am reassessing my position." Four days later, with loving wife and ten children at his side, he held a press conference on Capitol Hill. He announced that he was running.

In making this move, RFK bucked both the Democratic Party establishment and the gentlemen's agreements delineating acceptable political behavior. He was not only challenging a sitting president of his own party, but also trampling all over Eugene McCarthy's attempt to become the candidate of the antiwar movement. "This is the cheapest sort of opportunism," blasted the conservative *Chicago Tribune*. "Not since the days of Aaron Burr has the country been treated to such an example of unbridled personal ambition." Liberal columnist Murray Kempton was even more harsh on Kennedy: "He has, in the naked display of his rage at Eugene McCarthy for having survived on the lonely road he dared not walk himself, done with a single great gesture something very few public men have ever been able to do: in one day he managed to confirm the worst things his enemies have ever said about him."[37]

Although the press might have howled, the entry of the charismatic Kennedy began to erode the candidacy of the sober, poetry-quoting Eugene McCarthy. The next big primary was Wisconsin, where the president was running far behind McCarthy in the polls. Johnson announced his withdrawal from the race two days before the Wisconsin vote, and it was a good thing he did. McCarthy won over 400,000 votes, edging out the president by more than 150,000. Robert Kennedy was not on the ballot, but got over 46,000 votes as a write-in.[38]

With Wisconsin, things became more complicated. Johnson was gone, but McCarthy was showing himself to be a serious opponent to Kennedy. The young people who had mobilized for McCarthy felt that he, not RFK, was the authentic antiwar candidate. Yet the liberal power brokers who had worked so hard behind the scenes to get a Johnson challenger were experiencing a bit of buyer's remorse when it came to Gene McCarthy. An outsider and an iconoclast, and more conservative at heart than some of his bleeding-heart liberal allies liked, McCarthy was an imperfect candidate for an antiwar faction who wanted victory in November. For some of them, Kennedy had been their first choice. Now that Kennedy was officially in, their enthusiasm for McCarthy became several degrees cooler. Allard Lowenstein, chief architect of the "Dump Johnson" movement in 1967 and passionate Robert Kennedy loyalist, tried to broker a deal where Kennedy and McCarthy would agree to split the remaining candidates so the antiwar vote would not have to be shared between the two of them. Deeply irritated, McCarthy turned the deal down. On the stump, his jabs at Kennedy became personal. "He plays touch football," scoffed McCarthy to one crowd. "I play football."[39]

Then, to further complicate the Democrats' civil war, there was Johnson's vice president, Hubert Humphrey. Humphrey had been among the first to learn that Johnson was not running, and on hearing the news had burst into tears—for Johnson, and for his own political prospects. He had long had White House ambitions, but being Johnson's number-two was not an electoral advantage this turbulent season. "Hubert has always been in trouble because he was ahead of his time," commented Washington pundit James "Scotty" Reston, "but now, for once, he seems to be late and out of luck. He has been punished for playing a role he didn't like and couldn't avoid." Off the record, Humphrey's Democratic colleagues were blunter in their assessment. "He has all the disabilities without any of the strengths that Johnson has," one grumbled. Undeterred, Humphrey started to work the phones, asking his friends in the Democratic establishment to refrain from committing to either of the antiwar candidates just yet.[40]

The political reforms that had introduced the direct primary system were more than five decades old, but the system of choosing party nominees still remained a game insiders could dominate if they so chose. There were still 33 states that did not have binding primaries, meaning their delegates were not locked into support for any particular candidates until the convention. The exhaustive press coverage of the primary battles had not increased transparency, but instead created more opportunities for political spin. Media-saturated primaries had become "costly battles between the candidates for cards to play when the backroom dealing starts." This was all good news for Hubert Humphrey. He was not on the ballot in any primary states, and didn't have to be. He could still win the nomination if the party regulars were with him. Instead he ran proxy candidates in primary states, so that his opponents couldn't get enough delegates to win.[41]

So it was a real three-way race, not the simple path for which Kennedy and his supporters might have hoped. However, RFK was certainly number one when it came to attention from the press. Reporters who covered both Kennedys observed that their politics was an artful combination of grassroots constituency-building and charismatic image-making. Robert Kennedy's 1968 campaign involved both, but the charismatic side of things dominated. As he told a student audience, "The contest in 1968 is not for the rule of America, but for its heart."[42]

Kennedy's grasp of this politics of the heart showed itself on the day Martin Luther King, Jr., was assassinated. Coming on the heels of events at home and abroad that already had rocked the nation since the New Year, King's death on 4 April triggered violent convulsions of destruction and looting in cities like Detroit, Chicago, and Washington. On that dreadful day, Robert Kennedy was campaigning in Indianapolis. The state was a tough one for Democrats. Gritty steel towns in the north filled with racial tensions and growing white working-class resentment; its southern hill country was home to a mix of conservative and populist politics, and only forty years earlier had been home to some of the nation's largest chapters of the Ku Klux Klan. Pure liberalism did not go over well in Indiana. Kennedy started the campaign painfully, giving earnest speeches on poverty to small-town civic clubs that didn't want to hear about it. McCarthy, too, found his antiwar message had far less steam in Indiana than elsewhere.[43]

Kennedy was campaigning in a black neighborhood as the news of King's death came over the wire. Recognizing the potential for the moment to turn violent, Kennedy's advisors urged him to stay in his hotel room. Indianapolis police did the same. Instead, Kennedy went ahead as planned with a nighttime rally, rising up before the large crowd and breaking the news. After the gasps from the audience had died down, Kennedy stood in the cold and dark, and delivered an ad-lib and very personal speech. "I can only say that I feel in my heart the same kind of feeling," he said, and as if anyone needed reminding, "I had a member of my own family killed." Then he pleaded for peace. "Let us dedicate ourselves to what the Greeks wrote so many years ago: to tame the savageness of man and to make gentle the life of this world." Rioting did not break out in Indianapolis that night, and reporters broadcast

Figure 20. Eugene McCarthy at Campaign Headquarters Opening, Manhattan,
23 April 1968. Once Robert F. Kennedy entered the race, he siphoned off both
supporters and media attention from McCarthy. As McCarthy geared up for
the New York State primary, he could not escape the looming presence of student
activists who now backed RFK. Bettman/Corbis/AP Images.

news of Kennedy's eloquence across the nation. At last, the younger Kennedy
seemed to be rising to the greatness of his mourned older brother. He won
Indiana, and the momentum grew from there.[44]

The reputation of Kennedy grew, especially among the under twenty-
five generation. Many college students still gravitated to McCarthy, but
Kennedy had the star power McCarthy lacked. Posters of RFK became a
dorm room staple. One sign in the crowd at a Kennedy rally proclaimed,
"Bobby is Groovy." He held fundraisers featuring the Byrds and Sonny and
Cher. Crowds surged around him at his appearances, reaching grasping
hands toward him, to touch him, to feel the magic. Kennedy started to knit
together the different groups who were turning their back on big politics
and embracing identity politics. He was no longer a consensus liberal. He
was a standard-bearer for the New Left. He had the youth and charisma
to glue together these anxious and agitated interest groups into a larger
cause.[45]

The primary season was full of tightly fought contests. Kennedy won Indiana and Nebraska and South Dakota. McCarthy won Pennsylvania and Massachusetts and Oregon. By April, Humphrey had officially thrown his hat into the ring and was zinging his Democratic rivals relentlessly. "I do believe," Humphrey said of Kennedy, "there is such a thing as too much ambition." He decried both of his opponents for their dour assessments of America's trajectory. "You won't make this country better by leading from fear, despair and doubt," said the vice president. Instead, Humphrey made his campaign theme "the spirit of happiness." Yet Hubert Humphrey, for all his intelligence and likability, was such a workmanlike politician his optimistic urgings had little of the emotional pull of Robert Kennedy's poetics or even Gene McCarthy's low-key persuasion. "There's very little poetry in him," one Democratic senator confided of Humphrey. "He says very few things you want to remember, let alone quote."[46]

With the Democratic establishment behind him, however, Humphrey was still the man for McCarthy and Kennedy to beat. By late spring, all the key elements of the Democratic power structure forged by the New Deal order had come down on the side of Humphrey: the labor unions, business leaders, and big-city political bosses. It all came down to the California primary on 5 June. The winner of that would be the person who would take on Humphrey for the nomination.

Kennedy won, narrowly. He gave a rousing victory speech just before midnight at the Ambassador Hotel in Los Angeles. Then, as he exited through the hotel kitchen, six shots fired out. Robert Kennedy was dead, killed by a gunman angry about Kennedy's support of Israel.

The nation once again went into mourning. Crowds lined the tracks as the train bearing Kennedy's body rolled across the country, from California back east for burial in Arlington National Cemetery. Before that, his body lay in state in New York City's St. Patrick's Cathedral, where more than 150,000 people waited up to six hours to file through, paying their respects to their fallen hero. With Bobby Kennedy's death, the constellation of factions that was the New Left lost their most compelling leader, the glue that stuck them together, the man who had seized the mantle from McCarthy to become *the* antiwar candidate. The rest of the country mourned as well. The cover of *Newsweek* asked, "Has Violence Become an American Way of Life?" One newspaper columnist declared, "The country does not work anymore." The candidates suspended their campaigns for two weeks.[47]

From 1963 to 1968, three icons—two Kennedys and one King—perished in a hail of assassins' bullets. The men to whom many Americans had turned to make sense of a rapidly changing world were all killed in their prime. The depths of this trauma spilled through politics, making some people want to abandon formal politics altogether. It made others look for bolder, more radical political solutions. The fracturing of America, and the fracturing of the Democratic Party, were well underway before Robert Kennedy died, but his killing seemed to fracture things further. For the worst days of the Democratic Party's election season were still to come.

CHAPTER 6

*

Improbable Victories

In early January 1968, Democratic National Committee Chairman John Bailey made a prediction. No matter how unpopular Lyndon Johnson had become, Eugene McCarthy was a mere irritant who posed no real challenge to the president: "we know who our nominees will be." Instead, chuckled Bailey, "I'm happy to be able to say the Republicans have all their bloody infighting to look forward to."[1] Bailey was spinning the party line, but it resonated with the conventional wisdom in Washington at the start of the election year. The Republican Party remained a house divided between Rockefeller-style moderates and Goldwater-Reagan conservatives. Before the GOP could make a credible challenge for the White House, it needed to come to terms with which side of the party would prevail in nominating a candidate. Whoever won the nomination would, in turn, need a message that could win nationally.

In finding this candidate and this message, the Republican Party began to shift itself rightward, beginning a process that fundamentally recast the GOP, its constituencies, and its leadership. This rightward shift was not wholly visible to observers in 1968, but it found its direction and gained its momentum from gut-wrenching changes experienced by Americans of the New Deal generation that turbulent year. The causes of all these changes became conflated in voters' minds—war, youth in revolt, and ghettos on fire all seemed symptoms of the same national illness. Politics followed society, not the other way around. The disintegration of big-politics America pulled citizens to the outer edges. And it was the rightward edge, rather than the leftward, that ultimately won the battle for the Republican Party's soul.

The construction of a new conservatism was not the GOP's doing alone, but also came from the fractures within the Democratic Party in the post-civil rights era. For the Democrats of 1968 were not all liberals or peaceniks, campaigning on an end to war and the end of poverty. Some of them were very, very conservative, and the journey of these voters and their leaders out of the Democratic Party and toward the GOP turned conventional wisdom on its head, redrew the electoral map, and reshaped the two parties going forward.

The Southern Question

The Republican Party had a numbers problem in the mid-1960s. Nationally, only 27 percent of Americans identified themselves as Republican while 48 percent called themselves Democrats. Yet much of that Democratic margin came from Southern states where federal action on civil rights had begun to break down white voters' formerly rock-solid allegiance to the Democratic Party. Outside his home state of Arizona, the only states conservative Barry Goldwater won in 1964 were in the Deep South. More important, the changes in the South's population and economic geography since World War II profoundly altered who voted, why they voted, and what sorts of political messages resonated. The region was exploding in population, and the areas that were growing the fastest were middle-class suburbs ringing cities like Atlanta and Charlotte and Dallas and Houston. The emergence of what came to be called the New South moved the region from one-party rule to a two-party system. The South had been a critical bloc in nearly every presidential election since Jefferson and Adams, but the bigger, bolder, richer New South mattered more than ever before.[2]

Yet the Old South persisted. The disintegration of the old racial order had fueled the rise of a set of fiercely segregationist politicians who spoke about states' rights and law and order in ways that appealed to the rural white constituencies who felt both economically and politically marginalized in the Space Age, suburbanized South of the 1960s. South Carolinian Strom Thurmond had been the first of these politicians to use segregation as a platform to challenge the status quo, breaking from the Democrats in 1948 over their pro-civil rights platform plank and running an insurgent campaign as candidate of the States' Rights Democratic Party, known as the "Dixiecrats."

By the mid-1960s, Alabama governor George Wallace had emerged as the inheritor to Thurmond's states rights throne. A Democrat, Wallace first ran for Alabama governor in 1958 as a racial moderate. He rejected the endorsement of the Ku Klux Klan and accepted that of the NAACP. He lost, badly. After that defeat, Wallace's racial attitudes transformed. In 1962 he ran again for governor, and won. He became a staunch defender of segregation. And he had a flair for theatrical gestures that generated media attention and increased his national profile.

At his inauguration in 1963, Wallace proclaimed: "In the name of the greatest people that have ever trod this earth, I draw the line in the dust and toss the gauntlet before the feet of tyranny. And I say, Segregation now! Segregation tomorrow! Segregation forever!" Shortly after that, he protested integration by literally standing at the door of a University of Alabama building to block its first two black students from registering, giving a fiery speech that made the national television newscasts. He first ran for the Democratic nomination for president in 1964.[3]

Wallace played off 1960s-era white voters' fears of the changes that came in the wake of federal integration orders, but in his methods and his message he was a classic populist, fighting for the people against powerful, far-off, faceless interests who sought to unfairly constrain their lives. It was a message that had resonated with beleaguered small farmers in the 1880s Middle West, radicals and Socialists in the Progressive Era, and unemployed laborers in the Great Depression. It had been a language that historically had pressed toward left-wing political solutions, but by the time it got to Wallace, it had turned sharply toward the right. Wallace realized that only the South cared so deeply about preserving segregation, but voters across the nation could relate to the broader populist idea, especially at a moment when an intrusive and untrustworthy big government was becoming so unpopular. Wallace was a Democrat, but a dramatically different sort of Democrat than Gene McCarthy, or Bobby Kennedy, or the Great Society-era Lyndon Johnson. He started thinking about another try for the White House.[4]

Meanwhile, Republicans saw the electoral opportunity that lay in Southern states, but they also recognized that uncompromising opposition to civil rights could alienate the constituencies of the New South. In the 1950s Dwight Eisenhower had won significant inroads into the region, in large part because of the appeal of the GOP's pro-business message to urban and suburban white-collar professionals. Another part of the Southern opportunity lay in shoring up support of African Americans who had

Figure 21. Governor George Wallace attempting to block integration at the University
of Alabama. Warren K. Leffler, photographer. As governor of Alabama, Wallace
fiercely defended the continuation of the Southern segregationist order, calling it a
matter of protecting "states' rights" against an intrusive national government.
In an attempt to stop integration of the University of Alabama in 1963, Wallace stood
at the door of a university building, surrounded by the National Guard. Standing
opposite is the Kennedy administration representative dispatched to confront him,
Deputy U.S. Attorney General Nicholas Katzenbach. Library of Congress.

once had such a strong allegiance to the Party of Lincoln. In 1960, Richard
Nixon had won the support of more than half of Atlanta's black population.
In 1964, Barry Goldwater had come out swinging against civil rights, reasoning that to win the region he needed to be more like Strom Thurmond
than Dwight Eisenhower, and go "hunting where the ducks are." The strategy had won him 71 percent of the vote in the Deep-South states but only
49 percent in the upper South. He had lost support among the Eisenhower
Republicans in metropolitan areas as well as losing the black vote. In contrast, in Arkansas in 1966, moderate Winthrop Rockefeller (brother of Nelson) won over 90 percent of the African American vote and became the
state's first Republican governor since Reconstruction.[5]

To the moderates in the GOP, all these seemed proof points for a Southern strategy focusing on the moderate middle, not the racial extremists. Yet there also was growing evidence that a third path could be carved out that appealed to both. In 1966, the same year Win Rockefeller was elected in Arkansas, a Democrat-turned-Republican named Claude Kirk won the governorship of Florida.

Kirk's key to victory was a message that went straight to the racial anxieties of Southern whites, but did it in a way that spoke to both the rural hardliners and the suburban middle. Florida cities like Tampa and Miami and Jacksonville were now filled with migrants who brought with them a habit of voting Republican and a dislike of strongly racist language. So Kirk started talking in code. Like Reagan in California, he spoke the language of law and order, and of the protection of individual rights and economic opportunity. He talked about the rights of homeowners and of independence from intrusive government mandates. He appealed to the fears whites had about the new world of court-ordered integration, civil rights, youth power. Appealing to this new, anxious homeowning class, Kirk revolved his campaign around the slogan "Your home is your castle—protect it." It was devastatingly effective.[6]

The GOP task in 1968 was to find a strategy—and a candidate—able to woo the segregationists away from Wallace, speak to the concerns of the new suburbanites, and not alienate everyone else in the process. The party needed not simply a Southern strategy, but a national strategy. The code words used by politicians like Regan and Kirk provided, just perhaps, the way to do that.

The Road to "The One"

For the moderates and Rockefeller-Republican types, as well as for the national media, the most appealing candidate of 1966 and 1967 was Michigan governor George Romney. A sixty-year-old Mormon, handsome and filled with "high-compression energy," Romney was an auto industry CEO who had become a politician with bipartisan appeal.[7] He had won repeatedly in Michigan, a heavily Democratic state. Sometimes he even sounded like a Democrat. He was one of the few Republicans who had survived the bloodbath of 1964, because he actively distanced himself from the party's nominee, Goldwater, and his conservative politics. He called America's worship of individualism "nothing but a political banner to cover up greed." Jack Kennedy considered Romney a formidable opponent, telling a confidant that in 1964 "the fellow I don't want to run against is Romney." In the run-up to the 1968 election, Nelson Rockefeller had taken himself out of presidential contention and had, instead, endorsed Romney as heir to the moderate Republican throne. By late 1966, polls showed Romney winning a hypothetical matchup with Johnson by 6 percentage points.[8]

However, it turned out that Romney was not quite ready for prime time. When he started hitting the road to lay the groundwork for a presidential run, he started getting questions on policy matters he could not answer very well. Especially on issue number one: Vietnam. At first, he said he wouldn't comment on the war until he had studied the issue further. But Romney was a man who said what he thought; he never had mastered the dark arts of political spin. Journalist Theodore White once described him as having "a sincerity so profound that, in conversation, one was almost embarrassed."[9] On the trail, Romney made some offhand comments about how Republicans would handle Vietnam better because Johnson was "locked in" to certain approaches. Reporters pounced. What did Romney mean? What was his position on the war? Romney didn't have a good answer. Eventually, at the tail end of a summer of nonstop fundraising and glad-handing, Romney's weariness got him to make a mistake.

In late August 1967, he told a television interviewer his earlier support for the war was the result of what generals and diplomats had told him when he visited there in 1965. They were wrong, he concluded. In fact, they'd given him "the greatest brainwashing that anybody can get." He continued, quite thoughtfully, that when he dug deeper into the history and complexities of the conflict (something few politicians or diplomats had actually done), it was clear this was a disastrous endeavor. Romney's observation was utterly honest, nuanced, and prescient, but in the hothouse atmosphere of the presidential election cycle, all the press corps heard was "brainwashing." It ultimately became the mistake that came back to haunt his candidacy. By the time Romney formally announced that he'd run in November 1967, the journalists who once had embraced him had become dismissive. On top of being gaffe-prone, Romney turned out to be rather boring. He didn't have the magnetism to sustain the attention of a press corps in search of drama and a television news machine looking for a compelling three-minute lead story.[10]

The other significant candidate in the GOP race was becoming worthy of sustained press attention, however. And it was the unlikeliest of people: Richard M. Nixon. The poor boy from Whittier, California, already had lived an extraordinary life and remarkable career. Soon after being elected to Congress, Nixon had skyrocketed to national prominence by becoming one of the earliest and fiercest anti-Communist crusaders in politics. His House Un-American Activities Committee relentlessly pursued those it suspected to be Communist spies, and he parlayed this notoriety into a run for Senate, mercilessly attacking his liberal female opponent as "pink" and soft on Communism. Tapped as Dwight Eisenhower's vice president in 1952, Nixon went from partisan attack dog to Cold War insider. Motivated by an intensely competitive spirit and a visceral dislike of the Ivy League educated intellectual establishment, Nixon was a man of action and risk. "I can't understand people who won't take the chance of failure," he once remarked.[11] Failure came. He narrowly lost to John F. Kennedy in 1960, felled in part by an unlikable public persona that translated awkwardly into the powerful new political medium of television.[12]

After his California gubernatorial defeat in 1962, Nixon had left public life and joined a New York law firm. His name was floated as a possible presidential nominee in 1964, and his presidential ambitions began to reignite. Yet Republicans of all stripes worried that Nixon was not electable. The moderates didn't like him. One, Senator Ed Brooke of Massachusetts, said if Nixon was the nominee "it wouldn't be a contest in '68—we'd give it away." The conservatives didn't like his chances much either. Colorado Senator Pete Dominick, a close friend of Goldwater's, said, "he's the most qualified man, but can we win with a man who's lost twice?"[13]

Perhaps they had not been paying attention to what Nixon had been doing for the past several years. After Johnson's 1964 landslide, Nixon had started a quiet campaign to win over the hearts of the Republican establishment and its new conservative flank, including the young people who had campaigned so fiercely for Barry Goldwater. He enlisted the help of key advisors. He made his law partner John Mitchell his top advisor and fund-raiser, calling Mitchell "the heavyweight."

Others who later made an important mark in national politics joined the team. A young press aide named Patrick Buchanan started planting stories in the national media that tried to change the narrative that Nixon was a political loser. He brought on a savvy communications director named William Safire, who had a talent for crafting punchy speeches and memorable sound bites. He recruited the producer of the hit *Mike Douglas Show*, a brash twenty-eight-year-old named Roger Ailes, who started thinking about how to win over hearts and minds through television. "This is an electronic election," Ailes told his new colleagues. "The first there's ever been. TV has the power now."[14]

The campaign included other future political power brokers as well. Nixon's head of economic research, Alan Greenspan, crafted a policy platform advocating for free and untrammeled markets. "Sure I'm a liberal," Greenspan remarked, "but I'm a nineteenth century liberal." The key to saving America, he argued, was to liberate businesses from high taxes and burdensome regulations.[15]

Nixon started to make himself indispensable. In the 1966 midterm election, Nixon campaigned energetically for Republican congressional and gubernatorial candidates, helping the GOP win a wave of victories. Democrats noticed Nixon's emerging respectability, and tried to tear it down. Scoffed DNC Chair Bailey, "there is no 'new Nixon,' only a retread of the old slasher of the '50s." Safire complained that the mainstream press paid little attention; Nixon barely made "the furniture pages of the *New York Times*."[16]

Other "glamor boys" like Romney got the spotlight in the early months, and Nixon let them have it. He traveled on assignment for *Reader's Digest* and worked the politics out of the spotlight, biding his time as the media fell in love—and then out of love—with other Republican contenders. Then, as the election season got underway in earnest, Nixon proved formidable. The network he had built steadily over the past several years started to pay dividends. The ardent support he had from ordinary folk away from the coastal power centers buoyed his popularity. He was more conservative than Rockefeller, more intellectual than Reagan, more strategic than Romney or Goldwater. His straddling of the GOP divide was precisely what was needed in a year when the general political spirit leaned to the left, but where primary-state sensibilities demanded careful political maneuvering on hot-button issues like the war and civil rights. Richard Nixon had done the math. A survey of Republican delegates in 1968 had found that 75 percent identified themselves as conservatives. To win the nomination, he needed to tack right, but carefully.

Nixon's response to the assassination of Martin Luther King, Jr., provides one example. After the killing, conservatives roared that King's death was something he brought on himself. Strom Thurmond waxed biblical as he wrote supporters, "we are now witnessing the whirlwind sowed years ago when some preachers and teachers began telling people that each man could be his own judge in his own case." Ronald Reagan linked King's death to the greater breakdown in law and order, a "great tragedy that began when . . . people started choosing which laws they'd break." Nixon and his aides debated whether he should attend the funeral. He went to Atlanta—to privately pay his respects to the King family and attend the funeral service. When the funeral procession rolled through the streets of the city, Nixon was nowhere to be seen. The next day, Nixon's Southern campaign director Brad Hayes did some retail politics, making telephone calls to every key Southern Republican who might be worried that Nixon was kowtowing to the family of a liberal icon. "Yes, I'm as concerned as you are about this," he assured them, "but it was something the candidate felt he had to do."[17]

Two months later, Nixon flew once again to Atlanta, but this time he met with a very different group: South Carolina's Strom Thurmond, Texas senator John Tower, and key Republican Party leaders from the South. Nixon assured them that he agreed school busing to achieve integration was wrong. He promised Southerners key roles in his future Administration. He spoke of his commitment to a strong military—an important issue for a conservative region that also was highly dependent on defense spending. Leaving the meeting, Nixon and his aides were confident that they had the Southern delegates locked up.[18]

Through the primary season, the other Republican contenders fell by the wayside. Reagan toyed with putting his name in the mix, but held back. Romney dropped out in April. Nelson Rockefeller jumped in, then out, then in again after Romney's withdrawal.

Rockefeller's bid employed expensive high-tech tools to make his case. He commissioned a New York ad agency to do intensive market research on his chances against Nixon. Rich and powerful friends urged him on, arguing that while Nixon might appeal to the conservative base, only a moderate like Rockefeller could win in November. With the primaries nearly done, Rockefeller had to appeal to the influencers outside the party machinery. Drawing on his own deep pockets and those of his family and friends, he launched a high-priced media campaign and commissioned poll after poll to make the case that he was more electable than Nixon. Perhaps money, and sheer force of will, could convince GOP delegates that their future lay in the moderate, not the conservative, direction.[19]

At the end of July, however, days before the opening of the GOP convention in Miami, Rockefeller's poll- and media-driven strategy ran out of air. A Gallup Poll concluded that Nixon would beat Humphrey by 7 points in a national matchup, while Rockefeller and Humphrey were dead even. Another poll a few days later showed Rockefeller ahead—and was more meaningful, as it focused on key industrial swing states—but the blow had been dealt. Without being the clear-cut leader in the polls, Rockefeller didn't have a strong case to make to party delegates.

By the Miami convention, Richard Nixon was, as his campaign slogan put it, "the One." As he accepted the nomination, he acknowledged his vanquished rivals—Romney, Rockefeller, Reagan—and gave one of his most stirring speeches. In 1932, Franklin Roosevelt had spoken of "the forgotten man." In 1968, Nixon addressed the convention hall, and the millions of television viewers at home, and presented himself as the candidate of "the forgotten Americans—the non-shouters; the non-demonstrators. . . . They are not racists or sick; they are not guilty of the crime that plagues the land. . . . They are good people, they are decent people; they work, and they save, and they pay their taxes, and they care." This was the message Nixon took forth as the Republican nominee. Yet the historical resonance of this pivotal election came not just from the messages Nixon delivered, but the tools he employed to deliver them.[20]

The Whole World Was Watching

From Tet to global countercultural protests to the assassinations of King and Kennedy, television had not only delivered the news of the year but also shaped how people understood it. Television had been the stage on which presidential elections played since the medium's infancy. Networks covered the conventions starting in 1948, and the first political ads appeared in 1952. In 1960 the televised debates between John Kennedy and Richard Nixon had proved to be a pivotal moment in a tight campaign, the bright studio lights framing a starkly contrasting pair of candidates: a sweaty and shifty-eyed Nixon and a smooth and telegenic Kennedy. Those who heard the first debate on the radio concluded that Nixon had won; those who saw it on television considered the event a big win for Kennedy.[21] By 1968 television had become the beating heart of a massive and technologically sophisticated political machine of media, polling, and professional campaign management that reporter James Perry termed "the new politics." In a book of the same name published at the start of 1968, Perry gave a dour assessment of what this new approach meant, fearing it would "dehumanize" politics. By allowing candidates to appeal directly to the people rather than through partisan machinery, Perry argued, the new politics destabilized the party system to a dangerous extent, and bestowed great advantages on candidates with the most money.[22]

Some of Perry's insights were prophetic, including the rising importance of polling and the engagement of media professionals to sell candidates to the American public using the same techniques used to sell cars or ketchup. The use of increasingly more refined tools to slice, dice, and measure public interest all fed into candidates' ability to use the medium of television to reach out to different blocs of voters as well as to reach millions of people at once. Although presidential contenders had been on television for two decades, political advertising lagged far behind Madison Avenue in its skill in crafting persuasive and sophisticated campaigns. 1968 was the year that politics caught up.

The other reason television mattered to this pivotal election was when the campaign went off script. Television could be the ultimate vehicle of political spin for a candidate, but it had as much, or more, power to derail the master narrative of a campaign or party. With television cameras on, groups that otherwise could not get their message out to a national audience could grab mass attention, co-opting media events on their own terms, beaming *their* message into American living rooms. These events were unscripted, they were raw, and they shaped the outcome of the campaign.

Exhibit number one was the Democratic Convention in Chicago. Since early in 1968, the antiwar left had been thinking and planning about how to use television to take on the Establishment. The activists' flagship enterprise, the National Mobilization Committee to End the War in Vietnam (or Mobe) identified the Democratic Convention in late August as a prime opportunity. Network producers and reporters would descend in a swarm on Chicago, setting up a complex network of live television feeds that provided a ripe opportunity for disruption. In a confidential memorandum, antiwar activists Tom Hayden and Rennie Davis outlined the Left's strategic opportunity:

To the average Democrat who wants a say on the widening war, high taxes, and urban squalor, the "choice" will appear desperate.

Many, for the first time, will wake up to the fact that in the wheeling and dealing of the democratic process the average person does not count. . . . His choices are limited to which of the stars he least dislikes. This summer, millions of anxious Democrats will ask, what now?[23]

Hayden and his compatriots seemed the sober, rule-abiding wing of the Left when compared to the other group planning to make mischief in Chicago, the Yippies. Led by two outsized personalities, Jerry Rubin and Abbie Hoffman, the Yippies specialized in theatrical, outrageous, and made-for-television moments. Fueled by LSD and marijuana, propelled by the counterculture but drawing their understanding of political protest from their own personal histories in the civil rights and antiwar movements, Rubin and Hoffman made the alternate reality of hippiedom into a political act. At an antiwar march in 1967, Hoffman famously urged a group to sing and chant until the Pentagon levitated 300 feet in the air and turned orange. Another morning, Rubin and Hoffman sidled into the gallery of the New York Stock Exchange and started dropping money down on the floor below. Traders scrambled over one another to grab the cash, creating a scene that led the newscasts that evening.

In January, the Yippies issued their first manifesto and told their followers to mark their calendars for good times in Chicago: "Come all you rebels, youth spirits, rock minstrels, truth seekers, peacock freaks, poets, barricade jumpers, dancers, lovers, and artists. It is summer. It is the last week in August and the NATIONAL DEATH PARTY meets to bless Johnson. We are there!"[24]

Even though Johnson didn't make it to the Convention, the Mobe and the Yippies did. As Democrats converged on Chicago, 10,000 college kids and peaceniks and lefties and hippies gathered on the streets outside. Meeting them there: 20,000 police officers and soldiers tasked with keeping the peace. Democratic Chicago Mayor Richard J. Daley had twisted many arms to win the hosting rights for the Convention, and he didn't want the long-haired kids disrupting it. Thus, Chicago refused to issue permits allowing protesters to march or sleep in city parks, and passed a new disorderly conduct ordinance that gave Daley's police the power to stop "any unreasonable or offensive act, utterance, gesture, or display." It provided an extraordinary amount of leeway for law enforcement to target anyone—protestor, reporter—who threatened to disrupt the proceedings or bring

Figure 22. Yippie holds up burning draft card, Chicago, 27 August 1968. As Democrats converged on Chicago for their nominating convention in 1968, so did antiwar activists. In response to night-long demonstrations and massive encampments in city parks, Chicago Mayor Richard Daley dispatched city police to curb the demonstrations with brute force, as reporters looked on. The nationally televised melee created a public relations debacle for a deeply divided Democratic Party.
Bettman/Corbis/AP Images.

unrest to city streets. Daley called up nearly every possible officer at his disposal, from regular beat cops to riot police, and surrounded the convention hall with barbed wire-topped fencing.

To top all this off, Chicago's bus drivers and telephone workers went on strike. Stalled mass transit was an inconvenience to the convention-goers, but the inability to get many telephone calls through was a disaster. Instead of being able to build elaborate communication networks to beam live video, television networks were stuck with having to hand-carry videotape to central broadcast facilities. The only place they could broadcast live was in the convention hall itself. Everything else had to be broadcast with a couple of hours' delay, changing what audiences saw and when they saw it.

It was a tinderbox waiting to explode, and it did. As student activist and historian Todd Gitlin later put it, "the movement's irresistible force collided with Mayor Daley's immovable object, while the television cameras floodlit the clash into national theater."[25] A later congressional investigation called the events "a police riot" and blamed the mayor for "unrestrained and indiscriminate police violence." [26] Given the awful scenes beamed into American homes, it was hard for Congress to come to any other conclusion.

The first battles were innocuous, and even a little humorous. The Friday before the Convention's start, the Yippies gathered in a park to nominate a 150-pound pig named Pigasus for president. The cops arrested six protesters and took Pigasus to the Chicago Humane Society. By Sunday night, however, "the mood had . . . turned nasty" and dangerous. Five hundred protestors defied a police curfew and remained camped in Lincoln Park. Batons started to swing. The slow burn began, exploding into violent chaos on Wednesday, the last evening of the Convention.[27]

In the early evening hours, a column of protestors marched down Michigan Avenue, to be met by a wall of blue-helmeted police officers at the front steps of the two convention hotels. The crowd pushed forward, the police pushed back. The police threw tear gas; the fumes wafted up to the hotel rooms above. On the 25th floor, Hubert Humphrey rubbed his eyes and had to take a shower. On the 23rd floor, Gene McCarthy looked down in horror as police batons began to hammer down on the college kids who had followed him since New Hampshire.

Things got ugly very quickly, and the reporters swarming over the convention hotels grabbed their notebooks and cameras, recording as protesters' chants of "Fuck you, LBJ!" turned to screams for help as the police clubbed through the crowd and dragged people across the asphalt. Paper and other objects rained down from the hotel rooms below, launched by convention-goers trying to stop the police. Blood was on the sidewalks as the crowed yelled, "The Whole World is Watching, The Whole World is Watching."

And the world *was* watching. What made it so powerful and politically consequential, however, was that the world saw this happen on television a couple of hours after it happened because the telephone workers' strike meant the television footage could not beam live. Instead, tape of what had happened at 8:00 P.M. got woven into the live coverage of the Convention proceedings at 10:00, giving the impression the two things were happening simultaneously. Both presented grim scenes. For the primary season blood-bath had left deep divisions and resentments in the Democratic Party.

Kennedy's assassination had taken the wind out of the Left's sails, and paved the way for Hubert Humphrey—the man who had not been on a single primary ballot—to secure the nomination. The rules governing the Democratic Convention had changed little since 1912 or 1932. Delegates were not obliged to go with their state's primary winner, and "favorite son" candidates stood for election in many states as a way to gain votes that were merely placeholders for candidates aiming to work their way to the top at the convention. By late June, the *Wall Street Journal* sighed resignedly that the likely nominees of both parties would be "favorites of the party profes-sionals" after all. "The pundits contend that the public wants a choice, but the political system gives it an echo."[28]

McCarthy was still in, but diminished. His singular identification with the antiwar cause had left him scrambling for support among key Demo-cratic constituencies. "It is almost as if McCarthy has identified himself so completely with one facet of national concern—policy in Vietnam—that no one, including the black man, thinks he stands for anything else," com-mented the *Chicago Daily Defender*.[29] McCarthy still had his ardent follow-ers, but by this point they seemed more committed to his being president than McCarthy was himself. Another prominent antiwar senator from the Midwest, George McGovern, entered the race a few weeks before the con-vention in a last-ditch effort to provide the Democrats an antiwar standard-bearer. The aching gap created by Robert Kennedy's death prompted a boomlet of support in the Convention's first days for his brother Teddy, but by late Tuesday night it was clear Humphrey had a lock on the nomination.

On that deadly Wednesday evening, reporters roamed the convention floor and interviewed antiwar delegates whose words undercut every attempt the party made to show unity. Delegates burst into tears on national television. They denounced their party's leaders and its position on the war. They stood on chairs and sang "We Shall Overcome." Mean-while, Mayor Daley appeared on the convention floor, turning purple with rage and spouting expletives as he was denounced for his "Gestapo tactics" by one speaker at the podium. All the while, the networks interspersed the video of what had happened on the street earlier that evening.

Humphrey was furious, and he turned his fury on the television report-ers. Far above the melee on the street, and not fully understanding the extent of the violence, he could not believe that the night of his political coronation was playing out so badly. Sitting in his hotel room watching NBC, he reportedly shook his fist at the reporter on the screen, saying: "Don't forget . . . I'm going to be president someday. I'm going to appoint the FCC—we're going to look into all this." Genial, liberal, kind, intelligent Humphrey came out of Chicago as the Democrats' nominee, but forever tarnished by the violence and infighting that played out on network television. "The average voter may resign himself, uneasily, to Vietnam," commented *Life* magazine. "But he is not likely to forget Democratic delegates crying shame at their own leaders or the paroxysms of brutality by which Daley's blue-helmeted police bloodied brigades of ragged hippies and earnest McCarthyites in full view of the American living room."[30]

Mad Men

While the Democrats' televised campaign spun out of control, the Republicans' narrative became even more tightly crafted and polished as Richard Nixon took his message to a national audience.

In addition to playing smart politics during the primaries, Nixon had started in early 1968 to tap into the cultural *zeitgeist* in ways few politicians had grasped. Always suspicious of the Eastern Establishment and attuned to the concerns of Middle America, Nixon and his team saw that grassroots activism was not only a product of the left, but an emerging force on the right. For the 1960s saw the birth of other kinds of youth movements, where hair wasn't long but stayed short. Where no one was dropping out of college or taking drugs. Where students marched in favor of the war, not against it. These young people listened to and participated in Up with People, the clean-cut singing troupe. They joined Young Americans for Freedom, the campus conservative organization.

Nixon's team also saw how the changes of the decade created potential to mobilize the New Deal generation, who watched in bewilderment as old certainties dissolved. Their children were growing their hair long and rebelling; people with black and brown skin were moving into their neighborhoods. Taxes were going up to pay for the war, yet ordinary people weren't seeing visible benefits. Jobs once done by people were now done with high-tech computers and automated machinery. They were anxious about lots of things, and feeling powerless to stop them. Some were Southerners who felt abandoned by the Democrats' embrace of civil rights. Yet a good many lived beyond the South, in electoral vote-rich states like Nixon's native California, or Michigan, or Illinois.

Richard Nixon took note of all this, and played it to win. In early 1968, a memo started circulating around the Nixon campaign written by a young campaign worker named Kevin Phillips. Titled "Middle America and the Emerging Republican Majority," it explained how the great social upheavals of the 1960s had created a new enemy. Phillips pointed out that the New Deal was successful by focusing people's anger on the economic elites who had so much when the rest had so little.[31]

Franklin Roosevelt, despite being an elite himself, artfully appealed to those fears in the 1930s and created an alternative vision. Now, people were angry at *cultural* elites: the "experts" in Washington who were telling ordinary people to put their kids on buses and ride to integrated schools across town, who were tolerating drug use and bad behavior from insolent college students, who weren't cracking down on crime on city streets. Phillips's "Middle America" listened to Lawrence Welk, not to Motown or the Doors. They went to church, not to antiwar demonstrations.

In May, Nixon gave a national radio address in which he gave these people a name. He called them the "silent center." He told them: "A great many quiet Americans have become committed to answers to social problems that preserve personal freedom." Later, as president, he would label this group the "great silent majority." Liberals in Washington had trampled on individual freedoms and ignored these silent Americans. Nixon, poor boy from Whittier, the anti-Communist crusader, would give them a voice.[32]

Yet as Nixon approached the fall campaign, he needed to find ways to deliver this message without reinforcing his old reputation as a conservative hatchet man. The conventional wisdom among the mainstream political press and in moderate-Republican circles—and Democratic ones as well—was that politics that pitted different groups against one another would not work at the national level. America had fragmented in 1968; it was the job of the next president to put it back together. Sage Washington commentator Scotty Reston reflected in April, "neither Nixon nor [Robert] Kennedy, despite their advantage in the popularity polls, has a good chance of uniting the country. They are at the radical extremes of foreign and domestic policy, and the mood of the country seems to be for moderation and compromise."

The new media-driven politics also demanded approaches that brought people together rather than splitting them apart, the political establishment reasoned. In the age of network television and mass culture, where millions of people watched the same newscasts and sitcoms, personality-driven politics had trumped the old partisan machines. It stood to reason that a successful candidate would be one who could knit people together through the force of charisma and compelling ideas. Success would come from a healer, not a divider. Nixon's use of television in 1968 played off of this conventional wisdom, but also proved a good chunk of it wrong.

The debacle of Nixon's televised debates against John F. Kennedy in 1960 has become a staple of history textbooks. But another critical part of the television story of 1960 was how well Kennedy employed the tools of corporate advertising in his television commercials. He used snappy jingles and slogans that sold the candidate the same way Kellogg's might sell a box of cereal. He had celebrities like Harry Belafonte and Henry Fonda attesting to his patriotism, his intelligence, and his support of civil rights. He had his beautiful wife Jacqueline speaking in Spanish to woo Latino voters.

In contrast, 1960-era Nixon played by the rules. His TV spots were similar to those by most candidates who had come before him: one minute or more of the candidate awkwardly leaning against a desk, talking directly to the camera. In the increasingly snazzy and hyperkinetic world of television advertising, they were dull. They were made even more problematic by the fact that their star, Richard Nixon, lacked the geniality of Dwight Eisenhower or the charisma of the Kennedys. He was Nixon: serious, substantive, stern, scolding.

Nixon wanted 1968 to be different, and turned to Madison Avenue to help him transform his public image. Nixon was not the first to do so— both Democrats and Republicans had done it for years—but the effort was extraordinary for the meticulousness with which the admen took on a complete image turnaround for their client. At the head of the team was a former J. Walter Thompson pro named Harry Treleaven, who set himself to the task of how to play down Nixon's disadvantages and play up his strengths. Treleavan was bullish, writing of Nixon: "Not always loved, he is universally respected. He does have a certain star quality going for him." The candidate didn't have a great sense of humor, Treleaven acknowledged, which "could be corrected to a degree, but let's not be too obvious about it." Media aide Roger Ailes was more dismissive: "He's a funny-looking guy. He looks like somebody hung him in a closet overnight and he jumps out in the morning with his suit all bunched up and starts running around saying, 'I want to be president.'"[33]

The answer to this image problem was to carefully manage any and all times Nixon appeared on television. They held televised forums in which the audience was hand-picked, the questions were scripted, and the questioners pre-selected. They placed him in informal settings. They heeded Treleaven's call to "avoid closeups." In September, the new, television-friendly Nixon made a surprise cameo appearance on the hugely popular NBC comedic variety show *Rowan & Martin's Laugh-In*, cleverly making fun of his stiff image and making his rival Humphrey seem unhip by comparison.

Yet encased in this polish, the messages of the Nixon campaign were hard-hitting and tough, playing on the fears of the "silent majority." This came through clearly in the fall campaign, when Nixon launched a series of slickly produced ads that were unlike nearly any other political commercial in history.

Nixon never appeared in these ads; they featured only his disembodied voice, which provided simple and sonorous narration to a series of fast-paced, jarring, gripping images. They hit all the key issues: Vietnam, law and order, youth culture. They said little of substance, but featured images that were impossible to ignore—of bloody battles in Vietnam, of violence on the streets, of Democrats at war with each other in Chicago. In one ad, images of campus protesters and urban rioters flashed back and forth in rapid succession, while Nixon's voice read:

> It is time for an honest look at the problem of order in the United States. Dissent is a necessary ingredient of change, but in a system of government that provides for peaceful change, there is no cause that justifies resort to violence. Let us recognize that the first civil right of every American is to be free from domestic violence. So I pledge to you, we shall have order in the United States.

"This time," flashed the words on the screen, "vote like your whole world depended on it."[34]

Even though Nixon was speaking to a very different set of concerns and constituencies, his campaign was one that played off the same interest group and identity politics emerging on the Left. Just like activists on campus and in the inner cities, middle-America conservatives no longer believed what the leaders in Washington, or Wall Street, or corporate boardrooms were selling them. They no longer believed we were "all in it

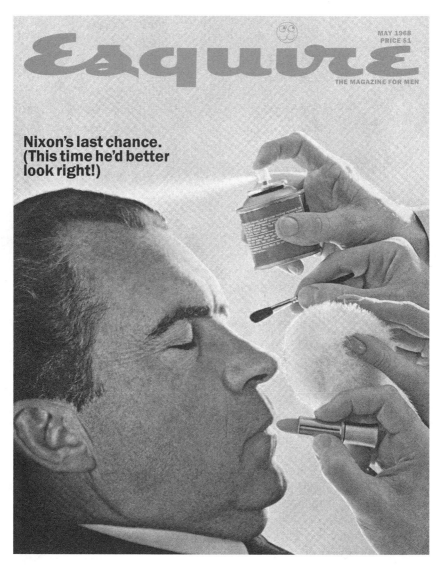

Figure 23. *Esquire*, May 1968. George Lois, designer. After stumbling in televised appearances in his 1960 presidential run against John F. Kennedy, Richard Nixon hired advertising industry professionals to help craft a fresh public image. National publications noticed and satirized his media makeover, but the results proved highly effective. Courtesy of George Lois.

together." Just like the young people protesting the war and fighting for equal rights, Nixon raged against the consensus liberal Establishment. He packaged this rage in phrases and images derived after intensive research and attuned to the finer points of demographic change. Television had helped give Richard Nixon the charisma he lacked and allowed him to widen his appeal far beyond what the pundits ever expected. And it worked.

The Sound and the Fury

In the middle of all this, there still were a great many Americans who felt that no major party candidate—from Rockefeller and Nixon to McCarthy and Humphrey—spoke to their wants and needs. Only one person did: George Wallace. While liberal and moderate Democrats fought, Wallace had split from the Democrats and set out as the standard-bearer of the American Independent Party, bringing a legion of disillusioned working-class whites along with him. "Our middle class," Wallace later wrote, "ignored and neglected by the Democratic and Republican Parties, would now be represented."[35]

Wallace's platform was a harsher and more undiluted version of Nixon's message to the "silent majority." He positioned himself as the candidate of the "little man," and he was careful to steer away from the stridently racist rhetoric he had employed as governor of Alabama. "Both national parties . . . have kowtowed to every anarchist that has roamed the streets," he thundered to a campaign crowd in Madison Square Garden. "I'm not talking about race. The overwhelming majority of all races in this country are against the breakdown of law and order." Wallace talked about how elitist Ph.D. types were stomping on the rights of the ordinary folks. He talked about crime, school busing, and unemployment. He spoke of all the things working-class Americans—in the South and in the North—were worrying about. He wasn't talking about race, he assured his audiences. But, really, he was.[36]

The Wallace third-party insurgency was damaging to both Nixon and Humphrey. It pulled away some disaffected Southerners and disgruntled members of the "silent majority" who might have otherwise voted for the Republican, as well as presenting an alternative for the Democrats who felt their party had given in on civil rights. More important, it demonstrated the power of a particular kind of message on a particular kind of voter. The white ethnics from New York City's outer boroughs and Chicago's South and West sides, the small farmers from rural Alabama and North Carolina and Texas and Indiana, the churchgoing folk from small towns and the proud homeowners from working-class suburbs: these were the voters who had gone for FDR in the 1930s, but who were anxious and angry about all the changes the 1960s had wrought. They saw a Democratic Party that had allowed chaos to be unleashed, and they weren't yet convinced the Republicans had an answer. George Wallace spoke to them. It wasn't just about Southern "states' rights" anymore. It was about freedom, opportunity, and *individual* rights.

Wallace's campaign pulls two things into focus about the election of 1968. First, it wasn't all about the new politics and the new media. George Wallace did remarkably well without employing any Madison Avenue ad men or commissioning expensive polls or crunching demographic data. The unfiltered rhetoric was part of Wallace's appeal. He gave traditional, red-meat speeches to big crowds, and because of his outrageousness the media covered him extensively without his having to buy many minutes of air time. In election cycles to come, this "free media" became a critical tool for candidates on the ideological fringe and short of campaign cash.

Wallace's candidacy also reveals how moderate, even liberal, the Richard Nixon of 1968 was in comparison to the Republicans who followed him. Nixon's strain of conservatism was one that advocated ending the war in Vietnam, extending civil rights, and supporting the expansion of welfare programs and enhancing environmental protection. Nixon said little in public about social issues like homosexuality or abortion. Nixon's talk of the "silent majority" was kinder and gentler than Wallace's strident talk of "rights" and "freedoms." Yet, in the decades to come, the terms Wallace used, his vilification of big government, and his disparagement of the "cultural elite" came to be central tenets of the way Republicans of all stripes ran for office. It was Wallace, not Nixon, who presaged where politics was headed.

Two Novembers

The voters made their ultimate choice on 5 November. Richard Nixon at last won the job he had been seeking for so many years, and that so many people had thought he'd never get. His message resonated from coast to coast; in contrast to the sea of blue states Johnson had won in 1964, Nixon won the upper South, much of the Midwest, the Great Plains and West, California, and Texas. Hubert Humphrey was more than 100 electoral votes behind. His candidacy had never recovered from the disaster of Chicago. The antiwar liberals saw him not only as a proxy for Johnson but as a symbol of all that was wrong and crony-ridden about the Democratic Party nomination process. All the passion on the Democratic side had existed in the insurgent campaigns of McCarthy and Kennedy. With those two men gone, the fire went out. George Wallace hacked away at the Solid South, winning five Deep-Southern states and their 45 electoral votes.

The popular vote was much closer, reflecting the generally leftward tilt of the country and revealing the true impact of Wallace's third-party insurgency. Less than 1 percentage point separated Nixon and Humphrey in the popular vote: Nixon got 43.4 and Humphrey 42.7 percent. Meanwhile, Wallace got 13.5 percent, a number achieved by siphoning off Southern Democrats and conservative Republicans. The electoral math was such that, unlike 1912, the presence of a third-party candidate did not change the ultimate electoral outcome. In fact, the Wallace voters would most likely have voted for Nixon. Yet the popular vote totals reflected the shakiness of Richard Nixon's victory. Despite Democratic implosion, an unpopular incumbent, and the slick and expensive television makeover of the candidate, Nixon didn't win over that many more voters than his chief rival.

The results laid bare the degree to which the New Deal Democratic coalition fell apart in 1968. In its place was a fractured and often antagonistic identity politics divided along lines of race, class, and region. Americans on both left and right were questioning mainstream "big" party politics, just as they were questioning big science, big business, and big government. This was not the first time such impulses had risen to the fore. Earlier times of tumult had revealed similar processes. In 1912, the inequalities of industrialization had propelled a new progressive politics and a third-party charge that split the Republican Party in two. In 1932, massive economic crisis led Americans of all political stripes to question old assumptions and traditional leadership, making way for a reconstituted Democratic Party and a new conception of the role of government. Republicans had been on the losing side in these moments of political change. In 1968, the chief victims of the fracturing of America were the Democratic Party leaders who had been in charge.

With this fracturing, the broad-based, business conservatism of the postwar Republican Party started to morph into the cultural conservatism

Figure 24. Richard M. Nixon campaign rally, 1968. Oliver F. Atkins, photographer.
At the end of a tumultuous election and a violent, momentous year, Richard Nixon
emerged victorious in his quest for the White House. His win derived partly from
savvy marketing and campaign strategy, and substantially from the implosion of the
Democratic Party. The dynamics of 1968, however, foreshadowed the transformation
of politics in the Reagan era and beyond. National Archives.

of a post-civil rights era. The Religious Right was not yet a significant force,
but the rhetoric and issues driving the 1968 election started to make cultural and moral topics fair game in politics in new and powerful ways.
Similarly, trends in white working-class voting began to shift in important
ways. In the 1930s, Franklin Roosevelt appealed to these voters' identity as
Americans. He promised them jobs and homes and economic security—
and they faithfully voted Democratic in return. Starting in the late 1960s,
Republicans appealed to their identities as homeowners, suburbanites, or
churchgoers. They promised the white working class law and order and a
return to traditional values and protection of individual rights, and they
began to vote Republican in return.

So, ultimately, the story of 1968 doesn't just explain 1968. It explains
what comes afterward. In 1972, the wounds of the last election were still
visible throughout the Democratic Party. In the post-civil rights era, the

party had become a much bigger tent, and much more open to new voices. African Americans, women, gays and lesbians, and other minority groups had more prominent roles in the Democratic Party than they ever had before. Yet the Democrats had lost the establishment power they had enjoyed from the New Deal through the Johnson years. They faced increasing dissent from the ranks of white working-class voters who had been the bedrock of the national party since the 1930s. George McGovern tried to be the glue that could bind these different factions together, but he couldn't pull it off.

Meanwhile, the Republican Party had found a new way to talk to voters, and had made inroads into critical parts of the old Democratic base. The real end point of the 1968 election, then, is not 5 November 1968 but 4 November 1980. Ronald Reagan's landslide victory over Democratic incumbent Jimmy Carter was a triumph of all the politics tested by Richard Nixon in 1968. Reagan had extraordinary powers of communication and ability to persuade and inspire voters. He picked up the Democratic voters disaffected by civil rights and cultural change. And he added Democrats in blue-collar manufacturing regions who had devastated by the economic malaise of the 1970s. Together, these voting blocs made the Reagan Revolution happen.

The outlines of the twenty-first century's red-state and blue-state map started to emerge in 1968. They solidified in 1980. In the thirty years since the election of Reagan, however, many other things happened to change the political landscape—and the personalities and issues driving the two major political parties. That is what the next two chapters will explore.

PART IV

*   *   *

1992

CHAPTER 7

*

Reagan Revolutionaries
and New Democrats

At 5:00 p.m. Eastern Standard Time on Sunday, 1 June 1980, the Cable News Network, also known as CNN, came on the air. The first words heard on the new network came from its owner, brash and boastful Atlanta cable operator Ted Turner, who proclaimed CNN "the news channel for America" and promised its 24-hour coverage would follow both national and international news like no other network before it. Turner had raided the three broadcast networks for reporting talent and set up full-time bureaus in six cities as well as stringers around the world, doing all of it on a $25 million budget, only a fraction of what the major television networks spent on their news divisions. The bootstrapping showed in the first newscast that followed Turner's appearance, memorable for its technical glitches and bland reporting. It was clear, however, that something new was afoot in television news.[1]

Six weeks later, Ronald Reagan stood before the Republican National Convention in Detroit as his party's new nominee for president. Accepting the nomination, he promised a new beginning for a country that had been battered by a decade of foreign crises, economic malaise, and social turbulence. He condemned the Democrats as irresponsible tax-and-spenders who had made America less safe by their compromises with the Soviet Union. "It is time to put America back to work; to make our cities and towns resound with the confident voices of men and women of all races, nationalities and faiths bringing home to their families a decent paycheck they can cash for honest money," Reagan said. "For those who have abandoned hope, we'll restore hope and we'll welcome them into a great national crusade to make America great again!"[2]

Figure 25. The Cable News Network, created in 1980 by Atlanta entrepreneur Ted
Turner, transformed the television news business and fundamentally altered the
rhythms and media strategies of national politics. Here, network president Reese
Schoenfeld and weekend anchor Reynelda Nuse prepare for the first broadcast.
CNN Cable News Studio, 31 May 1980. AP Photo.

Twelve years later, Turner's scrappy enterprise had turned into a media
juggernaut with a worldwide audience of millions. Reagan's two terms in
office had redefined American politics and reshaped national government.
The New Deal Order that had held steady since the days of Franklin Roosevelt became replaced by a new politics of free markets and free enterprise,
of government cuts and privatization, and of social issues and "family values." The Democratic Party lost three presidential elections in a row. It had
morphed from a party of liberal consensus to an expansive and chaotic
combination of identity-focused interest groups, Southern populists,
tradition-bound labor union bosses, and an economically beleaguered
working class. A new generation of leaders within the Democratic Party,
hailing from Southern and Western states, had started to argue that the

party must move to the political center to stay viable; Democratic liberals strongly disagreed. Meanwhile, the GOP had become more disciplined in its message, more charismatic in its leadership, and more conservative in its politics. Always the party of business, the Republicans had also become the party of evangelical Christians, who were taking a more visible and instrumental role in political affairs than ever before.

The cable news revolution and the Reagan Revolution culminated in the presidential election of 1992. The Democratic nominee, Bill Clinton, a Southern governor and standard-bearer of the Democratic centrists, gave speeches about hope and opportunity that sounded less like a typical Democrat and more like 1980-vintage Reagan. The Republican nominee and White House incumbent, George H. W. Bush, was a politician who had been conservative in an earlier political generation but who, in the increasingly rightward-leaning 1990s, seemed like a throwback moderate, and an ineffectual one at that. Both candidates operated on an ideological playing field that ranged from moderate to strongly conservative, far from the liberal tilt of the late 1960s. Both talked of curbing spending and cutting taxes, balancing budgets, reinventing government, and reforming welfare.

Cable news became the great definer, and the great disrupter, of the contest between the two major parties. Its relentless 24-hour rhythm pulled professional consultants and communications gurus to the forefront of the campaign machinery in ways they had never been before, and it demanded constant care and feeding with sound bites, scandal, and spin. CNN, the undisputed king of the medium, became the platform for an outsider candidate, Ross Perot, to launch and run the most successful third-party effort since Teddy Roosevelt's 1912 Bull Moose campaign. The popular success of the erratic and iconoclastic Perot attested not only to the power of new media to bypass and disrupt campaign narratives, but to the deep dissatisfaction American voters had with both major parties, and with the political system itself.

It took a great deal of money to play in such an intensely competitive national political game, with its relentless news cycle and need for television buys, media consultants, and sophisticated technologies. The cost of campaigns had been spiraling upward for years, and by 1992 it had become a staggeringly expensive political-industrial complex that demanded perpetual fundraising. Those with money had the advantage, whether they were deep-pocketed interest groups who could buy access to a candidate, or individuals rich enough to funnel millions of dollars of personal wealth into their own campaigns. Ross Perot fell in the latter category. He became the first self-financed outsider to alter the outcome of a major election, but he was hardly the last.

The Democrats' rightward tilt, the cable news spin cycle, and relentless demand for campaign cash all defined 1992 as a pivotal election. Playing out against a backdrop of economic and social transformation, and channeling the liberal energies of the 1960s rights revolution as well as new impulses of neoliberalism and neoconservatism, the presidential election of 1992 created a roadmap future elections would follow. At his second inauguration, Bill Clinton spoke of the "bridge to the twenty-first century." The election that brought him to the White House was the contest that moved presidential politics out of one century and into the next.

Rightward Bound

The fracturing of America that had contributed to Richard Nixon's improbable 1968 victory continued to have profound repercussions on the political landscape three decades later. The 1960s rights revolution had opened national politics to an extraordinary extent, giving racial minorities, women, and young people an influence on partisan politics that never had existed before. While the radical Left had imploded into infighting and violent extremism after the end of the Vietnam War, liberals of the baby boom and post-civil rights generations found a home in the Democratic Party.

Ironically, the prosperity set in motion by Franklin Roosevelt's New Deal helped weaken the ties working-class constituencies had to the Democrats. Families who were blue-collar working class in one generation became white-collar middle class in the next. They were more likely to be college educated and less likely to belong to a union. The bread-and-butter issues that had wedded them to the Democratic Party in the Great Depression now mattered less. South of the Mason-Dixon line, the New Deal had set in motion an economic transformation, but had allowed the old racial order to stay intact. When the civil rights revolution of the 1960s broke down that order, the fealty of many Southerners to the New Deal and its Democratic architects dissolved along with it. Many who remained in the working class started to feel the Democrats had left them behind, becoming a party of intellectual elites and cultural permissiveness. To these voters, as well as to the growing numbers of Americans who embraced evangelical

Christianity in the 1970s, '80s, and '90s, social issues like abortion, homosexuality, or gun rights started to matter more. Liberal voters, too, made social issues litmus tests of whether they would support a particular candidate on Election Day.

The divergence in political views occurred in a context of consumer abundance, a burgeoning and diverse popular culture, and an emphasis on individual "lifestyle choices" over shared values and sacrifice. Journalist and cultural observer Tom Wolfe famously labeled the 1970s the "Me Generation," and while the label tended to overstate the vacuous and aimless nature of the decade, many Americans at the time were acutely conscious of the lost sense of higher purpose and collective action that had catalyzed so much change only a few years before.[3]

The lost promise of the 1960s seemed particularly acute when it came to politics. In the 1960s, Americans had the Kennedys and King, all of whose reputations had become more giant and idealized after their martyrdom. The political heros weren't all liberals: Goldwater and Reagan lived on in the hearts and minds of conservatives as true believers, unswerving in their beliefs in limited government, a strong military, and individual freedoms. The Watergate scandal that brought down Richard Nixon not only discredited the more temperate Republicanism he ultimately came to represent—as president he ended a war, beefed up social programs, and visited Communist China—but left Americans of all political stripes deeply disillusioned by the political system. A wave of reform-minded young legislators, most of them Democrats, came into office in the wake of Nixon's resignation in 1974. Despite the changes they wrought, many American voters continued to feel that Washington was irrevocably broken.[4]

The 1976 presidential contest between colorless Republican incumbent Gerald Ford and largely unknown Democratic governor of Georgia Jimmy Carter left voters uninspired and drove down turnout to less than 55 percent, one of the lowest levels in history. "I'm not apathetic about nonvoting," said one who stayed home. "I'm emphatic about it."[5] Even though Carter was a more moderate Democratic voice, and even though the Republican Party remained deeply unpopular, his victory over Ford was a squeaker. The popular vote was nearly evenly split, with Carter winning 50.1 percent to Ford's 48 percent. Party loyalty diminished. Only 15 percent of American voters identified themselves as strong Democrats in 1976, and only 14 percent strong Republicans. Over a third considered themselves Independents.[6]

The disillusionment with politics also became so deep, and so bitter, because political leaders seemed powerless to halt the drastic economic changes that played out painfully throughout American communities in the 1970s. By the late 1960s, the things that had contributed to the country's unprecedented run of economic prosperity after World War II were starting to come loose from their moorings. Within months of taking office, Richard Nixon found himself struggling with a growing economic recession. Unemployment climbed to 6 percent, the highest in years. Since the New Deal, moderates of both parties had turned to government-sponsored economic stimulus programs as the obvious answer to economic bumps, following the theories of liberal economist John Maynard Keynes. Looking at the dire numbers, Nixon became persuaded. In early 1971, he went on network news to announce a program of stimulus, wage adjustments, and inflation curbs, remarking "I am now a Keynesian in economics." Journalist Howard K. Smith commented in response that it was "a little like a Christian crusader saying, 'All things considered, I think Mohammed was right.'"[7]

Economic malaise had multiple structural causes and no easy solutions. After more than two decades of rebuilding from postwar devastation (an endeavor financed chiefly with U.S. aid), the economies of Japan and Germany came roaring back to life, joined by new East Asian nations like Taiwan and Korea, presenting formidable competition to American industries that had enjoyed unchallenged global dominance for years. Employing newer technologies and production processes, overseas factories were able to manufacture goods like cars and steel more efficiently and cheaply than Americans could.

In the absence of foreign competition, American companies had not needed to build for efficiency. They could afford to pay their workers well and provide robust pension packages, and more workers belonged to labor unions than at any other time in history. Now, with shrinking profit margins, U.S. companies began to cut union jobs or move their factories to union-free Southern states or overseas. At the same time, increasing reliance on computer technologies and white-collar service industries made a college degree a prerequisite for more and more professions. The well-paying blue-collar jobs that had provided stable economic foundations for working-class families started disappearing.[8]

The cracks in the economic foundation broke open in 1973, when the Organization of Petroleum Exporting Countries (OPEC) enacted an embargo in protest of U.S. support of Israel during the Yom Kippur War.

Gas prices spiraled, leading to long lines at the pump and rising consumer demand for foreign compact cars rather than American-made gas guzzlers. The combination of this with other economic forces pushed the nation into a combination of economic stagnation and inflation—stagflation—that strained family pocketbooks and led to sharp partisan divisions over how to fix the economy. While the 1970s were an era of increased consumer choice, personal freedoms, and huge technological advances, the economic malaise gave everyone the feeling that the good times were gone for good.

By the late 1970s, a new wave of Republican leaders—many of them from the Sunbelt states and Far West—started to shape the national understanding of what was wrong with America and where the solutions might lie. Chief among them was Ronald Reagan, who had continued to be a leading voice of the conservative wing of his party through his time as California governor and beyond. In 1976 he ran against Ford in the Republican primaries, and he had his sights on another run in 1980. Reagan had honed his free market, law-and-order message into a powerful indictment of the government-centered approaches of Democratic liberalism.

Social policies aimed at the poorest of the poor became a ripe and effective target for Reagan. On the stump in 1976, he told the story of a woman in Chicago who was milking government welfare programs for all they were worth through outrageous fraud: "she has 80 names, 30 addresses, 12 Social Security cards, and is collecting veterans' benefits on four nonexisting deceased husbands." Allegedly raking in "$150,000 a year," Reagan's "welfare queen" was a symbol of liberalism run amok. Despite the fact that little about the story was true, Reagan repeated it again and again on the campaign trail. The anti-welfare rhetoric was a new, and devastatingly effective, variation of the political code that 1960s politicians like George Wallace had used to speak to white working-class audiences. Reagan never mentioned that the "woman in Chicago" was black, but in his exaggerated descriptions of her fur coats and gold Cadillacs he played off racist stereotypes and white assumptions about ghetto culture.[9]

The combination of ineffectual leadership and anti-government rhetoric meant that by 1980, voters laid the blame for economic malaise squarely on the shoulders of the Democratic Party. After a combative primary season, Reagan triumphed over more moderate rivals to become the 1980 GOP nominee. Many in both parties still found him an intellectual lightweight and an ideologue, but his conservative-tinged message of hope and opportunity resonated with many voters who felt squeezed by the new economy, threatened by newly empowered minorities, and abandoned by the party of FDR. So many of these core members of the New Deal coalition voted for the former movie star that they came to be known as "Reagan Democrats." Ronald Reagan was their first Republican vote, and he would not be their last. Adding insult to Democratic injury, the Republicans took control of the Senate and won more House seats then they had held in nearly three decades.[10]

Reagan had a rocky first term. The economy was still in the doldrums. His solution had been a bold program of tax cuts and spending cuts that came to be called "Reaganomics." The one area in which he beefed up government spending was on defense. As his reelection campaign loomed, Reaganomics didn't seem to be doing much to bring the economy back. Tensions with the Soviets were rising. Democratic liberals charged that Reagan was a warmongering president who favored the rich and punished the poor. Many threw their hat in the ring for the 1984 race. The crowded Democratic field in the primaries attested to the fact that many considered Reagan beatable, and also reflected how much the party's makeup had changed since the civil rights revolution. Prominent among the contenders was the first African American man to seek the presidency, Reverend Jesse Jackson. A magnetic civil rights activist from Chicago, in the previous decade Jackson had become a major figure in the national Democratic Party and a fierce and stirring critic of both Carter's centrism and Reagan's conservatism. Pushing a hard-hitting message of social justice and economic fairness, Jackson won more votes and political traction than any black candidate until Barack Obama.

Just as both parties started mobilizing for the 1984 race, however, the economy started turning around.[11] By the time the election was in full swing, Reagan was able to campaign on the slogan of "Morning in America," running gauzily filmed television ads that were light on policy details and heavy on emotion. In the most iconic of these, a warm male voice spoke as images of families, neighborhoods, and flag-raisings filled the screen:

> It's morning again in America. Today, more men and women will go to work than ever before in our country's history. With interest rates at about half the record highs of 1980, nearly 2,000 families today will buy new homes, more than at any time in the past four years. This afternoon, 6,500 young men and women will be married.

And with inflation at less than half of what it was just four years ago, they can look forward with confidence to the future. It's morning again in America. And, under the leadership of President Reagan, our country is prouder and stronger and better. Why would we ever want to return to where we were less than four short years ago?[12]

The economy still hobbled, and American upward mobility would never return to where it was in the 1960s, but Reagan's message of hope triumphed decisively over the pessimistic and fractious message the Democrats put forth to counter it. The Democratic nominee in 1984 was Carter's vice president and an old protégé of Hubert Humphrey, liberal Minnesotan Walter Mondale. Reagan trounced him in the biggest landslide since Johnson-Goldwater.

The smooth message discipline of the Republican Party, coupled with its embrace of conservative ideology and the marginalization of its moderate wing, moved it from the disaster of Watergate to the triumph of Reagan's reelection in a mere ten years. In contrast, the Democrats' diverse liberal coalition had difficulty speaking with one voice. "The trouble with the Democratic Party," wrote *Time* a few months after Mondale's defeat, "is that to many voters its national leadership appears to be no more than a collection of shrill special-interest groups."[13]

Yet the generally conservative temperament of the American electorate aided the GOP revival. Since the birth of opinion polling in the early twentieth century, Americans had made it clear that they were generally disinclined toward big-government solutions and wary of rapid social change. The New Deal's ambitious reformulation of the government's role in American life only became politically feasible because of the crises of depression and war, and fiscally conservative, small-government views continued to hold steady even amid the heyday of the New Deal Order. The failures of political leadership since Vietnam and Watergate, and the failure of government to deliver on its promises to end poverty and restore law and order, had made Americans even more distrustful of liberal solutions.[14]

Shifting economic and social geography also aided the rise of the right. The New South, already a force to be reckoned with in the late 1960s, now played a critical role in any national political context. The region had exploded in population, most of it in the suburbs of large metropolitan areas. It had become wealthier. In 1960, the South's per capita income was only 60 percent of the national average; in 1980, it was 80 percent. Reapportionment of Congressional districts in the 1960s had given the suburban South an increasingly powerful voice in national politics, moving the region away from staunch defense of white racial supremacy but toward an equally strong support of individual "freedoms" and "traditional" family structures.[15]

Over the course of several decades, factories had decamped from cities like Cleveland and Pittsburgh and Detroit for the green fields and cheaper, non-union labor of the Southern states. Farmland turned into industrial parks; small towns became manufacturing hubs making electronics, cars, and clothing. Small family farms gave way to large-scale agricultural enterprises producing cotton, chickens, and catfish. With the spread of air-conditioning, the hot and languid South became a feasible location for advanced manufacturing and a desirable destination for Northern migrants. The phenomenon was not limited to the former Confederacy, but extended westward into the West and Southwest. Cities like Phoenix and Las Vegas exploded in size; in California, metropolitan areas grew so large that they collided into each other, creating "megalopolises" of suburban homes and office parks that stretched from Los Angeles to San Diego, from San Francisco to San Jose.[16]

New Democrats

The rise of the Sunbelt paved the way for the rise of new Democratic leaders, most of whom—like the conservative icons of the Republican Party—hailed from the South and West. Some of them were literal heirs to an earlier generation of Southern Democrats who had ruled over the House and Senate in the Cold War years. Sam Nunn, grandnephew of powerful Georgia Representative Carl Vinson, won the Senate seat vacated by legendary Richard B. Russell in 1972, winning conservative votes by distancing himself from Democratic nominee George McGovern and accepting the endorsement of George Wallace. Al Gore, handsome son of the former Tennessee senator, won a House seat in 1976 at twenty-eight.[17]

Others were "Watergate babies," young men elected to Congress after Nixon's disgrace. Former McGovern campaign manager Gary Hart ran and won a Senate seat from Colorado in 1974, and soon became a vocal advocate for the high-tech "sunrise industries" that were so important to his state. Tim Wirth, another Coloradan, pushed forward organizational reforms in the House and took over Hart's Senate seat in 1986. Massachusetts was another hub of high-tech industry, and in 1978 a young and cerebral liberal named Paul Tsongas defeated venerable but scandal-plagued Republican moderate Ed Brooke. The advocacy of Wirth, Tsongas, and others of this generation for investment in new technology led the press to call them the "Atari Democrats."[18]

Governors as well as members of Congress were among those worried about their party's political marginalization, and they went to work at the national level to shift the Democrats in a more moderate direction. It wasn't easy. After the 1980 election, Louisiana Representative Gillis Long brought together a new House Democratic caucus committee of Sunbelt moderates "to reassess our Party's direction and redefine our message." Yet the reports issued by the group contained "few, if any, startling ideas," and failed to ignite much excitement.[19] Virginia governor Chuck Robb and Arizona governor Bruce Babbitt tried and failed to get a Sunbelt moderate installed as chair of the Democratic National Committee in 1984. Mondale's subsequent defeat validated the moderates' argument that the Democrats couldn't win back the White House through its current interest-group politics. And, as many commentators pointed out at the time, many centrist Democrats had White House aspirations.

In early 1985, all these impulses came together in the formation of a new group, the Democratic Leadership Council (DLC), headed by Nunn, Robb, Babbitt, and others, and led by executive director Al From, who had run the earlier House effort to redefine the Democratic agenda. "There is a perception our party has moved away from mainstream America in the 1970s," said Nunn. "We view the council not as a rival to any other party entity," remarked another young leader, Missouri Representative Richard Gephardt, "but as a way station or bridge back into the party for elected Democrats."[20]

The DLC drew its intellectual firepower from an ideology already circulating among Washington think tanks and journalists, whose founding document of sorts was an essay published two years earlier in the *Washington Monthly* titled "A Neoliberal's Manifesto." Written by the *Monthly*'s founding editor, Charles Peters, the essay laid out a new vision for political leaders who supported the broad goals of modern liberalism but were disillusioned with current orthodoxy. "We still believe in liberty and justice and a fair chance for all . . . but we no longer automatically favor unions and big government or oppose the military and big business," wrote Peters. Neither traditional liberal nor traditional conservative responses had been adequate to tackle the crises of the 1970s. What was needed was a new brand of liberalism that forged a middle ground.

Peters wrote of encouraging entrepreneurship through tax and regulatory reform, instituting performance standards for unionized workers like teachers and government employees, and establishing time limits and stricter income limits on welfare programs. Just like Reagan, Peters portrayed government bureaucracy as a problem rather than a solution. Unlike Reagan, he saw government having a critical role to play—still intervening in markets, but more strategically and entrepreneurially. This was not an abandonment of Progressive and Rooseveltian principles, but, rather, a reinvention: big government reformulated for the age of the high-tech startup and the Sunbelt suburb.[21]

In many respects, the revolutionary aspect of this neoliberalism was not in the substance of what it proposed to do, but in the way it talked about these goals.[22] The importance of style and language became clear as the DLC took these precepts and began to build a movement, going into the Southern and Western heartland to urge Democrats to "fight, don't switch." They gained plenty of critics on the way. Jesse Jackson, noting the all-white, all-male makeup of the group as well as its preponderance of new-style Dixiecrats, scoffed that DLC stood for "Democratic Leisure Class." In an op-ed, historian and JFK advisor Arthur Schlesinger, Jr., derided the approach as "me-too Reaganism." Liberals argued that Reagan's 1984 triumph came from his likability, not his politics; after all, Democrats still made up close to 40 percent of the electorate. Undaunted, Al From countered that such arguments "have been advanced by the stand-patters in our party," and that "we cannot be constrained by policies that no longer work and labels that no longer apply."[23]

The defeat of Massachusetts governor Michael Dukakis in the 1988 election further fueled the DLC's sense of mission. Neither a strident liberal nor a core member of the DLC alliance, "Dukakis erased the graffiti on the wall but put nothing on it," said From. In the vacuum, Dukakis's rival George H. W. Bush was able to blast him as an out-of-touch liberal. The DLC had proved ineffective in getting its preferred candidates to the top of the ticket in either 1984 or 1988. The group began to subtly advance the presidential aspirations of Robb, Babbitt, and Nunn. It revved up its policy operations, churning out one white paper after another. Its membership increased to over 200, including leaders who had previously avoided affiliating themselves for fear of alienating the Democrats' liberal constituencies.[24]

One of these newcomers was the young governor of Arkansas, Bill Clinton. Clinton was born in a small town in Arkansas to a single mother with few resources. He was very smart, very outgoing, and with an astounding ability to connect on a personal level with a range of people. From a very early age, Clinton had his eyes on a political career, and he had teachers and mentors who nurtured this ambition. He went to Georgetown University, using scholarships and part-time jobs to pay his tuition, then on to Oxford as a Rhodes Scholar. Returning to attend Yale Law School, he met another extraordinary young person, Hillary Rodham.

Hillary went back with him to Arkansas, where he ran for Congress in 1974 at twenty-eight. He lost, but made a strong showing, and Democratic leaders in Arkansas pegged him as a young man to watch. He won the post of attorney general in 1976, and two years later—at thirty-two—he became governor of Arkansas.

In Clinton's first term, he got ahead of himself. Young and idealistic, filled with liberal fervor, he brought in a great many young people like him to mix things up and do a lot of reform in a short period of time. Conservative, tradition-bound Arkansas was not ready for this change. They looked at the long-haired young governor. They looked at his scholarly, feminist wife, who hadn't changed her last name when she got married.

Up for reelection in 1980, Clinton lost. Chastened, he returned to run two years later as a more centrist candidate. He cut his hair short, and Hillary changed her last name to Clinton. They both understood that he wasn't going to appeal to everyone. With the right message, however, he could get enough Arkansas voters on his side to win.

Clinton was reelected again and again, blending old-style liberal populism with business-friendly approaches and neoliberal rhetoric. He was particularly effective at winning support from the black community while still getting strong support from whites. Arkansas was perfect for Clinton's style of intensive, personal retail politics, being a small state with a population of about two million people. Its largest city, Little Rock, had a population not too much more than 100,000 at the time Clinton was governor.

Figure 26. Bill and Hillary Clinton on their wedding day, Fayetteville, Arkansas, 1978. Elected governor at thirty-two and a candidate for president at forty-five, Bill Clinton became the first major-party nominee from the Baby Boom generation. With a high-powered career of her own, his wife Hillary was an unconventional political spouse, and bewildered a conservative Arkansas electorate by not changing her last name after their marriage. Courtesy William J. Clinton Presidential Library.

By 1988, Clinton's national star was rising. He became chair of the National Governors' Association and played a major role in advancing support for the Reagan administration welfare reform bill, the Family Support Act. Welfare reform became a signature issue for Clinton, who found a compelling way to talk about the importance of providing aid without fostering dependency. He talked about his childhood as the son of a struggling single mother, he talked about the empowerment that came through work, he talked about giving poor people "a hand up, not a hand out." His only setback came at the 1988 Democratic Convention, when he gave such a long-winded speech that the biggest applause came when he finally said, "in conclusion." He bounced back. In 1990, Clinton became the DLC's first chair from outside Washington.[25]

As the next election cycle neared, more people in the party agreed that it was time for new blood. It was time for New Democrats. First, however, they had to defeat a sitting president who looked pretty hard to beat.

The Incumbent

Born into power and economic privilege, George H. W. Bush's upbringing could not have been more different from that of Bill Clinton. His father, Prescott Bush, was a Wall Street banker who went on to serve as a U.S. senator from Connecticut. A classic Northeastern Republican, Prescott Bush was a patrician politician of the old style who passed on to his son his decorous manner and belief in the honor of public service. From his mother, Bush inherited a ferociously competitive streak that came out in games of sports and games of politics.

George Bush turned eighteen the day of his prep school graduation, in spring 1942. The next day, against his parents' wishes, he enlisted in the U.S. navy and became its youngest pilot. He served three years and went on 58 combat missions. On one of these, he was shot down by the Japanese and had to bail out over the Pacific. Eventually rescued by a U.S. submarine, he was awarded the Distinguished Flying Cross for his heroism under fire.

Graduating from Yale after the war, Bush chose to leave New England behind and moved his family to Texas to seek his fortune in the oil industry. His move to Texas gave him a front-row seat in witnessing the Sunbelt revolution and the changes it wrought on the Republican Party. When he first ran for Congress in 1964, he was criticized as a carpetbagger from the North, and lost. Yet the changing demographics of 1960s Texas started to work in Bush's favor. More Republicans were moving from North to South. The strength of the Democratic Party was weakening in Texas in the wake of civil rights. Bush ran again in 1966 as a Republican moderate. Lifted by votes from his fellow transplanted Northerners, he won.

In the 1970s, Bush worked in a series of jobs in Washington that demonstrated his great party loyalty and helped him develop a strong reputation as a leader in foreign policy. He served as Nixon's ambassador to the UN, Ford's ambassador to China, and director of the CIA. In between, he took on the thankless job of head of the Republican National Committee in the thick of Watergate. He first ran for president in 1980, as a more moderate alternative to Reagan. But 1980 was not the moderates' year, so he ended up accepting the vice presidential post.[26]

Bush did not have Reagan's masterful communication skills, nor did he share his straightforward conservative ideology. Yet he and Reagan became close to each other during their eight years in the White House, and Bush had some significant influence on the Reagan agenda, particularly when it came to foreign policy. Foreign policy was certainly the defining realm of Reagan's second term and Bush's first term, as the two men presided over the end of the Cold War and the rise of a new world order.

Reagan came into office with an aggressive stance against the Soviets, beefing up defense and referring to the USSR as an "evil empire." He supported efforts to curb the spread of Marxist and socialist-leaning governments around the world. This included Nicaragua, where a scheme to funnel arms to a conservative counterinsurgency would result in the Iran-Contra scandal—an affair in which both Reagan and Bush were implicated.[27]

By the time Reagan left office, however, the U.S.-Soviet relationship had changed profoundly. Reformist Soviet leader Mikhail Gorbachev had instituted policies of openness and economic change, glasnost and perestroika. Reagan's and Gorbachev's summit meetings in the late 1980s were headline-grabbing moments that foreshadowed the end of the Cold War. The breakup of the Soviet Union and tearing down of the Iron Curtain happened in Bush's first year in office. But with the old Soviet enemy gone, a new set of threats rose to the forefront.

In August 1990, Iraq invaded the small but oil-rich nation of Kuwait in an attempt to gain the smaller nation's resources and strategic position on the Persian Gulf. Bush mobilized an international coalition—including the Soviets—to halt the invasion and beat back Saddam Hussein's forces. Framing this as a critical moment for the international community of nations, "not another Vietnam,"[28] Bush and his military commanders were determined for this to be a war conducted chiefly by air and long-distance missile strikes, not by American boots on the ground. "Operation Desert Storm" was a huge military and political triumph. It was smooth, aggressive, and quick. It showed off all the high-tech wonders of the modern U.S. military.

The war also showcased the sophistication of the political message machine the Republicans had built over the previous decade. Remembering how much negative press attention hurt the American effort in Vietnam,

Figure 27. President George H. W. Bush talks with troops in Saudi Arabia,
22 November 1990. Fought aggressively with high-tech weaponry and carefully
managed press coverage, the Gulf War was a huge political victory for Bush. As his
popularity soared, many prominent Democrats concluded his reelection was
inevitable, and chose to stay out of the 1992 race. Courtesy George Bush
Presidential Library.

the White House put strong restrictions on how the war could be reported.
Journalists were embedded in military units and their movements were
strictly contained. Most reporters didn't even get to go into Iraq at all, but
had to report from U.S. government facilities in Kuwait. When the war
ended in March 1991, President Bush had approval ratings as high as 90
percent. The president rejoiced, "By God, we've kicked the Vietnam Syn-
drome once and for all."[29]

What Bush and the Republicans did not fully internalize, however, was
the degree to which the Cold War had provided the rhetorical and ideological glue for the Republican conservative ascendance. Reagan had been masterful at turning the struggle with the Soviet Union into a Wild West

parable of good guys versus bad guys, "us" versus "them." His tough talk about the Soviets in the early years of his presidency gave him the political cover to enter into a new, less belligerent dialogue with Gorbachev later. Reagan and his supporters continued to claim credit for the fall of the Iron Curtain and disintegration of the Soviet Union, even though it was clear that the end of the Cold War sprang from many causes.

The quick and effective Gulf War helped keep the jingoistic spirit alive, but amid the chants of "USA! USA!" it was clear that the Republican Party needed a fresh way to articulate what it stood for, and whom it stood against. Many conservatives—particularly evangelical Christians—had already concluded they had identified the new enemy, and "it was us." As many conservatives saw it, the cultural relativism and permissiveness set in motion by the 1960s had created a culture of "political correctness" that permeated American schools and universities, boardrooms and bureaucracies. In their desire for social equality, liberals had become soft on crime. In their promotion of rights for women and sexual minorities, they had contributed to the breakdown of the family. In the opinion of these conservatives, the 1960s had not been an era of progress and increased individual rights. Instead, it had ushered in an era of cultural permissiveness and government intrusion that had trampled on these rights. There was a war going on in America between the people who wanted to preserve traditional cultural values, and those who wanted to destroy them. It was time to fight back.

Bush had tested this theme of a "culture war" in the 1988 election with great success. The New England Ivy Leaguer and his similarly preppy vice presidential nominee, Dan Quayle, went populist, courting evangelicals and lashing out at intellectual elites and out-of-touch Washington types. The genteel Bush had no hesitation going dirty. He hired as his campaign manager Lee Atwater, a young and steely South Carolinian operative known for his relentless and sophisticated political attacks. Atwater crafted a series of hard-hitting television ads portraying Mike Dukakis as a weak-kneed failure and poster child for the cultural elite. One ad showed Dukakis sitting awkwardly in a tank, a helmet propped on his head, looking more like a child playing GI Joe than a commander-in-chief. Atwater exploited this unfortunate photo op to the hilt. There was the infamous "Willie Horton" ad, which showed a menacing mug shot of a black felon let out of prison on a Massachusetts furlough program. Atwater perfected the art of playing on voters' fears about race, the economy, and pointy-headed intellectuals stomping on individual rights. He took George Wallace's message and updated it for the 1980s, and in the process, made George H. W. Bush president.

If the 1992 election had been about foreign policy, Bush would have been the stronger candidate. He still glowed in the aftermath of the Gulf War. Yet that glow wore off quickly, and 1992 turned out to be an election that hinged on the economy and the domestic agenda. Within a few months of the end of Desert Storm, the U.S. economy started to struggle. For liberals, the slump seemed proof that Republican economic politics didn't help the little guy. For conservatives, it reminded them that Bush had promised not to raise taxes, and had gone back on that promise. Bush had never been an undiluted conservative like Reagan, and he didn't have the communication skills to turn a sour-economy story into a Morning in America. The worsening economy started to hack at Bush's approval ratings, but they were still at 60 percent by fall 1991.

This happened to be the critical moment when Democratic contenders needed to decide whether to throw their hats in the ring. Waiting much longer would put them behind on fundraising, and would disadvantage them in the early primaries. Looking at the boost the Gulf War had given Bush in the polls, the biggest Democratic names—Dick Gephardt, Al Gore, Sam Nunn—concluded that the president was not going to be beatable. Yes, the economy was slowing, but the conventional wisdom concluded the election would still be won or lost on foreign policy.

This situation opened things for a fresh crop of candidates who had not run before. There were three senators, all identified with DLC-style centrism: Bob Kerrey of Nebraska, Paul Tsongas of Massachusetts, and Tom Harkin of Iowa. There were two Sunbelt governors: Douglas Wilder of Virginia and Jerry Brown of California.

Then, in early October, there was another governor: Bill Clinton. He stood in front of the Old State House in Little Rock and announced he was running for president. "You'd expect a governor of Arkansas to become president of the United States about as soon as a great world statesman would emerge from Bolivia or Portugal," cracked Washington commentator Morton Kondracke. Yet even Kondracke recognized that Clinton now delivered a compelling message in a charismatic package. He had taken the neoliberal and centrist creed and redefined it, calling for "every last American citizen to assume personal responsibility for the future of this country."[30]

George Bush was the inheritor of the Reagan mantle on the Republican side, but the career and ascendance of Bill Clinton, the New Democrat, is really where one can see the culmination of the Reagan Revolution. Clinton's centrist Democratic ideas bore the influence of Reagan's beliefs about cutting government spending, about individual responsibility, about less regulation. And, just as important, Clinton also learned from Reagan the importance of communicating your message in an inspiring way, and from hammering that message home every day, every hour, and every minute of a presidential campaign.

CHAPTER 8

The CNN President

I hear you're the smartest guy in the race. That's sorta like
saying that Moe's the smartest of the Three Stooges.
—New Hampshire voter to Bill Clinton, January 1992

By 1992, CNN had gone from being Ted Turner's outlandish idea to a
serious news outlet whose influence radiated far beyond the size of its
viewer audience. It had become regarded as "the fourth network" that presented a formidable challenge to the business model of network nightly
news.[1] The Gulf War of 1990 and 1991 was CNN's breakout moment, a
fast-moving and highly visual war that matched the fast-paced rhythm of
cable news. On air 24 hours a day, CNN was able to break stories before
the broadcast networks could get them, and the cable network could pro
vide video content to local news outlets that were in fierce competition for
ratings. It became a global power, setting up different international feeds
that beamed out of its Atlanta headquarters into nearly every continent. On
ordinary news days, the networks still ruled; CNN mustered only about 10
percent of the U.S. viewership NBC, ABC, and CBS could draw. Yet in the
opening days of the conflict in the Gulf, CNN scooped its competition by
being the only news outlet with reporters on the ground in Baghdad as the
U.S.-led Coalition forces began their high-intensity barrage of air bombing.
CNN's American audience surged to 150 percent of the usual network news
share; millions more watched around the world.[2]

The network continued to be a news-breaker and newsmaker in 1992,
even though its audience share never quite returned to the dizzying heights
of Desert Storm. Domestic crises garnered high ratings. In late April, Los

Angeles exploded into violence. An all-white jury had acquitted police officers accused of beating a black motorist, Rodney King. Angry residents
lashed out at the injustice, turning their anger on local businesses, most
of which had white or Asian American owners. The images of a burning
neighborhood, of looting and violence on the streets, flashed across TV
screens and newspapers. The network's audience share doubled. Two
months later, earthquakes in Southern California triggered a surge in CNN
audience, and in late August the devastation of a major storm, Hurricane
Andrew, caused an even bigger spike. CNN was event-driven television,
and in its pursuit of ratings it helped turn the ordinary processes of a presidential election year into suspenseful, personality-driven media events. And
if a bad story about a candidate started running on CNN, campaign staff
needed to stop it—immediately—or else it would spread like a virus to the
rest of the media universe.[3]

In February, Texas billionaire H. Ross Perot went on the network's mar-
quee interview program, *Larry King Live*, to announce that if his supporters
got him on the ballot in all fifty states, he'd run for president as a third-
party candidate. Perot and CNN were tailor-made for each other. Both
presented themselves as independent iconoclasts, in the business of speaking truth to power, and not beholden to any particular political interests.
CNN's audience was more affluent, older, and had a higher percentage of
male viewers than the major networks. It was an audience not only more
inclined to be interested in national politics, but also to be receptive to
Perot's no-nonsense style and hard-hitting message. CNN styled itself as
the home of crusading television journalism. Perot believed he was on "a
crusade for America itself."[4]

The Straight Talker

For over two decades, American voters had become increasingly suspicious
of Washington and the political insiders that filled it. After the construction
of the interstate highway ringing Washington, the term "inside the Beltway" became shorthand for political business in the nation's capital. By the
early 1990s, the term had morphed into an insult. With the country in an
anti-government mood, partisan infighting on the rise, and an increasing
number of voters identifying themselves as political independents, being a
Washington insider had turned from asset to liability. Teddy Roosevelt and

Figure 28. H. Ross Perot on Larry King. Attesting to the power of CNN not only to report the news but to make headlines on its own, Perot became a major presidential contender through a series of appearances on the network's evening talk show, *Larry King Live*. AP Photo.

Woodrow Wilson had urged Americans to embrace rule by bureaucratic experts as the path to true reform. Franklin Roosevelt and his advisors had argued successfully that only a large and strong central government could steer the modern nation. Even Richard Nixon had overseen the expansion of social programs and government regulatory powers. Now, political reformers found the bureaucrats and experts the source of the problem.

Ross Perot capitalized on this sentiment to great effect, positioning himself as 1992's ultimate outsider. He condemned career politicians for not understanding the issues, for being beholden to special interests, for forgetting the real America. In reality, however, Perot was a creature of Washington, a man who had grown wealthy after securing government contracts, and gotten wealthier through savvy lobbying of Congress to get more contracts and favors. One frustrated Bush campaign official complained Perot "was everything in real life that he was railing against in politics."[5]

Perot was born in 1930 in Texarkana, Texas, only about thirty miles away from the small town of Hope, Arkansas, where Bill Clinton came into the world sixteen years later. Although his parents weren't poor, growing up in Depression-era East Texas was a struggle. Perot wrangled horses and delivered newspapers to make an extra dollar. When his boss at the newspaper cut his commission, Perot confronted him until the boss, amused by this determined, big-eared kid, gave in. He went to the U.S. Naval Academy and then served four years of military service, leaving to sell computers for IBM.

On the day he turned thirty-two, the maverick Perot founded his own high-tech startup, Electronic Data Systems (EDS). Most of the big money to be made those days by computer companies that weren't IBM came through government contracts, and at first the company went nowhere. Then Perot got hugely lucky. Lyndon Johnson signed Medicare and Medicaid into law in 1965. These huge government health care programs required big data management and the kind of sophisticated computer systems that Perot's company could provide. He won prime contracts to service Texas Medicare and Medicaid claims; then Governor Ronald Reagan awarded him California's. Along the way, EDS faced charges of perpetuating an East-Texas-style racial order, firing and demoting black workers. EDS went public in 1968, turning Perot into what the leftist magazine *Ramparts* called the first "welfare billionaire."[6]

As his wealth and reputation grew, Perot turned himself into a folksy, down-home business hero who mixed populist plain-talk with corporate aphorisms. Despite government having made him rich, he cultivated a persona built around the triumph of free-market capitalism, about a little-guy entrepreneur who used his smarts and pluck to compete with corporate giants.[7]

Perot ardently believed that private businessmen like him were better equipped than the government to solve America's problems, and he made a number of audacious ventures in the 1970s and 80s that played this out. The first was orchestrating the successful rescue of two EDS employees jailed in Iran shortly after the Islamic Revolution. Next, he tried to push for the return of American POWs in Vietnam, and offered unsolicited advice to the Carter administration in their quest to free the U.S. Embassy hostages in Iran. He funneled money to the secret Iran-Contra operation headed by Lt. Col. Oliver North. Single-minded and hot-headed, Perot became frustrated that people in power never paid as much attention to his advice as he thought they should. Many considered his efforts mere publicity stunts; Perot knew he was fighting to make things better. In the meantime, he had become "America's most intriguing—and most publicized—businessman."[8]

Perot spent a good thirty years building this legend before he ran for president, and the mythos served him well, particularly for voters comparing him to his fellow Texan, George H.W. Bush. Positioning his quest for the presidency as a pure grassroots campaign, called upon by the "everyday folks" who were "writing me in longhand" to urge him to run. "I don't want to fail them." Even though he had neither government experience nor a particularly clear policy platform, Perot's populism struck a nerve. "George Bush is a good ol' boy from Texas who made a lot of money in oil and has lost touch," said 43-year-old Marilyn Johnson. "I suppose Mr. Perot may be a good ol' boy, but he went out and made his own money, started from nothing. God bless him. Bush was born into money."[9]

The response to Perot reflected the deep disillusionment with party politics and big institutions of all kinds in 1992 America, the upending of political truisms that made robber barons into the populist heroes. While not entirely spontaneous or truly bottom-up—Perot seeded the idea and used his considerable fortune to bankroll statewide operations—the engagement of a wide array of ordinary people in Perot's campaign made it a third-party campaign like no other. Theodore Roosevelt had run as a third party candidate after two terms as president and with the support of powerful business and intellectual leaders. George Wallace had been a four-term governor and gained his strength from the disaffection of Southern whites with the Democrats' support of civil rights. Third party candidates in other years had championed single issues, interest groups, or regions. Perot drew support from men and women, working-class and middle-class, North, South, East, and West. The only thing his supporters had in common—aside from their disdain for the major-party offerings—was that the vast majority of them were white.[10]

These voters disliked the mainstream press nearly as much as they disliked mainstream politicians, and CNN became the "alternative" place both for Perot to deliver his message and for his candidacy to be endlessly analyzed and dissected. "What Perot did," commented conservative journalist Mona Charen on another CNN program later that spring, "is he absolutely leapfrogged [over] the major media." Noted a more liberal CNN talking head a few days later, "everybody thinks that [Perot] agrees with them. Moderates think he's moderate; liberals think he's liberal; conservatives think he's conservative."[11]

Third-party candidates in earlier elections didn't have CNN. They didn't have a way to get their message directly to the voters, and a way to control the news cycle. But they also didn't have to weather the scrutiny Perot—and all his fellow candidates—faced in the cable-news age.

The Spin Cycle

With 24 hours to fill, CNN provided airtime to people and stories that the others didn't have time to cover. And with 24 hours to fill, it was able to dig deeper into all aspects of the people running for president, including their personal lives. Over the course of many decades, changing media technologies and political communications made the relationship between candidate and voter more personal. From Wilson's limericks to FDR's fireside chats to Nixon's polished television commercials, candidates and presidents carefully crafted their "personal side" to win votes and cement political loyalties.

After Vietnam and Watergate, voters realized that behind this friendly, paternal façade national leaders had dirty secrets: waging war, building "enemies lists," breaking into rival campaign headquarters, covering it up. The press seemed complicit in the cover-ups, failing to ask the hard questions and looking the other way when leaders behaved badly. Although the nineteenth-century press hadn't hesitated to dive deep into presidents' sexual sins, the twentieth-century D.C. press corps kept what they knew about extramarital dalliances to themselves.[12]

After Watergate, the press never again wanted to be caught flat-footed. Their swing toward investigative journalism occurred simultaneously with the rise of a sex-saturated and celebrity-driven pop culture. Youth culture, gay liberation, and feminism had brought discussions of sex out of the bedroom and into the public realm; at the same time, television and magazine outlets chronicling the lives of the rich, beautiful, and famous proliferated. Popular culture celebrated the rebels and the rule-breakers, from the bikers of *Easy Rider* to punk rockers and the frustrated news anchor in the satirical film *Network* who yelled, "I'm mad as hell, and I'm not going to take this anymore!"[13]

Politicians moved from being genial father figures to being living and breathing personalities, full of flaws and peccadillos. Relentless investigations into all dimensions of candidates' lives—from the cereal they ate for breakfast to the women they dated at night—became an integral part of presidential campaigns. In 1988, Gary Hart's presidential campaign received a fatal blow after a tabloid published photos of the married candidate enjoying the close company of a lovely blonde named Donna Rice. The Hart-Rice scandal got news outlets of every sort involved in the pursuit of political scandal. Political reporting was no longer the purview of the inside-the-Beltway establishment.

The rise of cable television intensified this hothouse environment. Many channels competed for viewers' attention, and this further privileged the sensational and salacious over the staid and serious. Reporters now had multiple deadlines per day, and multiple stories to follow. The result was the reporters had less time to work on long-term investigative reporting that involved a lot of research. Cable technology also contributed to a regulatory change that had a profound effect on balanced, informed journalistic debate on television. For years, the Federal Communications Commission had required television networks to present multiple views on controversial issues; if a station gave one side time to air its positions, it was required to give equal time to the opposing side. This "fairness doctrine" not only kept television news generally impartial but also kept the lid on the more outrageous strains of argument. If you were going to go on the attack, you needed to base it on facts that could withstand rebuttal.

In 1987, the Reagan-era FCC abolished this rule, responding in good part to arguments by conservatives that the mainstream press had a liberal bias. One of the most vocal supporters of the change was former Nixon aide Roger Ailes, who had long understood the power of cable television to reach new audiences and shift political conversations. Now, Ailes and his fellow conservatives could launch news programs of their own. The birth of Ailes's Fox News happened four years after the 1992 election, but the repercussions of the end of the fairness doctrine were already being felt in the early 1990s. Not only could journalists go on television telling one side of an issue, but campaign operatives also could go on air and repeat their messages again and again, without having rivals there to challenge them.[14] As one Clinton campaign advisor put it, the press is "just a giant monster that has . . . to be continually fed. Either you feed it or it feeds on you."[15]

The Democratic primaries showed just how powerful that giant monster could be. In late 1991, there were six declared candidates, but a great many Democrats were waiting for someone better to come along. Many of them pinned their hopes on Mario Cuomo, governor of New York. Cuomo was an unapologetic liberal with a common touch, cerebral and deft with the press, with the character and gravitas needed to run for president. He'd already made a run for the nomination in 1988, and his support and organization were even stronger four years later. He was charismatic, with an extraordinary ability to deliver mesmerizing speeches that rallied the party faithful in ways few other politicians could. Cuomo was big-time. Clinton and the rest of them were small-time.

For months, Cuomo had been sending signals about possibly running again. Yet he just wouldn't come out one way or another. His indecision gave him the nickname "Hamlet on the Hudson." As the fall months went by, Bush's approval ratings started dropping. When polls were taken about preferences for Democratic candidates, Cuomo came out ahead of the men already in the race. Even though he would have a late start, it seemed he had an opportunity to become the front-runner if he got himself on the ballot in the first primary state, New Hampshire.[16]

The deadline for filing for candidacy in that primary was December 20. And as luck would have it, right at that moment Cuomo was in final intense negotiations with the state legislature over the New York State budget. New York Republicans seized the opportunity to blast Cuomo over putting his political ambitions over the interests of his constituents. Cuomo deeply disliked the accusation; as he later recalled, "I felt, 'The state's in trouble— this is no time to leave.'" By the end of December 19, there was still no budget deal. And New Hampshire law required Cuomo to file for candidacy in person.

Reporters descended on Albany. CNN set up cameras on the tarmac at the airport, keeping watch on the plane Cuomo had chartered to fly himself to Manchester to file. The story dominated CNN all day. The hours ticked by. No budget deal. No Cuomo on the plane. At 3:30 P.M., Cuomo made a public statement. The budget had to take priority over his presidential ambitions. He was out. "If I had left for New Hampshire without a budget," Cuomo reflected, "just imagine what the media would have done. And they would have been right. . . . It would have been hopeless for me."[17]

The remaining candidates on the Democratic side soon learned the hazards of running for president in the age of the 24-news cycle. By January 1992, the race for New Hampshire was in full gear. Cuomo's departure had focused fresh attention on Bill Clinton, the up-and-coming Southerner. Unlike the other moderates in the race, he was from outside the Beltway. Unlike the other governors, he was a moderate. "Clinton is certainly no conservative, but he is a pragmatic middle-roader of the kind that won Democratic nominations in the pre-McGovern era," noted the eminent political reporters Rowland Evans and Robert Novak. "He is in step with the party's comers in Congress—typified by senators Joseph Lieberman of Connecticut and Richard Shelby of Alabama—who disdain ideology." Meanwhile, the other Democratic campaigns sputtered. Tom Harkin took a two-week Caribbean vacation. Bob Kerrey had trouble raising money and had a revolt of his top campaign staff.[18]

It was too good to last. In mid-January, the *Star* supermarket tabloid published a bombshell, telling the story of an Arkansas jazz singer and newscaster named Gennifer Flowers and her longtime affair with Bill Clinton. In Arkansas in the 1980s, rumors about Clinton's personal life were so common people didn't really pay a great deal of attention to them. They were rumors, and the people who supported Clinton didn't care too much about them. The people who cared didn't vote for him anyway. Nothing made its way into the local press. As he moved onto a national stage, Clinton continued to be surrounded with rumblings about his alleged affairs— the campaign staff called them "bimbo eruptions"—but nothing stuck.[19]

Now, the national media machine went into overdrive. Already deft at rapid response, the campaign came out swinging, telling reporters that Flowers's story was a lie. Bill and Hillary went in front of millions of television views of CBS's *60 Minutes* to talk about the strength of their marriage.

Flowers and the *Star* countered with a press conference at New York's Waldorf Astoria Hotel the next day. She played tapes of her phone calls with Clinton, including an excerpt where he encouraged her to deny their relationship if asked by curious reporters.

Like many stories in politics, the scandal became powerful because it substantiated a narrative that was emerging about Bill Clinton—not just about his sexual habits, but about his broader "character." One political wag in Arkansas had once called him "Slick Willie." The name stuck, because it fit an image of a candidate who would say anything to get elected, and who played fast and loose with the truth.[20]

The Flowers incident also was a powerful media moment because of the intersection between tabloid journalism and straight journalism never before seen in presidential politics. Gennifer Flowers went public because the *Star* reportedly paid her $100,000 for her story. She fielded questions from reporters from the *Wall Street Journal* and *New York Times*—as well as from a sidekick on the profane and sensational radio show of "shock jock" Howard Stern.

Clinton was still reeling from the Flowers debacle when another scandal hit. This time, it wasn't sex but the Vietnam draft. Clinton was among the first of the Vietnam generation to run for president, and like many men his age had worked hard to avoid being drafted. His lack of military service during the war already was a tricky element of his biography, but Clinton had assured everyone he hadn't pulled any strings; he was no draft dodger. But as the tough New Hampshire primary campaign came down to its final days, it became clear Clinton had "pulled strings" to obtain a coveted berth in the University of Arkansas ROTC program—and, making matters worse, had reneged on his commitment when the next draft lottery gave him a number that made it unlikely he would be sent to Vietnam. Once again, here was a story feeding the narrative that Clinton was a candidate who might not be trusted. To make it worse, his Democratic rival Kerrey was a war hero who had lost a leg in Vietnam.

The pundits said it was over for Clinton. They underestimated him. They also underestimated the audacity of the Clinton campaign spin machine. It included two tough political consultants, Paul Begala and James Carville, and a cool but equally tough thirty-year-old communications director named George Stephanopoulos. DLC policy chief Bruce Reed had come from Washington to run the policy shop. Campaign pollster Stan Greenberg provided relentless slice-and-dice opinion surveys and focus-group data that gave the campaign a daily sense of where their candidate stood in the pack.

Many around Clinton belonged to a breed of political professionals unknown before the television age, who made working on campaigns into a full-time career. Many had worked for Michael Dukakis in 1988, and had learned some tough lessons. When Republican strategist Lee Atwater hammered away, the Dukakis campaign had been slow to fight back. Four years later, these operatives learned that rapid response and message discipline were critical to winning modern presidential elections. The candidate had to take control of the story and of the spin cycle.

To halt the draft story, the campaign released a 1969 letter from Clinton to the ROTC commander that was damning in its admission of guilt. "Thank you for saving me from the draft," the twenty-three-year-old wrote with palpable relief. But the forty-five-year-old candidate was able to contextualize these words with his own message. It didn't end the story, but it slowed it down enough for the campaign to keep its traction. Clinton came in second in New Hampshire, behind Paul Tsongas. His campaign advisors had the audacity to spin it not as a loss, but as a win—calling Clinton the "Comeback Kid."[21]

It remained a tough battle. Kerrey fell away, but the sober and uncharismatic Tsongas gained momentum. Jerry Brown ran an anti-establishment campaign that proved remarkably resilient. "Character" remained a recurring issue, as baby boomer Clinton had to fend off stories about his past never faced by leaders of the World War II generation, like Bush. Stories swirled about his smoking marijuana while in graduate school. He acknowledged it, but countered that he had "never inhaled." The campaign tried to spin the story another way, and fed the media beast with stories of their own. "We were winning ugly," observed Stephanopoulos later. "Every week we'd snuff out an incipient scandal, grind out a majority, and watch Clinton grow more unpopular."[22]

The Democratic field as a whole was not doing well. Clinton as well as the other candidates consistently ran third in national polls, behind both Bush and Perot. Many Democratic primary voters told pollsters they'd rather vote for the maverick Texas businessman. Over at Bush reelection headquarters, campaign manager Fred Malek was pleased at the disorderly Democrats. "The clear message of the Democratic race is that the voters are not satisfied with any of the Democratic candidates in the field," he told a reporter. Clinton was furious: at his rivals, at Perot, at the press. "They

Figure 29. *The Arsenio Hall Show* taping, Paramount Studios, Hollywood, 3 June 1992.
Democratic candidate Bill Clinton also took advantage of free media, including
making appearances designed to appeal to young and minority voters. A
saxophone-playing Clinton appeared on the wildly popular late night talk show
hosted by comedian Arsenio Hall. AP Photo/Reed Saxon.

have not captured the essence of my economic message," he thundered to
his aides.[23]

Yet the way the Clinton campaign wrested control of the media story
reinforced this trend of style over substance, entertainment over news. Not
too long after the Los Angeles riots, Clinton appeared on African American
comedian Arsenio Hall's popular late night talk show, wearing sunglasses
and playing his saxophone. He went on MTV, answering questions from
twenty-somethings on both serious and un-serious topics. Bill and Hillary
wanted to talk about policy, but their media advisor Mandy Grunwald
warned, "if we don't do that in a sexy way, we will be eaten alive." This
approach reached new audiences, and it also solved a money problem. The
intensity of the primary battles had drained the campaign's war chest.
Unable to pay for their own commercials, the Clinton team found ways to
get on television—and make news—for free.[24]

It worked. It was risky, but it worked. Clinton's campaign had more message discipline and understanding of the spin cycle than the competitors. The people at the head of the campaign had spent lifetimes in politics, yet for many of them this was their first presidential campaign. Because they had been so far outside of the political establishment, they had little difficulty in breaking its rules. They took advantage of the intersection between tabloid journalism and serious journalism, they responded to the demands of cable television, and they weren't as beholden to traditional Democratic constituencies. But Clinton himself was the most important weapon. For all his personal flaws, he possessed an extraordinary blend of political talent: an encyclopedic grasp of the policy issues, capacity to deliver pungent sound bites and pointed attacks on his opponents, and ability to make anyone with whom he interacted feel like the most important person in the room.

As he stumped through state after state, Clinton was able to speak a language of government reinvention and social compassion that resonated with many different groups, conveyed with charm and sincerity that made audiences fall in love with him. Robert Kennedy had been the last politician able to build such an effective "black and blue" coalition between African American and working-class voters. As the primary season drew to a close, and rivals fell by the wayside, an exhausted and road-tested candidate and his aides realized that they at last had the nomination.

Clinton capped it off with another made-for-TV moment: the announcement of Tennessee Senator and DLC stalwart Al Gore as his running mate. The event was so smoothly choreographed that Bush campaign staffers watching on CNN cringed as they saw it. It was a beautiful summer day in Little Rock. Against the red brick background of the Arkansas governor's mansion, in front of a group of cheering supporters, the Clinton and Gore families stood together. They were picture-perfect, with wholesome children and smiling blonde wives, already seeming like the best of friends.

By picking Gore, Clinton was going against longstanding conventional wisdom: to pick a vice president who was different from the president and appealed to different constituencies. FDR had picked John Nance Garner, then Harry Truman—two men about as different from the patrician New Yorker in background, region, and politics as you could get. The same thing happened when Kennedy picked Johnson, Nixon picked Agnew, and Reagan picked Bush. In contrast, Al Gore was nearly the same age as Clinton, from the state next door, with the same centrist politics. The choice was a bet that voters cared less about factionalism and more about having leaders who were young, moderate, fresh faces. Perhaps most important, both were from the South, the region whose politics were most in flux, and whose support was ever more crucial to winning a national election. Few Democratic liberals liked to acknowledge that the segregated "Solid South" had been the key to the party's dominance of national politics through much of the twentieth century. Lyndon Johnson's signing of the Civil Rights Act of 1964 began the steady hemorrhaging of Southern support from the Democratic to the Republican column. By 1992, only mid-South states like Arkansas were continuing to elect Democrats on a regular basis. Young leaders like Clinton and Gore might persuade their fellow Southerners to return to the Democratic fold, even just for one election.

The week after the Gore announcement, the Clinton troops moved triumphantly to New York City for the convention. Unlike the other Democratic Conventions we've explored thus far, it was slickly stage-managed and largely controversy-free. Reforms instituted after the chaos of Chicago '68 had turned the primaries and caucuses into the places the nomination was decided; the convention no longer served as the moment of decision. The multiple balloting of yesteryear was a dim memory by 1992, but the wall-to-wall press coverage remained, and intensified in the cable-news era. Conventions turned into well-scripted political theater, rather than actually choosing a nominee: "the role of the assembled delegates instead was to serve as extras in the crowd scenes and finally to arrive at a long foregone conclusion."[25]

The 1992 Democratic Convention showcased the biography and vision of Bill Clinton, with the handsome Al Gore as his New Democrat sidekick. It was, *Newsweek* reported, "one long infomercial spread over four evenings of free prime television time, and Bill Clinton flung himself at it as hungrily as a starving man at a banquet table." And in the carefully choreographed program, with its audience-tested references to "working families" and "empowerment" instead of poverty or inequality, the Democrats "signaled [their] determination to win back the voters who have deserted them over the past 20 years."[26]

For the first time, the national polls put Clinton in first place, ahead of Bush and Perot. Afterward, the Clintons and Gores went on a multistate bus tour that extended their post-convention bump in the polls. They rolled through the heartland, holding euphoric rallies in front of thousands as the campaign theme song played again and again: "Don't stop thinking about tomorrow/don't stop, it'll be here soon . . . don't you look back." Things were looking up.

But Clinton still had image problems. People didn't like him or trust him. He had a 15 percent approval rating. The campaign ran focus groups to see what the problem was. In Allentown, Pennsylvania, one woman put it this way: "Look, if you asked Bill Clinton what his favorite color is, he'd tell you 'plaid.'" On top of that, James Carville mused, "we were not the insurgent candidate in an insurgent year. With Perot in the race, it was going to be hard to convince people that we were the ones with new ideas."[27]

The Elephants in the Room

George Bush had problems, too. First, the president had an unexpected primary challenge from conservative Patrick Buchanan. An aide to Nixon and Reagan who had become one of the most articulate defenders of "family values" and conservative ideology as a speechwriter and pundit, Buchanan had a formidable intellect and an ability to tap into the ardent conservative base. Bush had been Reagan's vice president, but conservative true believers still perceived him as a moderate. "He is constantly pandering to a conservative constituency, hoping to ward if off by throwing a bone or two," observed one columnist, but it never seemed authentic. In contrast, Buchanan was *all* red meat. He spoke of himself as a "paleoconservative" and styled his crusade as a movement of "peasants with pitchforks." He was isolationist, anti-immigrant, and anti-tax. "We love the old republic," Buchanan trumpeted, "and when we hear phrases like 'New World Order,' we release the safety catches on our revolvers."[28]

In the New Hampshire primary, Bush won, but Buchanan was competitive enough to make the media pay attention. The 24-hour news cycle played up the fact that the incumbent president might have weak support within his own party. Suddenly, a boring GOP primary season was getting newsworthy. So the Bush campaign fought back. The next big fight was in Michigan, and the Bush spin machine fed stories to the media about Buchanan owning a foreign car—a deadly sin in the Motor City. Bush trounced Buchanan in Michigan, and that was the end of the Buchanan campaign's chances.[29]

However, it wasn't the end of Buchanan. He gave a speech at the Republican Convention in August that hard-right conservatives applauded, but that alarmed nearly everyone else. He tore into both Hillary and Bill Clinton for promoting an agenda that was dangerously liberal, and he played on the culture-war anxieties that had been percolating through Republican rhetoric in the 1988 race. "There is a religious war going on in this country," he cried from the convention podium. "It is a cultural war, as critical to the kind of nation we shall be as the Cold War itself. For this war is for the soul of America. And in that struggle for the soul of America, Clinton & Clinton are on the other side, and George Bush is on our side."[30]

Other speakers at the GOP convention sounded similar themes. Yet they were playing to the base, not to the general voter. This was a fatal mistake in an era when political conventions had ceased to be business meetings and become televised sales pitches. The economy still struggled, and the Republicans seemed to be all about waging culture wars. Senate Minority Leader Bob Dole, a once and future presidential candidate, observed that after the Democratic Convention, "the Democrats turned Madison Square Garden into a giant repair shop, where old broken-down liberals became shiny new moderates."[31] In contrast, the Houston gathering of the Republican Party showcased the ugly underbelly of conservative politics, replacing Reagan's message of hope and uplift with adversarial and bitter themes. "George Bush, Prisoner of the Crazies," ran one post-convention op-ed headline.[32]

The divisive Houston convention came on the heels of a campaign that, even beyond the Buchanan challenge, seemed deeply uninspired. Running as an incumbent has advantages and disadvantages. For George Bush in 1992, it was a disadvantage. The modern presidency is a bubble. Every minute of a president's day is scheduled. Protocol dictates what can be said, and when the president can say it. People around the president may be reluctant to be fully honest. White House aides can't work directly on campaign business, meaning that a wholly separate campaign operation needs to be launched, and the president has to keep tabs on both. On top of it all, the president has to hold down a full-time job, and a time-consuming one at that.

While Bill Clinton was a born campaigner and Ross Perot delighted in the spotlight, George Bush deeply disliked having campaign business pull him away from doing the job of governing. On top of that, he had been in the White House bubble for twelve years. It was easy for him to seem out of touch. The two sets of Bush staff people—White House and campaign—argued more often than they agreed. Throughout the primary season and into the summer, they fought over message, over scheduling, over tactics. Bush let it happen. "The White House now is like Noah's Ark without Noah," chortled one Clinton advisor. "They've got two of everything except a leader."[33] The warring factions of the Bush campaign could not seem to get their footing in a race where the Cold War was no longer the big issue, and where the economy mattered rather than foreign policy, and where the media rules had changed.

But perhaps more than anything else, being the incumbent was George Bush's great disadvantage because 1992 was the year when *change* was topmost on voters' minds. Four decades of being let down by Washington, and three-plus decades of feeling squeezed by the economy and threatened by increasing crime, had left many voters—particularly the critical one-third that identified neither as Democrat nor as Republican—looking for a white knight.

Ross Perot became the focus of this populist energy for all the spring and early summer of 1992. The Texas businessman continued his Larry King appearances and carefully stage-managed press conferences. Thousands of people gave their signatures to petitions to get Perot on the November ballot. Former Johnson White House press secretary Bill Moyers remarked with some amazement, "the Perot phenomenon is certainly for real, and it's sustained."[34]

In mid-May, the first national poll came out that put Perot ahead of both Bush and Clinton in the presidential race. This turned him from TV star to serious candidate. He stunned both Democrats and Republicans by hiring two of their own to run his campaign. One of them, Hamilton Jordan, had worked for Jimmy Carter. The other, Ed Rollins, had been campaign manager for Ronald Reagan's 1984 "Morning in America" campaign.

Perot's campaign was remarkable on many levels, but perhaps the most important was that it was the beginning of a new phenomenon in politics: the self-financed candidate. Campaigns were so expensive, and the ability of a candidate to campaign using their own money was a huge advantage. They didn't have to spend all that time fundraising. And they could pitch themselves to voters as an outsider candidate—beholden to no one.

That's what Perot did. Both the Bush and Clinton teams thought that Perot's money would turn off middle-class voters. It didn't. CNN analyst William Schneider noted in amazement that June: "The fact that Perot is self-made, that he did it himself, is a source of admiration for most people and in fact they treat it as a virtue. They say, at least he won't be bought and paid for. . . . To an awful lot of voters, right now, the fact that he's an extraordinarily wealthy man is seen as an advantage."[35]

Clinton's people thought Perot was a quack, but took his effort quite seriously. On the other hand, Bush's friends and advisors from Texas had known Perot for a long time, and they firmly believed he was a crackpot. They thus did little to acknowledge his candidacy, figuring he would blow himself up at some point. The Republicans had Pat Buchanan to battle; Perot seemed like an unimportant sideshow. So they let his momentum go unchecked throughout the spring.[36]

Only one thing could stop Perot's surge: the candidate himself. As soon as Rollins and Jordan joined the team in late spring, they realized they had signed up for a campaign like none they'd ever experienced. Rollins thought he had the perfect campaign playbook in Reagan '84, and urged the Perot team to follow the lock-step communications plan that had brought Republicans such a huge victory. "It may have been perfect," another Perot staffer chided Rollins, "but you had a robot candidate." In contrast, Perot willfully resisted staying on script. He had gotten to the top of the polls by being himself, the straight talker, the antithesis of slick. As Clinton's poll numbers began to climb before the Democratic Convention, Perot stubbornly resisted launching a major television ad campaign to remind voters that he, Perot, was the real candidate of change. Perot didn't think he needed these kinds of expensive tactics, even though he could afford them. "You're a Rolls-Royce," he spat to one advisor. "All I need is a Volkswagen." Carolyn Cepaitis, a Perot organizer in Michigan, agreed. "The commercialism is unnecessary, and ineffective. A lot of people don't trust it anymore. . . . We'd much rather deal with the real person."[37]

At the very same time, Perot's honeymoon with the press began to end. When he was not a serious candidate, merely a talking head on *Larry King Live*, the regular media didn't look at Perot very closely. When he started to lead the polls and build a real campaign organization, reporters started digging deeper. They started asking tougher questions, seeking more details of his policy positions, and Perot couldn't provide satisfying answers. Their digging unveiled much of the kookiness Bush's Texas hands had seen for years. Perot appeared to have many of the same paranoid and authoritarian qualities that had felled Richard Nixon: keeping lists of enemies, paying private investigators to spy on his family and close associates. Former employees called him a "dictator."[38]

One day after the end of the Democratic Convention, the pressure cooker exploded. Over four days, Perot dropped ten points in the polls. He had been unable to persuade any heavy hitters to join on as his vice presidential nominee. He fired Rollins on 15 July. The next day, he abruptly announced he was dropping out of the race altogether. Why? His work was done, Perot said; he had gotten the political system to pay attention to his message of change. With a Democratic revival, Perot said, it was all but certain that his continued presence in the race would create a deadlocked result in November, and he didn't want to subject the American people to such chaos. It was a terrible blow to the many who had worked on the Perot movement. "I can't believe it," lamented one Florida woman. "I keep wanting to say it's a Republican tactic, but of course it's not. I am mortified. I am hurt." Said another Florida supporter in disgust, "he's a little spoiled billionaire, and he didn't have enough guts to stay in the race." "Ross Perot's supporters deserved better than Ross Perot," concluded one editorial.[39]

At first, the Bush campaign thought Perot's dropping out was a huge boon to their cause. It wasn't. People who supported Perot were the people who wanted change. With Perot gone, they mostly switched over to the other "change" candidate: Bill Clinton.

"For People, For a Change"

The buoyant Democratic Convention and Perot's retreat had left the Clinton team energized but worried. They would need even more message discipline and organization in the general campaign. They knew that Americans still had deep reservations about Bill Clinton, and that much of the campaign momentum came from voters' greater disillusionment with George Bush. The Clinton people also knew they were going up against some formidable campaign managers, with three White House victories under their belts. By summer, Bush had persuaded former secretary of state James Baker to come in and run his campaign, imposing organization and tamping down the infighting between the campaign and the White House. The GOP establishment started to mobilize money and support. The president was going to be a formidable competitor.

The Clinton team also needed to get its house in order. Too many people had the ear of the candidate: old friends from Arkansas, staff from the governor's office, friends from New York and Washington, and paid campaign strategists and consultants. It wasn't quite Noah's Ark, but they needed focus and organization. The Clintons decided to keep the campaign headquartered in Little Rock—partly because of their daughter's school and sports schedule, and partly because putting campaign staff in Little Rock would reduce distractions. Meanwhile, the Bush people were in Washington, where the campaign was just a regular job.

Working on a modern presidential campaign demands all-consuming devotion and singular focus, and Little Rock provided that in a way Washington did not. The Clinton people were far from their homes and social lives in a small Southern city. So they worked all the time. When they weren't working, they went to dinner together, and talked about work. When that was over, they went back to the office. They lived together in barely furnished apartments. They ate from vending machines. They were young and had a high tolerance for little sleep, bad food, and no work-life balance. They lived and breathed the 24-hour news cycle.

For decades, the business of politics and policy had become increasingly professionalized and hermetically sealed in the corridors of power in Washington, with occasional detours up the Northeast Corridor to New York and Boston. The Little Rock operations reproduced a miniature version of that ecosystem in the Clinton campaign headquarters, but it permitted a good deal more of the "real world" to seep in. It communicated to voters that this was an "outsider" effort (despite being run by people who had spent their lives in politics), and it got the campaign staff to think of themselves as scrappy underdogs as well. "This is a very interesting place to be engineering the peaceful takeover of the Free World," campaign advisor Bob Boorstin remarked drily. "Because Little Rock is America."[40]

The other critical decision the Clintons made after the convention was to establish a campaign nerve center where all parts of the operation could mobilize to rapidly respond to any breaking news. Rapid response had saved them during the grim march through the primary season; it would keep them hungry and aggressive in the fall campaign. They tapped their firebrand campaign strategist, James Carville, to run the operation. Hillary gave it a name: the War Room.

George H. W. Bush's staff invented modern message discipline with the orchestration of war reportage during the Gulf War, embedding reporters and tightly controlling the story. In 1992, the roles were reversed. The Bush campaign lost control of the story again and again. The Clinton War Room was all about message discipline. Carville posted a whiteboard in the middle of the War Room with the three main messages of the campaign scrawled on it:

1. Change versus more of the same.
2. It's the economy, stupid.
3. Don't forget health care.

The Clintons built a whole operation to serve these messages.

The War Room also was about opposition research. Its staff performed the investigations on the other candidate that the press didn't have the time to do. Sleep-deprived twenty-something researchers dug up facts about the Bush campaign and presidency that senior staffers leaked to reporters. Young staff shadowed the Bush campaign on the road and in the media, and kept track of everything said and promised. They relentlessly followed the news, with two staffers staying up all night to put together a daily briefing book of news clips from papers all over the country. Across the hall from the War Room, a windowless office featured a wall of television sets, each tuned to a different network—CNN, NBC, CBS, ABC, C-SPAN— always on, day or night, scraping up every bit of campaign-related news. Fax machines buzzed. Beepers vibrated. A few lucky members of the team had shoebox-sized cellular phones, for quick communication on the road. "Everyone at the Clinton campaign has a CNN tan," teased *The Washington Post*.[41]

The exhaustive attention to information and to message discipline became even more critical in late September. A mere 33 days before the election, Ross Perot got back in the race. He said he was coming back in response to the pleas of his supporters. He also thought Clinton and Bush weren't addressing the real issues. Drawing on his personal wealth, he went on television but, once again, on his own terms. Telling his ad men to spend "whatever it takes," Perot bought 30-minute slots of time on the major TV networks for infomercials delivering his message. In a world of sound bites and talking points, Perot gave extended policy talks to his audience, armed with a pointer and a series of charts displaying key data.[42]

He talked about the looming problem of the budget deficit, and assailed both Bush and Clinton for ignoring the problem. He talked about jobs going overseas and the need to change American trade policy. He slammed Republican trickle-down economics. He said that Clinton was going to raise taxes on ordinary Americans. Despite the worries of his advisors that no one would pay attention to such dry presentation—delivered by a big-eared and self-important candidate with dangerously low favorability ratings— the infomercials were a hit. Sixteen million people watched Perot and his charts. "Perot had discovered an unmet hunger for hard information and candid talk instead of the usual cant of politics."[43] Perot remained a distant third in the race, but his presence forced the two major candidates to address new issues—the budget deficit chief among them.

October Surprises

The race remained extremely close between Clinton and Bush, two imperfect candidates for an imperfect era. Compounding all of it was Perot's reentry, which threw all the rituals of modern campaigning off-kilter in the last campaign weeks. Chief among these were the presidential and vice-presidential debates, events that had become the centerpieces of the general election season in the television era. In 1992, all the debates were compressed into nine short days in October, putting immense pressure on already exhausted candidates. The Texan's folksy presence threw the usual format off-kilter. Despite their hoarse voices and sleep-deprived brains, Bush and Clinton had smoothly prepared answers. Perot spoke informally and without regard for typical political platitudes. In contrast to prior televised debates, the un-prepped approach proved effective. The debate format rewarded one-liners and "zingers" over long-winded matters of substance. When asked a question, the jug-eared Perot smiled, "I'm all ears." When challenged on his lack of government experience, Perot observed "I *don't* have any experience in running up a $4 trillion debt." The audience loved it.[44]

The Perot effort continued to disrupt. James Stockdale, the retired admiral Perot had recruited as his vice presidential running mate, gave a performance in the debate with Gore and Quayle that was so unscripted that it became rather disturbingly odd, turning the war hero into comical fodder for *Saturday Night Live* skits and diverting attention from much of what the other two candidates had to say. "Who am I? Why am I here?" Stockdale asked rhetorically, as his two rivals looked on in silent bafflement.

In a world where campaign communications had become so slick, the Perot insurgency broke through the clutter with something that was the opposite of slick.[45]

Perot continued to be an unpredictable variable in the final weeks, although his polling numbers didn't improve considerably. His erratic personality began to shine through. He went on *60 Minutes* and said his withdrawal in the summer had been the result of Republican operatives plotting to disrupt his daughter's wedding. He didn't provide any evidence. He started to seem rather paranoid. Yet Perot was a lifeline to voters who didn't like either of the choices the major parties put before them. Clinton still had trust issues. In one focus group, a Michigan man sighed of Clinton, "he's one of the most polished bullshitters I've ever seen." George Bush fared even worse: "he's status quo," said another voter.[46]

President Bush was already deeply frustrated by the campaign. Here he was, a war hero, a deeply experienced policy leader, a sitting president, and he was lagging behind a draft-evading, double-talking small-time governor of a small-time state. The return of Perot had made it even worse. His insiders in Texas knew Perot was a little loony, but he was being treated as a political equal. "That son of a bitch is a psychiatric case," the president said to one close advisor.[47] On 15 October, at a debate with a town hall format, Bush was listening as Clinton ran overtime answering a question. Perhaps trying to send a signal to the moderator, and perhaps quite annoyed at having to share the stage with two undisciplined and unworthy competitors, Bush glanced at his watch.

The media beast pounced on this one. Here was an incumbent who already seemed out of touch, whose campaign seemed to running on autopilot, who didn't seem to care about Americans' economic woes. And he was checking his watch during the debate, as if to say, "when can I get out of here?"

Bush got tired and testy during those last weeks on the road. In one speech he called Clinton and Gore "bozos." When some pro-Clinton hecklers interrupted another event, he said, "I wish those draft dodgers would shut up so I could deliver my speech." He attacked the media as well, bashing them for covering Clinton so uncritically. He held up a favorite bumper sticker, reading "Annoy the Media: Re-Elect Bush." Bashing the mainstream media became such a theme for the campaign that audiences started hissing at reporters when they showed up at Bush rallies. As the campaign came into its final week, however, Bush eased off. A poll had come out showing him only one point behind Clinton. It seemed reelection was possible after all.[48]

However, the view from the White House was quite different from the view from Little Rock. The Clinton people were closer to the sea change. A country where a good deal of people wanted to vote for an odd and mysterious billionaire was a country that was not likely to reelect a man whose party had held the White House for over a decade. Yet the outcome remained uncertain; many states, many electoral votes remained in play in the final days of the race. Field teams hit the ground with a vengeance in Michigan, Wisconsin, California, Georgia. Clinton and Gore gave speech after speech; the Arkansas governor would lose his voice before it was all over.

On the Friday before the election, however, the Bush campaign was dealt a fatal blow. Independent prosecutor Lawrence Walsh, who had been investigating the Iran-Contra affair, came out with a report implicating President Bush in the scandal. It was the classic October surprise. The Bush team was convinced the timing had political motives (although no evidence exists that it was), but there was nothing to do.

Both sides sensed then that the election was over. The mood in Little Rock became celebratory. Supporters and reporters and all sorts of political hangers-on streamed into the Southern city in the very last days of the campaign. The Democrats had been out of the White House for twelve long years, and they were ready for a big party on election night.

What a party it was. Bill Clinton won 370 electoral votes, while Bush won 168. Perot did not win a single electoral vote, but grabbed a bigger chunk of the popular vote than any third party candidate since Teddy Roosevelt: 18.9 percent. Like Woodrow Wilson eighty years earlier, Clinton won with a plurality, not a majority, getting 43 percent of the popular vote while the incumbent president got 37.4 percent. The electoral map shifted decisively. Clinton won California—home of Nixon and Reagan, and long a swing state—by more than two million votes.

Bush spent election night in Houston, home of that fateful GOP convention, in the state that had given him his entry into politics just as the South was turning from blue to red. The angry campaigner of the previous weeks was nowhere to be seen; in his place was the patrician, polite, rueful man who sounded resigned to his forced retirement. "We have been in an extraordinarily difficult period," he said. "But," he urged the young people in the audience, "do not be deterred, kept away from public service by the

Figure 30. New Administration, Little Rock, Arkansas, 3 November 1992. Thousands of supporters crowded in front of the Arkansas Old State House to greet newly elected Bill Clinton and Al Gore and their families on Election Night 1992. The Democratic victory brought not only a new party, but a new generation, into power in the White House. AP Photo/Susan Ragan.

smoke and fire of a campaign year or the ugliness of politics. . . . I urge you, the young people of this country, to participate in the political process. It needs your idealism. It needs your drive. It needs your conviction."[49]

Bill Clinton also was thinking about the next generation as he gave his victory speech at the front of Little Rock's Old State House, the same place he had announced his run 13 months earlier. The city had been turned into a giant street party, with 16 square blocks of downtown closed to accommodate the thousands of Democrats from near and far. More than 2,000 news organization from around the world descended on Little Rock to document the momentous occasion, their satellite dishes spiking up from hotel rooftops and parking lots. The War Room had turned into a jubilant pre-party, with staffers sitting on their desks and breaking out bottles of bourbon.

Shortly after 10:00 p.m., the news became official that the Democrats had won enough electoral votes to go over the top. The Clintons and Gores came out on the Old State House steps, into the cool and crisp fall evening, to cries of "We love you, Bill!" and "Hill-a-ry! Hill-a-ry!" Clinton gave a speech that sounded like the liberal Robert Kennedy, speaking of "bring[ing] our people together like never before . . . where everyone counts and everyone is part of America's family." He also talked of reaching out to independents and Republicans, and of "empowerment" and "strength" in ways that evoked Ronald Reagan. Afterward he and Gore came forward and leaned into the crowd of staff and supporters like youthful rock stars, exuberant and heady with the glow of victory, thinking little about the hard road that lay ahead.[50]

＊

Conclusion: Hope and Change

The redefinition of party. The role of the press. The reconstitution of left, right, and center. The things that had defined and determined pivotal elections in the twentieth century continued to hold true in the twenty-first.

Eight years after Bill Clinton's triumphal election night in Little Rock, the nation's attention focused on two neighboring state capitals—Nashville and Austin—where the major-party candidates had gathered with their respective campaigns to see who would win the 2000 election. Vice President Al Gore, the Democratic nominee, had returned to his home state of Tennessee to watch the returns. He had sought the presidency for more than two decades. Now he would find out whether the American voters would give him the job.

Gore's Republican opponent, Texas Governor George W. Bush, sat in the Austin governor's mansion and watched the same election night television coverage. Bush was a relative newcomer to elected office, having won the governorship only six years earlier, but he had a lifetime of exposure to politics as the eldest son of ex-President George H.W. Bush. The governor was fiercely ambitious and had positioned himself as a more overtly conservative candidate than his father. Yet he and his aides relished the idea of vanquishing a man who had helped deny the elder Bush a second term in office.

The race had been tight, and election night was supposed to be the moment of decision. Little did Gore and Bush realize that it would be only the beginning of the greatest electoral drama of the modern presidency.

As vice president, Gore had enjoyed a higher profile than many of his predecessors, serving as a key member of the president's inner circle as well as leading major policy initiatives. By the time Clinton ran for reelection in 1996, it was clear that Gore had his sights set on taking over once his boss left office. The buttoned-down veep gave raucous speeches at black churches and deepened his friendships with deep-pocketed Silicon Valley titans and Hollywood power brokers. Yet by the time Gore became the frontrunner for the 2000 nomination, Clinton had become mired in scandal as the result of his dalliance with a college-aged White House intern, Monica Lewinsky.

The media and political uproar over the Lewinsky affair—and Clinton's ham-handed attempts to cover it up—nearly sank the Clinton presidency and deeply damaged Gore's candidacy. Cable news had become an even more powerful arbiter of political discourse since the CNN glory days of the early 1990s. Now, more pointedly partisan cable news networks like the right-wing Fox News (founded by Richard Nixon's 1968 advisor Roger Ailes) devoted hours of air time to the scandal, fueling calls on both left and right for action against the president. As a Republican-led Congress took steps to impeach Clinton for his moral and professional failings, Gore did his best to distance himself from his boss's scandals. In doing so, he found himself unable to take credit for the Clinton administration's accomplishments, including successful deficit reduction and steady economic growth.

Keeping a politically damaged Clinton off the campaign stump also deprived Gore of the Democratic Party's most powerful and persuasive voice. Although often witty and warm in person, Gore lacked Clinton's remarkable ability to connect with voters on the campaign trail. His speeches often seemed stiff, his policy vision sounded poll-tested rather than heartfelt. Exhausted from eight years in a scandal-plagued White House, Gore's aides ran a gaffe-prone campaign, full of backbiting and leaks to the press. In an effort to recapture the spirit of 1992, Gore relocated his campaign headquarters from Washington to Nashville. It was not enough.

Anti-Washington sentiment still ran strong. About 35 percent of American voters identified as independents, a larger chunk of the electorate than those who called themselves either Democrats or Republicans.[1] Though, at the end of the day, many of the self-styled independents tended to vote for a major-party candidate, their fickle mood raised the stakes for candidates to be "authentic" figures who bucked the party line. This time, Gore could no longer position himself as an outsider candidate as he and Clinton had done so effectively in their first run for the White House. He was the sitting vice president, barnstorming the country in Air Force Two, surrounded by

Secret Service officers and White House aides. Like the elder George Bush in 1992, he lived and worked in a bubble.

George W. Bush—despite being son of a president, grandson of a U.S. senator, and governor of one of the largest states in the nation—seized the "outsider" mantle and positioned himself as a fresh face, ready to take on the establishment and fight for ordinary men and women. Just as Gore distanced himself from Clinton, Bush distanced himself from his father. Folksy instead of preppy, rough-edged instead of genial, and possessing a genuine Texas twang, the younger Bush appealed to both conservatives and independents. He also appealed to the Southern voters who had left the Democrats for the Republicans in the years since 1968. He called himself a "compassionate conservative," willing to take on tough social issues like immigration and poverty. As Reagan had conveyed so effectively twenty years before, Bush promised independent-minded voters that he'd get an intrusive federal government out of their lives. "He's getting us back to the importance of the individual person," said one Wisconsin voter on the eve of the election. "He's saying that we can do our own thinking, that we don't have to depend on Washington."[2]

By 2000, both the Democratic and the Republican parties had become more conservative than they had been at any point since the New Deal. The language of limited government and individual rights articulated by figures like Barry Goldwater, George Wallace, and Ronald Reagan since the 1960s had become mainstream. As president, Clinton had burnished his New Democrat credentials—and horrified liberals—by signing into law a massive welfare overhaul. Gore had overseen a major effort to "reinvent government" by streamlining regulation and reorganizing executive branch programs. The "Rockefeller Republicans" who had dominated the GOP through much of the twentieth century had become a dying breed. Some of the loudest and most influential voices in the party in the 1990s were Sunbelt conservatives like Georgia's Newt Gingrich, who commandeered a Republican takeover of the House of Representatives in 1994.

Given the conservative tack of both major parties, it was perhaps unsurprising that the most potent third-party challenge of the 2000 campaign came from the left, not the right. Frustrated by the influence of business and conservative forces in politics, consumer advocate Ralph Nader ran for president under the banner of the Green Party, positioning himself as a fighter for the common worker like Debs, an iconoclastic independent like Perot.

Unlike Perot, however, Nader drew much of his support from disillusioned liberals who felt abandoned by the Democratic Party of Clinton and
Gore. Nader and his supporters had little illusion he would actually win
anything, and he rejected accusations that his run would spoil Gore's fragile
chances for election. "You can't spoil a system spoiled to the core," he said
to his cheering supporters on election night.[3]

Yet the 2000 election proved to be one with a razor-thin margin, and
the votes garnered by Nader turned out to have a decisive influence. Nader
siphoned most of his support from Gore voters. "More than half of
Nader voters said in exit polls that they would have voted for Gore if Nader
weren't on the ballot," noted the *Washington Post*, "and only one in five
said they would have voted for Bush."[4]

As election night wore on, the electoral map became more uncertain, and
the outlook more grim for the Gore campaign. By 2000, the polling and
electronic slicing-and-dicing of the electorate had become a sophisticated art
employing advanced technology. That wizardry was cobbled onto an archaic
electoral system that dated from the era of Washington and Adams. The
result was campaigns that focused their energies on a small number of states
which, because of their demographic and ideological diversity, could swing
to either the Democratic or Republican column. The greatest prizes were the
big swing states. And the biggest and most elusive of these was Florida, whose
governor was none other than George W. Bush's kid brother Jeb.

As in 1968 and 1992, the great drama of election night played out on
television. All of the network news divisions had created sophisticated polling systems of their own, and had set up elaborate technological operations
to analyze the data coming in from counties and cities, towns and precincts.
In 2000, despite this deluge of information, the television networks made
the wrong calls—not just once, but twice and thrice, taking the candidates
and voters on an all-night roller-coaster ride.

At 7:00 P.M., the networks called the swing states of Florida, Pennsylvania, and Michigan for Gore. The mood in Austin was despondent. Yet as
more results rolled in, signs of trouble emerged for Gore. States that had
remained safely Democratic in the Clinton years began to go Republican.
Gore lost West Virginia and Arkansas, and then—unbelievably—lost his
home state of Tennessee. The networks then took back an earlier call. Florida, it turned out, was too close to call.

Through the night, the verdict ricocheted back and forth. Florida was
in Gore's column. No, it was in Bush's. Amid all the high-tech gadgetry,

NBC anchor Tim Russert scribbled the ever-changing results on a smudged and decidedly low-tech dry erase board. Chaos reigned. By 10:00 P.M., CBS anchor Dan Rather referred to Bush's lead as "shakier than cafeteria jello."[5] By 1:00 A.M., Florida was in Bush's column and the networks called the election for the Republican. Gore called Bush to concede.

No sooner had the call been made when Gore operatives noticed a sudden shrinking in Bush's Florida lead, as more votes came in from heavily Democratic precincts. At 2:30 A.M., the vice president called his rival once again, to take back his concession. Bush was incredulous. "You don't have to be snippy about it," responded Gore.[6] Election night ended without a winner. It took 36 days and a decision by the Supreme Court to decide the election in Bush's favor.

Disrupted by a third-party spoiler, altered by shifting social demographics, and occurring in a media hothouse, the 2000 election had quite a few things in common with earlier pivotal elections. However, its cliffhanger results were fueled by phenomena quite different from those that shaped the eras of Teddy Roosevelt, Herbert Hoover, or Richard Nixon.

The American economy had changed profoundly by the turn of the twenty-first century, dominated by the money of Wall Street and the computer companies of Silicon Valley instead of the automakers of Detroit and the steel mills of Pittsburgh. More Americans lived in suburbs than in cities or rural areas. Waves of immigration from Latin America and Asia had changed the demographics of the electorate and destabilized old ethnic and racial coalitions. Multiple media outlets—including the vast and bewildering landscape of the Internet—had created a cacophony of commentary that stymied campaigns' ability to control the story. There was a level of unpredictability and instability in politics as a result. Conservatives and liberals alike were skeptical about the abilities of Washington politicians and the power of government to effect positive change. The self-styled independent voter was now a permanent fixture in the political landscape.

Most significantly, the costs of 24-hour media and the demands for the advice of highly paid professional campaign consultants had turned national elections into extraordinarily expensive affairs. Candidates and elected officials now had to engage in almost perpetual fundraising, and had to spend an inordinate amount of time asking wealthy donors for money. Millionaires and billionaires followed the lead of Ross Perot and financed their own runs for office. For those coming into politics without fat bank accounts, getting elected became a far more daunting task.

After 2000, Al Gore left politics behind. George Bush moved into the White House, and despite his unpopularity among liberal and moderate voters, won reelection in 2004. Eager to regain the White House, the Democrats looked toward a new generation of politicians who might provide the message and the substance to lead. Some thought the answer was a return to the politics and personalities of the Clinton years. In the wake of her husband's public disgrace, Hillary Clinton made a remarkable transition from First Lady to politician, getting elected U.S. senator from New York in 2000 and establishing a reputation as a collaborative and effective legislator. The political establishment buzzed with the possibility of a Hillary Clinton presidential run, and by the time the 2008 election season got into full swing, she had become a formidable candidate.

Other Democrats saw the answer in a figure unconnected to the Clinton years, a member of the next generation who—like Woodrow Wilson in 1912—had made an unexpected and meteoric rise to national prominence. Barack Obama was a Chicago law professor and state legislator making a long-shot run for the U.S. Senate when he was tapped to give the keynote at the Democratic Convention in 2004. Unlike Clinton, whose disastrous convention address in 1988 had nearly sunk his presidential aspirations, Obama gave a stirring speech that electrified an apathetic and disillusioned Democratic base. He talked about his personal history as the biracial son of a white Kansas mother and an African father. He talked about the frustration and disillusionment Americans had with politics, and politicians. It was time, Obama declared, to transcend these divisions: "There are those who are preparing to divide us, the spin masters and negative ad peddlers who embrace the politics of anything goes. Well, I say to them tonight, there's not a liberal America and a conservative America; there's the United States of America."[7]

By 2008, Obama had parlayed this ability to deliver powerful oratory into a presidential run that attracted a diverse group of supporters—including a cadre of young people whose fervent support recalled Gene McCarthy's 1968 campaign. He was not the first African American to run for president, but his campaign success eclipsed all candidates of color who had come before him.

Other opponents fell away in the early primaries, leaving just Clinton and Obama to battle it out for the nomination. While much of the attention focused on having two such strong candidates fighting it out for the Democratic nomination, what sometimes got lost was the most remarkable fact that the two leading presidential candidates were an African American and a woman. Neither candidacy would have been possible in 1912, 1932, or 1968. The rights revolution set in motion in the 1960s had paved the way for a more conservative politics, but it also had created a foundation for a more equitable politics in which race and gender no longer was an insurmountable obstacle to achieving high office.

However, the primary battle between Hillary Clinton and Barack Obama highlighted how far the political center had moved to the right. Unintentional hilarity ensued as the two Ivy-League-educated candidates battled it out for the conservative, working-class ethnic vote. Clinton did shots of whiskey with factory workers. Obama made a very bad attempt at bowling. Yet the primary fight also showed how the American political scene had made some peace with formerly divisive social issues. The nation was far from being a post-racial society, or one of gender equality, but it had come far enough that the idea of a black or female commander-in-chief seemed possible.[8]

Ultimately, Obama was the victor in both the nomination fight and the general election. He and Hillary Clinton morphed from rivals to allies, and as his secretary of state, Clinton once again reinvented herself as a master diplomat, and revived her presidential aspirations to become the most talked-about Democratic possibility for 2016.

Obama's 2008 victory had echoes of Franklin Roosevelt's in 1932. Like Roosevelt, Obama grasped the power of big ideas and oratorical flourishes to inspire and instill trust. He spoke boldly of unity, of transcending political divisions, and of hope and change. Like Roosevelt, he focused on inspiring rather than informing. He stayed rather skimpy on the details. And, like FDR, he effectively harnessed the power of new media—in this case, the Internet—to organize, fundraise, and communicate with voters.

In both 2000 and 2008, as in all the elections profiled in this book, the ultimate secret to the winners' electoral success was their opponents' failures. By the end of his second term, Bush had become miserably unpopular, his approval ratings sinking lower than Clinton's post-Lewinsky numbers. Barack Obama was a new face, a figure of promise, a path out of a decade of war. The hopes pinned on his candidacy were so high they were impossible to meet, yet despite not quite living up to all expectations Obama secured reelection in 2012. Like Wilson, both Roosevelts, Nixon, and Clinton, he became a two-term president.

As America moves into the second decade of the twenty-first century, the lessons of the elections of the twentieth century still resonate. They help us determine where American politics are now, and where they might go next. In 1912, the great progressive debates revolved around *how* to govern a large, messy, dynamic industrial capitalist democracy. In the twenty-first century the debate revolves over *whether* to govern. The Democrats, by and large, have become the party identified with government-centered policy solutions. The Republican Party has become identified as the party of free markets, of small government, and of curbs to government spending. The answer to policy problems, many Republican legislators and political figures argue, is to get rid of the policies and their associated programs altogether. The result has been legislative gridlock in Washington, significant austerity and cost-cutting measures, and plummeting approval ratings for both parties.

The reputations of tax-and-spend Democrats and free-market Republicans persist despite the fact that Democrats have presided over transformative deregulation and privatization measures during the past two decades, while Republican leadership has overseen military interventions and domestic security programs that have vastly expanded the reach of government into everyday life. Just as in the past, on both sides of the aisle there remain persistent contradictions between the language of politics and the actions of governance.

Yet while the independent voter bloc continues to grow—as of 2012, those identifying as independents hovered at 40 percent of the electorate—the two major parties manage to hold on. Their resilience is remarkable, yet not all that surprising in the context of the profound changes that have occurred in the parties and their major constituencies since the era of Roosevelt, Wilson, and Taft. Ironically, the Democrats and Republicans endure in part because of the fractious and fractured nature of modern media. The cable news hothouse is now intensely partisan; CNN, in fact, struggled in the Obama era because it lacked strong identification with either a liberal or conservative point of view. Voters pick and choose from many options for receiving their political news, and often choose to get it from sources that resonate with their existing political beliefs. Multiple Internet channels—some of them seriously journalistic, some barely credible—have intensified the echo chamber effect.

At the start of the twentieth century, the American political spectrum became animated by progressive ideas about an activist government that could serve as a counterweight to large corporations and the powerful men who ran them, and that could regulate the wild unpredictability of modern capitalist markets. These ideas became law in the 1930s. The liberal-progressive era of politics that followed in the New Deal's wake started to disintegrate in the late 1960s through a combination of economic transformation, technological and geographic changes, and cultural and generational transformations. They further receded with the landslide election of Ronald Reagan in 1980. After Reagan came new, right-to-moderate sets of politics from both parties. Democrats realized that New Deal liberalism no longer could win national elections. Republicans were pushed further to the right by cultural conservatism.

Yet at the same time, there were political undercurrents throughout the twentieth century that ran counter to the broader trends. In between the two progressive moments of the 1910s and 1930s was a more conservative and cautious Harding-Coolidge era of the prosperous and isolationist 1920s. Franklin Roosevelt's New Deal met with fierce critique from the right as well as from the left, and his broadest and most aggressive interventions into markets proved to be short-lived. The brand of conservatism that seemed to burst into the mainstream with Reagan's election had been gestating for nearly half a century before 1980.[9]

We see these contradictions still on display in the current political era. While ideas about the role and size of government, taxation, and regulation skew toward the right, notions of racial and gender and sex equality have gained more traction than ever before. As in the Progressive Era, cities and states have become the places where reformist ideas take root and gain traction. While Congresses and presidents have resisted joining global environmental treaties, mayors of large cities have joined together in low-carbon pledges of their own. While national debates around drug enforcement and gay rights have become increasingly conservative, states have begun to legalize same-sex marriage and recreational marijuana use. All these are signs that the center may be shifting once more, although not necessarily back toward the big-government liberalism of the New Deal era. Changing demographics, changing communication, and changing party structure point toward something new.

Despite the liberal turn in social attitudes, particularly among the younger generation, Democrats, Republicans, and the great independent middle seem increasingly unconvinced that big, central government programs are the answer. Potent third-party movements like the Tea Party and Occupy Wall Street articulate populist discontent on both left and right, echoing the chaotic swirl of ideas that shaped the elections of 1912, 1932,

1968, and 1992. The growth of the Internet has compromised message discipline, making it challenging for candidates and campaigns to stay on-message amid tweets and status updates and Reddit "ask me anything" sessions.

Will this produce more discord, or more democracy? Let us hope for the latter, and take what lessons we can from history. From the very start, Americans have argued over the same core values in election after election: the people versus the powerful, big government versus small government, the rights and responsibilities of citizenship. Elections have been the battleground on which these debates play out, but none of them have upended the basic premise of American democracy. For however fiercely we fight, the shared goal remains of turning this into a more perfect union. The best we can hope is that every four years, on the first Tuesday in November, we come a little closer to that goal.

NOTES

*

Introduction

1. Robert Goodloe Harper, *Virginia Gazette and General Advertiser*, 30 May 1800 and "Burleigh," *Connecticut Courant*, 1 August 1800, both quoted in Charles O. Lerche, "Jefferson and the Election of 1800: A Case Study in the Political Smear," *William and Mary Quarterly* 5, 4 (October 1948): 485; "Burleigh," *Connecticut Courant*, 20 September 1800, quoted in Michael Bellesiles, "'The Soil Will Be Soaked with Blood': Taking the Revolution of 1800 Seriously," in *The Revolution of 1800: Democracy, Race, and the New Republic*, ed. James P. P. Horn, Jan Lewis, and Peter S. Onuf (Charlottesville: University of Virginia Press, 2002), 59.

2. *Aurora*, 20 May, 24 April 1800, quoted in John E. Ferling, *Adams vs. Jefferson: The Tumultuous Election of 1800* (New York: Oxford University Press, 2004), 146, 148.

3. Ferling, *Adams vs. Jefferson*, 154, Lerche, "Jefferson and the Election of 1800," 487; James Roger Sharp, *The Deadlocked Election of 1800: Jefferson, Burr, and the Union in the Balance* (Lawrence: University Press of Kansas, 2010), 105–6.

4. George Washington, *Farewell Address*, 17 September 1796, 17, The Papers of George Washington, http://gwpapers.virginia.edu. Historian Joanne B. Freeman emphasizes the central importance of personal honor and reputation in understanding early clashes of faction and party, particularly in the election of 1800. See Freeman, *Affairs of Honor: National Politics in the New Republic* (New Haven, Conn.: Yale University Press, 2001).

5. Jefferson to Spencer Roane, 6 September 1819, in Merrill D. Peterson, ed., *The Portable Thomas Jefferson* (New York: Viking, 1975), 561–64.

6. For discussion of the debate over "the revolution of 1800," see Sharp, *The Deadlocked Election of 1800*, 169–78, as well as Horn et al., *The Revolution of 1800*.

7. Henry R. Luce, "The American Century," *Life*, 17 February 1941, 61–65.

8. V. O. Key, Jr., first advanced the theory of political realignments in "A Theory of Critical Elections," *Journal of Politics* 17 (1955): 3–18. E. E. Schattschneider put forth his own theory of realigning moments a few years later, followed in later decades by James L. Sundquist, Walter Dean Burnham, and others. A review and trenchant critique of the literature can be found in David R. Mayhew, *Electoral Realignments: A Critique of an American Genre* (New Haven, Conn.: Yale University Press, 2002). Another strand of

scholarship examines the realignment of the American presidency itself, locating a "big bang" between traditional and modern constructs of the executive around the time of the New Deal and Second World War. For discussion and critique, see Stephen Skowronek, "Presidency and American Political Development: A Third Look," *Presidential Studies Quarterly* 32, 4 (December 2002): 743–54. American political historians found the realignment idea a useful construct for periodization, and continued to do so after political scientists had begun to question the utility of this construct. See Richard L. McCormick, "The Realignment Synthesis in American History," *Journal of Interdisciplinary History* 13, 1 (Summer 1982): 85–105. The cyclic model of national politics is most closely associated with the two Arthur M. Schlesingers, the junior one in particular. For example, see Schlesinger, Jr., *The Cycles of American History* (Boston: Houghton Mifflin, 1986). The Schlesingerian pendulum may now be out of favor, but regimes and periods are not; a more recent and expansive update of this approach is Morton Keller, *America's Three Regimes: A New Political History* (New York: Oxford University Press, 2007).

9. Work exploring such connections has helped propel a revitalization of the field of American political history in the early twenty-first century. For a review, see Meg Jacobs, William J. Novak, and Julian Zelizer, eds., *The Democratic Experiment: New Directions in American Political History* (Princeton, N.J.: Princeton University Press, 2003), 1–19.

10. For discussion on Theodore Roosevelt and the power of the presidency, particularly his use of the media, see David Greenberg, "Theodore Roosevelt and the Image of American Activism," *Social Research* 78, 4 (Winter 2011): 1057–88. For a useful review of work discussing of the significance of the presidency and executive power in twentieth-century American politics, see Julian E. Zelizer, "Beyond the Presidential Synthesis: Reordering Political Time," in Zelizer, *Governing America: The Revival of Political History* (Princeton, N.J.: Princeton University Press, 2012), 11–40.

11. On the rise of interest groups, see Brian Balogh, "'Mirrors of Desires': Interest Groups, Elections, and the Targeted Style in Twentieth-Century America," in Jacobs, Novak, and Zelizer, *The Democratic Experiment*, 222–49. On the decline of parties and the rise of new forms of both organization and political communication, see Michael E. McGerr, *The Decline of Popular Politics: The American North, 1865–1928* (New York: Oxford University Press, 1986). On presidents' use of the media, see Kenneth Osgood and Andrew Frank, *Selling War: The Presidency and Public Opinion in the Twentieth Century* (Gainesville: University Press of Florida, 2010).

12. Jefferson to Adams, 21 January 1812, from Lester J. Cappon, ed., *The Adams-Jefferson Letters: The Complete Correspondence Between Thomas Jefferson and Abigail and John Adams* (Chapel Hill: University of North Carolina Press, 1959).

13. Jefferson to Adams, 15 February 1825, from Cappon, *The Adams-Jefferson Letters.*

Chapter 1. The Great Transformation

1. Additional accounts of Roosevelt's homecoming can be found in the collected letters of his longtime aide Archibald Willingham Butt, *Taft and Roosevelt: The Intimate Letters of Archie Butt, Military Aide* (Port Washington, N.Y.: Kennikat Press, 1930), as well as James Chace, *1912: Wilson, Roosevelt, Taft and Debs: The Election That Changed the Country* (New York: Simon and Schuster, 2004) and Lewis L. Gould, *Four Hats in the Ring: The 1912 Election and the Birth of Modern American Politics* (Lawrence: University Press of Kansas, 2008).

2. Taft, "A Welcome to Mr. Roosevelt: From the President," *Outlook* 95, 7 (18 June 1910): 342.

3. Roosevelt, "Letter to William Howard Taft," 20 June 1910, in *The Letters of Theodore Roosevelt*, ed. Elting E. Morison (Cambridge, Mass.: Harvard University Press, 1952), 7: 93.

4. For discussion of the Democratic gains and losses of the 1890s, see R. Hal Williams, *Realigning America: McKinley, Bryan, and the Remarkable Election of 1896* (Lawrence: University Press of Kansas, 2010), 21–45.

5. Arthur S. Link, *Woodrow Wilson and the Progressive Era, 1910–1917* (New York: Harper and Brothers, 1954), 8–9.

6. The biggest Democratic gain came in the House of Representatives, Republican-dominated since 1894, where Democrats not only regained control but won a 67-seat majority. Gould, *Four Hats in the Ring*, 20.

7. These and the demographic statistics that follow in this chapter can be found in U.S. Census Bureau, Selected Historical Decennial Population and Housing Counts (Washington, D.C.: U.S. Census, 1990), http://www.census.gov/population/www/censusdata/hiscendata.html.

8. Michael O'Malley, *Keeping Watch. A History of American Time* (New York. Viking, 1990). For more on migration and the role of the annihilation of space and time brought about by the railroads, see Richard White, *Railroaded: The Transcontinentals and the Making of Modern America* (New York: Norton, 2011).

9. Gavin Wright, *The Political Economy of the Cotton South: Households, Markets, and Wealth in the Nineteenth Century* (New York: Norton, 1978). This economy, while largely agricultural and technologically lagging, played a critical role in networks of global capital, supplying the overwhelming majority of cotton consumed by Great Britain, France, Germany, and Russia. See Sven Beckert, "Emancipation and Empire: Reconstructing the Worldwide Web of Cotton Production in the Age of the American Civil War," *American Historical Review* 109, 5 (2004): 1405.

10. This Southern upbringing informed how Wilson approached the politics of racial equity and civil rights as a candidate and as a president, believing that change should proceed slowly and states' rights ruled supreme. For discussions of white Southern antebellum culture, see Bertram Wyatt-Brown, *Southern Honor: Ethnics and Behavior in the Old South* (New York: Oxford University Press, 1982); for discussion of

Progressives and race, including the racial politics of the 1912 election, see David W. Southern, *The Progressive Era and Race: Reaction and Reform, 1900–1917* (Wheeling, Ill.: Harlan Davidson, 2005). Wilson's own segregation policies as president are explored in Nicholas Patler, *Jim Crow and the Wilson Administration: Protesting Federal Segregation in the Early Twentieth Century* (Boulder: University Press of Colorado, 2004).

11. James McPherson, *Battle Cry of Freedom: The Civil War Era* (New York: Oxford University Press, 1988). The transition was a long one, however, and the trauma of the war left its mark on multiple dimensions of American life from the personal to the institutional. As veterans aged and the war approached its fiftieth anniversary, however, a growing national consensus around sectional reconciliation made itself apparent in monuments, rituals, and political rhetoric that sought to at last put the Civil War in the past. The 1912 election occurred in this nationalist frame. See Drew Gilpin Faust, *This Republic of Suffering: Death and the American Civil War.* (New York: Knopf, 2008); David W. Blight, *Race and Reunion: The Civil War in American Memory* (Cambridge, Mass.: Belknap Press of Harvard University Press, 2001).

12. The literature on the urban-industrial transformation of nineteenth century America is voluminous. Important recent syntheses include Rebecca Edwards, *New Spirits: Americans in the Gilded Age, 1865–1905* (New York: Oxford University Press, 2007) and Nell Irvin Painter, *Standing at Armageddon: The United States, 1877–1919* (New York: Oxford University Press, 1997). For a survey of the urban immigrant experience, see John Bodnar, *The Transplanted: A History of Immigration in Urban America* (Bloomington: Indiana University Press, 1985).

13. Lincoln Steffens, *The Shame of the Cities* (New York: McClure, Philips, 1904), 9.

14. "Machine Politics in New York City," *The Century,* November 1886.

15. David Ray Papke, *The Pullman Case: The Clash of Labor and Capital in Industrial America* (Lawrence: University Press of Kansas, 1999); Richard Schneirov, Shelton Stromquist, and Nick Salvatore, eds., *The Pullman Strike and the Crisis of the 1890s: Essays on Labor and Politics* (Urbana: University of Illinois Press, 1999).

16. Jon C. Teaford, *The Unheralded Triumph: City Government in America, 1870–1900* (Baltimore: Johns Hopkins University Press, 1984).

17. Daniel Rodgers, *Atlantic Crossings: Social Politics in a Progressive Age* (Cambridge, Mass.: Belknap Press of Harvard University Press, 1998).

18. Croly, *The Promise of American Life* (New York: Macmillan, 1909), 59.

19. Quoted in David Henry Burton, *Taft, Roosevelt, and the Limits of Friendship* (Madison, N.J.: Fairleigh Dickinson University Press, 2005), 48.

20. Henry F. Pringle, *The Life and Times of William Howard Taft: A Biography* (New York: Farrar & Rinehart, 1939), 148.

21. "Lodge, Beveridge, Roosevelt, Spooner," *Wichita Daily Eagle,* 2 May 1900, 4.

22. Paul A. Kramer, *The Blood of Government: Race, Empire, the United States, and the Philippines* (Chapel Hill: University of North Carolina Press, 2006).

23. Pringle, *The Life and Times of William Howard Taft,* 238, 249.

24. Quoted in Frank Freidel and Hugh Sidey, "William Howard Taft," in Freidel and Sidey, *The Presidents of the United States of America* (Washington, D.C.: White House Historical Association, 1995).

25. Theodore Roosevelt, Letter to William Howard Taft (personal), 10 November 1908, in *Letters of Theodore Roosevelt*, 6: 1340.

26. Roosevelt to Mark Sullivan, 2 March 1909, quoted in Chace, *1912*, 13.

27. Sidney Milkis, *Theodore Roosevelt, the Progressive Party, and the Transformation of American Democracy* (Lawrence: University Press of Kansas, 2009), 34. Milkis's work provides an extended and nuanced analysis of Roosevelt's evolving Progressive philosophy during this period, see especially 1–37.

28. Helpful and analytically rich discussion of Taft's positions on the tariff issue and its role in the events of this election year can be found in Gould, *Four Hats in the Ring*. Gould notes, "1912 was the last presidential election in which the tariff played a significant role in the outcome" (xi) as the enactment of the national income tax in 1913 displaced the tariff as the federal government's chief source of revenue.

29. Archibald Butt, Letter to Mrs. Lewis F. (Clara) Butt, 28 March 1909, in Butt, *Taft and Roosevelt*, 1: 30.

30. "Roosevelt and Taft in a Warm Embrace," *New York Times*, 1 July 1910.

31. Milkis, *Theodore Roosevelt*, 40.

32. Roosevelt to White, 12 December 1910, *Letters of Theodore Roosevelt*, 7: 181.

33. Ibid.

Chapter 2. The Progressive Campaign

1. Lewis L. Gould, *Four Hats in the Ring: The 1912 Election and the Birth of Modern American Politics* (Lawrence: University Press of Kansas, 2008), 37–49; Sidney Milkis, *Theodore Roosevelt, the Progressive Party, and the Transformation of American Democracy* (Lawrence: University Press of Kansas, 2009), 44–54. For more on La Follette, see Nancy C. Unger, *Fighting Bob La Follette: The Righteous Reformer* (Chapel Hill: University of North Carolina Press, 2000).

2. Recent scholarship by historians and political scientists has countered this interpretation by showing the extent to which government institutions and national policy shaped markets and culture throughout the nineteenth century. See Brian Balogh, *A Government Out of Sight: The Mystery of National Authority in Nineteenth-Century America* (Cambridge: Cambridge University Press, 2009); Richard R. John, "Farewell to the 'Party Period': Political Economy in Nineteenth Century America," *Journal of Policy History* 16, 2 (2004): 117–25.

3. On McKinley's front porch campaign, see R. Hal Williams, *Realigning America: McKinley, Bryan, and the Remarkable Election of 1896* (Lawrence: University Press of Kansas, 2010), 129–45.

4. This term employed by Milkis, *Theodore Roosevelt*, 44–54. Richard L. Kaplan, *Politics and the American Press: The Rise of Objectivity, 1865–1920* (Cambridge: Cambridge University Press, 2002); Michael McGerr, *The Decline of Popular Politics: The American North, 1865–1928* (New York: Oxford University Press, 1986).

5. Gould, *Four Hats in the Ring*, 54; "La Follette Breaks Down, Quits Work," *New-York Tribune*, 4 February 1912, A1.

6. Taft to C. P. Taft, 6 September 1911, quoted in Henry F. Pringle, *The Life and Times of William Howard Taft: A Biography* (New York: Farrar & Rinehart, 1939) 761.

7. Roosevelt to Theodore Roosevelt, Jr., 22 August 1911, quoted in Gould, *Four Hats in the Ring*, 49–50.

8. Quoted in Gould, *Four Hats in the Ring*, 52.

9. "Roosevelt Back to Storm Boston," *New York Times*, 23 February 1912.

10. "Taft Opens Fire on Roosevelt," *New York Times*, 26 April 1912, quoted in Gould, *Four Hats in the Ring*, 63; Archibald Butt, letter to Mrs. Lewis F. (Clara) Butt, 4 April 1909, in *Taft and Roosevelt: The Intimate Letters of Archie Butt, Military Aide* (Port Washington, N.Y.: Garden Kennijkat Press, 1930).

11. Roosevelt to Andrew Carnegie, 5 March 1912, Theodore Roosevelt Papers, Manuscripts division, Library of Congress, http://www.theodorerooseveltcenter.org/Research/Digital-Library/Record.aspx?libID = 0224921. Theodore Roosevelt Digital Library, Dickinson State University (accessed 30 January 2013).

12. Taft to Horace D. Taft, 14 April 1912, quoted in Pringle, *The Life and Times of William Howard Taft*, 772.

13. Link, *Woodrow Wilson*, 10.

14. George E. Mowry, *The California Progressives* (Berkeley: University of California Press, 1951); Spencer C. Olin, *California's Prodigal Sons: Hiram Johnson and the Progressives, 1911–1917* (Berkeley: University of California Press, 1968). While both Mowry and Olin focus on white middle-class men like Johnson, the broad-based nature of California Progressivism—and the role of women and ethnic groups in advancing it—is explored in William Deverell and Tom Sitton, eds., *California Progressivism Revisited* (Berkeley: University of California Press, 1994).

15. Richard Hofstadter, *The Age of Reform: From Bryan to F.D.R.* (New York: Harper and Row, 1955), 257–59; Michael E. McGerr, *The Decline of Popular Politics: The American North, 1865–1928* (New York: Oxford University Press, 1986).

16. "President Taft's Increasing Strength," *Los Angeles Times*, 18 July 1912, 114. On Wilsonian progressivism, see Sidney M. Milkis, "Why the Election of 1912 Changed America," *Claremont Review of Books* 3, 1 (Winter 2002).

17. Pringle, *The Life and Times of William Howard Taft*, 756–74; Gould, *Four Hats in the Ring*, 46–49; Chace, *1912*, 93–123.

18. Roosevelt to Albert Cross, 4 June 1912, in *Letters of Theodore Roosevelt*, 7: 554.

19. Roosevelt to the Republican National Convention, 22 June 1912, *Letters*, 7: 562. For description of Roosevelt's journey to Chicago, see Gould, *Four Hats in the Ring*, 70.

20. Gould, *Four Hats in the Ring*, 70–73.

21. Gould, *Four Hats in the Ring*, 33–35, 76–89; also see Theodore Dreiser, "Champ Clark, The Man and His District," in *Theodore Dreiser's Uncollected Magazine Articles, 1897–1902* (Newark: University of Delaware Press, 2003), 66–77; Champ Clark, *My Quarter Century of American Politics* (New York: Harper, 1920).

22. Wilson to Mary Hulbert, 9 June 1912, quoted in Ray Stannard Baker, *Woodrow Wilson: Life and Letters*, vol. 3, *1910–1913* (Garden City, N.Y.: Doubleday, Doran, 1931), 321.

23. Quoted in Baker, *Woodrow Wilson*, 3: 334.

24. *Official Report of the Proceedings of the Democratic National Committee*, 13, quoted in Baker, *Woodrow Wilson*, 3: 341.

25. Baker, *Woodrow Wilson*, 3: 322–63; Gould, *Four Hats in the Ring*, 91–95.

26. Quoted in Gould, *Four Hats in the Ring*, 77.

27. "Roosevelt Named, Shows Emotion," *New York Times*, 8 August 1912, 1.

28. Roosevelt, "A Confession of Faith Before the National Convention of the Progressive Party," 6 August 1912 (New York: Allied Printing, 1912).

29. "Roosevelt Named, Shows Emotion."

30. Lewis L. Gould, ed., *Bull Moose on the Stump: The 1912 Campaign Speeches of Theodore Roosevelt* (Lawrence: University Press of Kansas, 2008).

31. Gould, *Four Hats in the Ring*, 35.

32. The definitive scholarly biography of Debs and his times is Nick Salvatore, *Eugene V. Debs: Citizen and Socialist* (Urbana: University of Illinois Press, 1982). For broader discussion of the Socialist movement as well as other leftist movements of the period, see Beverly Gage, *The Day Wall Street Exploded: A Story of America in its First Age of Terror* (New York: Oxford University Press, 2009).

33. Eugene V. Debs, "This Is Our Year," Chicago, 16 June 1912, reprinted in *Chicago Daily Socialist* pamphlet, 1912.

34. Eugene V. Debs, "Capitalism and Socialism," Fergus Falls, Minn., 27 August 1912, reprinted in Debs, *Labor and Freedom: The Voice and Pen of Eugene V. Debs* (St. Louis: Wagner, 1916), 167–75.

35. Wilson to Mary Hulbert, 25 August 1912, quoted in Baker, *Woodrow Wilson*, 3: 390.

36. Labor Day Speech, Buffalo, 2 September 1912, reprinted in John Well Davidson, *A Crossroads of Freedom: The 1912 Speeches of Woodrow Wilson* (New Haven, Conn.: Yale University Press, 1957), 78.

37. Taft to Helen H. Taft, 22 July 1912, quoted in Pringle, *The Life and Times of William Howard Taft*, 818; Taft to H. W. Taft, 18 September 1912, quoted in Pringle, 835.

38. On Bryan and modern liberalism, see Michael Kazin, "The Forgotten Forerunner," *Wilson Quarterly* 23, 4 (Autumn 1999): 24–34. For discussion of World War I's domestic impact, see David M. Kennedy, *Over Here: The First World War and American Society* (New York: Oxford University Press, 1980).

39. Hofstadter, *The Age of Reform*, 95.

Chapter 3. The Road to the New Deal

1. James A. Farley, *Behind the Ballots: The Personal History of a Politician* (New York: Harcourt, Brace, 1938), 59; Hoover, Speech Accepting the Republican Nomination, 11 August 1928, Palo Alto, California.

2. David M. Kennedy, *Freedom from Fear: The American People in Depression and War, 1929–1945* (New York: Oxford University Press, 1999), 51–52.

3. Herbert Hoover, *The Memoirs of Herbert Hoover*, vol. 3, *The Great Depression, 1929–1941* (New York: Macmillan, 1951), 3–4.

4. Quoted in Kennedy, *Freedom from Fear*, 53, who in turn quotes from Herbert Stein, *The Fiscal Revolution in America* (Chicago: University of Chicago Press, 1969), 16.

5. Kennedy, *Freedom from Fear*, 53–54. For broader discussion of the emerging importance of purchasing power to the economy and to politics during this period, see Meg Jacobs, *Pocketbook Politics: Economic Citizenship in Twentieth-Century America* (Princeton, N.J.: Princeton University Press, 2007), 53–135.

6. Kennedy, *Freedom from Fear*, 54; Roosevelt, Letter to Mrs. Caspar Whitney, 8 December 1930, reprinted in Franklin D. Roosevelt and Elliott Roosevelt, *F.D.R.: His Personal Letters* (New York: Duell, Sloan, and Pearce, 1947), 1: 161.

7. Hoover, *Memoirs*, 3: 29.

8. The economic crisis and 2008 election of Barack Obama intensified interest in the Great Depression and New Deal among political pundits on both left and on right. For an example of the liberal interpretation, see Jonathan Alter, *The Defining Moment: FDR's Hundred Days and the Triumph of Hope* (New York: Simon and Schuster, 2007). Conservative critiques sought both to rehabilitate Hoover's reputation and argue that government intervention (as practiced by both Hoover and Roosevelt) did little to alleviate the Great Depression, and likely prolonged it. See Amity Shlaes, *The Forgotten Man: A New History of the Great Depression* (New York: HarperPerennial, 2007). Critics of Shlaes and others have noted that such conclusions are based on selective reading of economic data. See Eric Rauchway, "FDR's Latest Critics: Was the New Deal Un-American?" *Slate*, 5 July 2007.

9. Eric Rauchway, *Blessed Among Nations: How the World Made America* (New York: Hill and Wang, 2006); David M. Kennedy, *Over Here: The First World War and American Society* (New York: Oxford University Press, 1980); William M. Tuttle, *Race Riot: Chicago in the Red Summer of 1919* (New York: Atheneum, 1970).

10. As in the earlier era, women (now newly enfranchised) were driving forces behind state and local reform movements; see Lorraine Gates Schuyler, *The Weight of Their Votes: Southern Women and Political Leverage in the 1920s* (Chapel Hill: University of North Carolina Press, 2006), 135–64.

11. Nancy MacLean, *Behind the Mask of Chivalry: The Making of the Second Ku Klux Klan* (New York: Oxford University Press, 1994). On immigration restrictions, see Mae M. Ngai, *Impossible Subjects: Illegal Aliens and the Making of Modern America* (Princeton, N.J.: Princeton University Press, 2004), 18–55.

12. Quoted in Kenneth S. Davis, *FDR, the New York Years, 1928–1933* (New York: Random House, 1985), 113.

13. Thomas Piketty and Emmanuel Saez, "Income Inequality in the United States, 1913–1998," *Quarterly Journal of Economics* 118, 1 (February 2003): 1–39; Gene Smiley, "A Note on New Estimates of the Distribution of Income in the 1920s," *Journal of Economic History* 60, 4 (2000): 1120–28; U.S. Bureau of Labor Statistics, *Handbook of Labor Statistics* (Washington, D.C.: GPO, 1936).

14. This was of course not just a rural phenomenon; see Matthew Avery Sutton, *Aimee Semple McPherson and the Resurrection of Christian America* (Cambridge, Mass.: Harvard University Press, 2007).

15. Deborah Kay Fitzgerald, *Every Farm a Factory: The Industrial Ideal in American Agriculture* (New Haven, Conn.: Yale University Press, 2003); Lee J. Alston, "Farm Foreclosures in the United States During the Interwar Period," *Journal of Economic History* 43, 4 (1983): 885–903.

16. Quoted in Hoover, *Memoirs*, 3: 6.

17. Eric Rauchway, *The Great Depression and the New Deal: A Very Short Introduction* (New York: Oxford University Press, 2008), 8–21.

18. Hoover, *Memoirs*, 3: 2–176. For discussion from an economic perspective see Brad DeLong, Reply to Alan Brinkley, Great Depression and New Deal History Forum, 4 April 2001, *History Matters.*

19. For example, Jay Tolson, "Worst Presidents: A Survey of Major Polls," *U.S. News and World Report* (online edition), 16 February 2007; Randy James, "Fail to the Chief: Herbert Hoover," in "Top 10 Forgettable Presidents," *Time* (online edition), 10 March 2009.

20. Quoted in Donald A. Ritchie, *Electing FDR: The New Deal Campaign of 1932* (Lawrence: University Press of Kansas, 2007), 18.

21. Kennedy, *Freedom from Fear*, 44 45; Ritchie, *Electing F.D.R.*, 18 19. As Ritchie observes (19), during his London years Hoover took to wearing the stiff, high shirt collar so in fashion at the time. He continued to sport it in his White House years and beyond, long after it was no longer fashionable and gave him a stiff and old-fashioned appearance.

22. Hoover quoted in Will Irwin, "The Autocrat of the Dinner Table," *Saturday Evening Post*, 23 June 1917, 56.

23. Quoted in Ritchie, *Electing FDR*, 20, quoting *Congressional Record*, 65th Cong., 1st Sess., 1917, vol. 55, Pt. 5, 5157 and Pt. 8, App. 372.

24. Ritchie, *Electing FDR*, 17–21. Also see Hoover, *Memoirs*, vol. 1, *Years of Adventure, 1874–1920* (New York: Macmillan, 1951); George H. Nash, *The Life of Herbert Hoover: Master of Emergencies, 1917–1918* (New York: Norton, 1996).

25. Quoted in Kennedy, *Over Here*, 119.

26. Richard Norton Smith and Timothy Welch, "The Ordeal of Herbert Hoover," *Prologue* 36, 2 (Summer 2004), http://www.archives.gov/publications/prologue/2004/summer/hoover-1.html (accessed 21 June 2013).

27. Herbert Hoover, *American Individualism* (Garden City, N.Y.: Doubleday, 1922). Also see Kennedy, *Freedom from Fear*, 46–48.

28. John M. Barry, *Rising Tide: The Great Mississippi Flood of 1927 and How It Changed America* (New York: Simon and Schuster, 1997). On this and other floods and flood control, see Ari Kelman, *A River and Its City: The Nature of Landscape in New Orleans* (Berkeley: University of California Press, 2006), 157–98. For detailed records of Red Cross aid, see American National Red Cross, *The Mississippi Valley Flood Disaster of 1927: Official Report of the Relief Operations* (Washington, D.C.: Red Cross, 1929).

29. Letter to Nicholas Roosevelt, 19 May 1930, quoted in Davis, *FDR, The New York Years*, 163.

30. Farley, *Behind the Ballots*, 61–62.

31. Alan Brinkley, *Franklin Delano Roosevelt* (New York: Oxford University Press, 2010), 6. For more on Roosevelt's early life, see Joseph Alsop, *FDR: A Centenary Remembrance* (New York: Random House, 1985), 15–42; and Kenneth S. Davis, *FDR: The Beckoning of Destiny, 1882–1928* (New York: Putnam, 1972).

32. Brinkley, *Franklin Delano Roosevelt*, 9.

33. Quoted in Arthur M. Schlesinger, *The Age of Roosevelt* (Boston: Houghton Mifflin, 1957), 1: 82.

34. Ritchie, *Electing F.D.R.*, 7–172; Kennedy, *Freedom from Fear*, 95–96. There is some debate as to how much polio shaped FDR's outlook on the government's role in ensuring economic security and social welfare, but it most certainly altered his life and personal relationships; see Brinkley, *Franklin Delano Roosevelt*, 19–20. His illness also had a transformative effect on his marriage, deepening and solidifying his estrangement between Roosevelt and his wife Eleanor, who over the 1920s turned toward increasing public pursuits as a social activist and political strategist. See Blanche Wiesen Cook, *Eleanor Roosevelt: A Life*, vol. 1, *1884–1933* (New York: Viking, 1992), 288–380.

35. Davis W. Houck and Amos Kiewe, *FDR's Body Politics: The Rhetoric of Disability* (College Station: Texas A&M University Press, 2003), 27. Houck and Kiewe argue that after 1921 Roosevelt's "unquenchable political ambition" was "everywhere informed by a disabled body" (8).

36. Quoted in Davis, *FDR, the New York Years*, 37.

37. The definitive works on these subjects are by Roland Marchand, *Advertising the American Dream: Making Way for Modernity, 1920–1940* (Berkeley: University of California Press, 1986) and *Creating the Corporate Soul: The Rise of Public Relations and Corporate Imagery in American Big Business* (Berkeley: University of California Press, 1998). Also see Alfred P. Sloan, *My Years with General Motors* (Garden City, N.Y.: Doubleday, 1964), especially chap. 4, "Product Policy and Its Origins."

38. Walter Lippmann, *Public Opinion* (New York: Macmillan, 1922), esp. chap. 10, "The Detection of Stereotypes."

39. Hoover quoted in William E. Leuchtenberg, *Herbert Hoover* (New York: Henry Holt, 2009), 35. On Hoover's "targeted style" and the new politics: Brian Balogh, " 'Mirrors of Desires': Interest Groups, Elections, and the Targeted Style in Twentieth Century

America," in *The Democratic Experiment: New Directions in American Political History*, ed. Meg Jacobs, William J. Novak, and Julian Zelizer (Princeton, N.J.: Princeton University Press, 2003), 222–49. Moviegoing statistics and observations on the connection between film and 1920s Republican politics can be found in Steven J. Ross, "How Hollywood Became Hollywood: Money, Politics, and Movies," in *Metropolis in the Making: Los Angeles in the 1920s*, ed. Tom Sitton and William Deverell (Berkeley: University of California Press, 2001), 255–76. Having the Irish Catholic Al Smith as his 1928 general election opponent was also a huge boon. Smith's candidacy had drained away Democratic support in Southern and rural areas where anti-Catholic sentiment ran strong and the KKK ran stronger. Biographers of Smith note the critical role of the Klan in his defeat; see Christopher Finan, *Alfred E. Smith: The Happy Warrior* (New York: Hill and Wang, 2002), 157–230; Robert A. Slayton, *Empire Statesman: The Rise and Redemption of Al Smith* (New York: Free Press, 2001), 299–318.

40. Charles Michelson, *The Ghost Talks* (New York: Putnam's, 1944).

41. Garner quoted in Kennedy, *Freedom from Fear*, 62.

42. Ritchie, *Electing F.D.R.*, 54; Rauchway, *The Great Depression and the New Deal*, 31.

43. "Aid to Farmers Urged by Senator Wheeler," *New York Times*, 25 May 1932, 34.

44. Ritchie, *Electing F.D.R.*, 52–53.

45. Ibid., 45.

46. Herbert Hoover, "Statement About Signing the Reconstruction Finance Corporation Act," 22 January 1932. Online by Gerhard Peters and John T. Woolley, The American Presidency Project, http://www.presidency.ucsb.edu/ws/?pid = 23210 (accessed 25 June 2014).

47. "Mrs. Caraway Hits at Hoover Program," *New York Times*, 6 September 1932, 5.

48. "President Hoover's Record," *Current History* 36 (July 1932): 387. Nevins later became a close advisor to John F. Kennedy, helping draft his acceptance speech at the 1960 Democratic Convention; Gerald L. Fetner, *Immersed in Great Affairs: Allan Nevins and the Heroic Age of American History* (Albany: State University of New York Press, 2004).

Chapter 4. The Promise of Change

1. Quote from Davis, *FDR: The New York Years, 1928–1933* (New York: Random House, 1985), 222. For discussion of Roosevelt's New York relief efforts, see David M. Kennedy, *Freedom from Fear: The American People in Depression and War, 1929–1945* (New York: Oxford University Press, 1999), 90–91.

2. Farley, *Behind the Ballots: The Personal History of a Politician* (New York: Harcourt, 1938), 65.

3. Ibid., 66, 67.

4. Farley quoted in "Portents & Prophecies," *Time*, 31 October 1932, 12. Also see Farley, *Behind the Ballots*, 71–72, 80–81.

5. Mrs. Jesse W. Nicholson quoted in "N.W.D.L.E.L. v. W.O.F.N.P.R.," *Time*, 27 April 1931, 20.

6. Earle Looker, "Is Franklin D. Roosevelt Physically Fit to Be President?" *Liberty Magazine*, 25 July 1931, 6–10. Interestingly, *Liberty*'s co-founder was "Colonel" Robert McCormick, publisher of the conservative-leaning *Chicago Tribune* and later a fierce Roosevelt critic. Author Earle Looker went on to write several books about Roosevelt and become his presidential speechwriter. For more on the rumors about FDR's disability and the campaign's efforts to counter them, see Davis W. Houck and Amos Kiewe, *FDR's Body Politics: The Rhetoric of Disability* (College Station, Texas A&M University Press, 2003), chap. 5.

7. John Dewey, "The Need for a New Party," *New Republic*, 18 March 1931.

8. Joel T. Boone oral history quoted in Donald A. Ritchie, *Electing FDR: The New Deal Campaign of 1932* (Lawrence: University Press of Kansas, 2007), 94; Theodore Joslin, diary entry of 27 April 1932, quoted in Houck and Kiewe, *FDR's Body Politics*, 82.

9. For more on the genesis of the Brains Trust, see Davis, *FDR, The New York Years*, chap. 10.

10. Roosevelt, "The Forgotten Man," 7 April 1932, Albany, reprinted in *The Public Papers and Addresses of Franklin D. Roosevelt*, vol. 1, *1928–32* (New York: Random House, 1938), 624; Address at Oglethorpe University, 22 May 1932, reprinted in *The Public Papers and Addresses*, 1: 639. For more on the ideas animating the campaign, see Kennedy, *Freedom from Fear*, 98–103. As Kennedy puts it, Roosevelt's campaign "defined an attitude, not a program" (101).

11. P. J. O'Brien, *Will Rogers, Ambassador of Good Will, Prince of Wit and Wisdom* (Philadelphia: Winston, 1935), 162.

12. Henry H. Vaughn, letter to the editor, "Wants Trust Busters," *Chicago Defender*, 4 September 1932, 14.

13. "A Catch-All Speech," *New York Times*, 20 April 1932, 22.

14. "Campaign Address on Progressive Government at the Commonwealth Club in San Francisco, California," 23 September 1932.

15. *New Republic*, 1 April 1931, 166, quoted in Kennedy, *Freedom from Fear*, 101; Walter Lippmann, *Interpretations, 1931–32* (New York: Macmillan, 1932), quoted in Kennedy, *Freedom from Fear*, 101; Harrison, letter to the editor, "Action Wanted Now: Governor Roosevelt Held to be Dealing Too Much with the Past," *New York Times*, 27 April 1932, 16.

16. Marshall McLuhan, *Understanding Media: The Extensions of Man* (New York: McGraw-Hill, 1964), 270–71.

17. Ritchie, *Electing F.D.R.*, 95–96.

18. Mrs. George H. Miles, President of the New Jersey State Women's Republican Club, quoted in "Mrs. Miles Deserts Republican Ranks," *New York Times*, 19 October 1932.

19. "The Land Stand of Days," *Baltimore Evening Sun*, 15 June 1932, reprinted in H. L. Mencken, *Making a President: A Footnote to the Saga of Democracy* (New York: Knopf, 1932), 50.

20. Sarah E. Igo, *The Averaged American: Surveys, Citizens, and the Making of a Mass Public* (Cambridge, Mass.: Harvard University Press, 2007), esp. chap. 3.

21. Mencken, *Making a President*, 105–6. Prohibition was on the minds of the Democrats as well in Chicago, yet the growth of the urban wing of the party over the previous decade was making it clear the "wets" had gained the advantage over the "drys." As Prohibition's rural and reformist advocates reluctantly sat back, the platform fight for the Democrats came down to how quickly, and decisively, the Volstead Act should be repealed. Scott Schaeffer argues that the 18th Amendment, more than the New Deal, ushered in the age of "big government"; see Schaeffer, "Legislative Rise and Populist Fall of the Eighteenth Amendment: Chicago and the Failure of Prohibition," *Journal of Law & Politics* 26 (2010): 385. For more on Prohibition, see Daniel Okrent, *Last Call: The Rise and Fall of Prohibition* (New York: Simon and Schuster, 2010).

22. L. F. Coles, letter to the editor, "Coles says G.O.P Leaders Are After Crumbs and That They Haven't the People's Welfare at Heart," *Afro-American*, 5 November 1932, 6.

23. Nomination Address, 2 July 1932, reprinted in *The Public Papers and Addresses*, 1: 647.

24. Lucy G. Barber, *Marching on Washington: The Forging of an American Political Tradition* (Berkeley: University of California Press, 2004), chap. 3. Not only was the Bonus Expeditionary Force separate from the Communist Party, but its organizers were also determined to keep the "Communist element" from influencing susceptible veterans; see Paul Dickson and Thomas B. Allen, *The Bonus Army: An American Epic* (New York: Walker, 2004), 82–85.

25. Joseph Carl Thomson quoted in "V.F.W. Assails Hoover on Bonus Evacuation," *New York Times*, 1 September 1932, 19; "Patman Assails Hoover," *New York Times*, 30 July 1932, 4; Ritchie, *Electing F.D.R.*, 119.

26. "To Spur up Interest," *New York Times*, 6 August 1932, 10.

27. Hoover, *Memoirs*, 3: 256, 259.

28. Brian Balogh, "'Mirrors of Desires': Interest Groups, Elections, and the Targeted Style in Twentieth Century America," in *The Democratic Experiment: New Directions in American Political History*, ed. Meg Jacobs, William J. Novak, and Julian Zelizer (Princeton, N.J.: Princeton University Press, 2003), 222–49, 231.

29. John Carlile, Production Director, Columbia System, quoted in "Personality on the Air," *New York Times*, 20 March 1932, X14.

30. Kathryn Cramer Brownell, *Showbiz Politics: Hollywood in American Politics, 1928–1980* (Ithaca, N.Y.: Cornell University Press, 2014).

31. Ritchie, *Electing F.D.R.*, 137–40, 143–44.

32. John A. Simpson quoted in Arthur Krock, "Republicans Facing Hard Fight in Iowa," *New York Times*, 5 October 1932, 3; "Los Angeles Republican Club for Roosevelt;

Poll Shows 70% of Members Back Governor," *New York Times*, 29 August 1932, 1; "Progressives Start a Roosevelt League," *New York Times*, 26 September 1932, 1; "Hoover or Roosevelt Which?" *Chicago Defender*, 22 October 1932, 14; "Roosevelt or Hoover?—Roosevelt," *Afro-American*, 29 October 1932, 6; Dr. Clarence True Wilson, Executive Secretary of the Methodist Board of Temperance, Prohibition and Public Morals, quoted in "Dr. Wilson to Cast Vote for Thomas," *New York Times*, 4 September 1932, 13.

33. Hoover, "The Success of Recovery," 22 October 1932; Hoover, *Memoirs*, 3: 255; Kennedy, *Freedom from Fear*, 102.

34. "The Roosevelt Campaign," *New York Times*, 6 November 1932, E1; Anne O'Hare McCormick, "The Two Men at the Big Moment," *New York Times*, 6 November 1932, M1.

35. Hoover, *Memoirs*, 3: 343. The African American electorate would become a solid Democratic constituency starting with the 1936 election. See Nancy Weiss, *Farewell to the Party of Lincoln: Back Politics in the Age of F.D.R.* (Princeton, N.J.: Princeton University Press, 1983).

36. In addition to the works cited in this chapter, some of the important contributions to this literature on the New Deal and its legacies include two classics: Richard Hofstadter, *The Age of Reform* (New York: Vintage, 1960) and William E. Leuchtenburg, *Franklin D. Roosevelt and the New Deal: 1932–1940* (New York: Harper & Row, 1963), and recent reinterpretations and elaborations including Alan Brinkley, *The End of Reform: New Deal Liberalism in Recession and War* (New York: Vintage, 1996); Jennifer Klein, *For All These Rights: Business, Labor, and the Shaping of America's Public-Private Welfare State* (Princeton, N.J.: Princeton University Press, 2004); Jason Scott Smith, *Building New Deal Liberalism: The Political Economy of Public Works, 1933–1956* (New York: Cambridge University Press, 2006); Ira Katznelson, *Fear Itself: The New Deal and the Origins of Our Time* (New York: Liveright, 2013). The New Deal has been commemorated as a fundamental shift in the compact between citizen and state: see, e.g., Steve Fraser and Gary Gerstle, eds., *The Rise and Fall of the New Deal Order* (Princeton, N.J.: Princeton University Press, 1989) and a temporary departure from a laissez faire norm, Jefferson Cowie and Nick Salvatore, "The Long Exception: Rethinking the Place of the New Deal in American History," *International Labor and Working-Class History* 74 (2010): 1–32.

37. Hoover, *Memoirs*, vol. 3; Gary Dean Best, *Herbert Hoover: The Postpresidential Years, 1933–1964* (Stanford, Calif.: Hoover Institution Press, 1983). Kim Philips-Fein traces the conservative mobilization in *Invisible Hands: The Businessmen's Crusade Against the New Deal* (New York: Norton, 2008).

Chapter 5. The Fracturing of America

1. Gerry Studds quoted in Lewis Chester, Godfrey Hodgson, and Bruce Page, *An American Melodrama: The Presidential Campaign of 1968* (New York: Viking, 1969), 93.

2. Douglas Brinkley, *Cronkite* (New York: HarperPerennial, 2013), 340–87; James T. Patterson, *Grand Expectations: The United States, 1945–1974* (New York: Oxford University Press, 1996), 678–81.

3. *Public Papers of the Presidents of the United States: Lyndon B. Johnson, 1968–69* (Washington, D.C.: GPO, 1970), 1: 469–76. Bruce Schulman notes: "LBJ, never a brilliant public speaker, looked terrible on the tube—his wordy, folksy style looked forced, phony." Schulman, *Lyndon B. Johnson and American Liberalism: A Brief Biography with Documents* (Boston: Bedford Books of St. Martin's, 1995), 155.

4. Barry Goldwater, "Peace Through Strength," Address to American Legion, Dallas, Texas, 23 September 1964, reprinted in Leonard Schlup and James Manley, *The Political Principles of Senator Barry M. Goldwater as Revealed in His Speeches and Writings: A Source Book* (Lewiston, N.Y.: Edwin Mellen, 2011), 233–38.

5. Among other things, Rockefeller had advanced a strongly pro-civil rights plank in the 1960 Republican Platform. Rick Perlstein, *Before the Storm: Barry Goldwater and the Unmaking of the American Consensus* (New York: Nation Books, 2009), 79–90.

6. Lisa McGirr, *Suburban Warriors: The Origins of the New American Right* (Princeton, N.J.: Princeton University Press, 2001); Jonathan M. Schoenwald, *A Time for Choosing: The Rise of Modern American Conservatism* (New York: Oxford University Press, 2002). Other scholars have traced the role of race in the emergent conservative movement, in both South and North; see Kevin Kruse, *White Flight: Atlanta and the Making of Modern Conservatism* (Princeton, N.J.: Princeton University Press, 2005); Matthew D. Lassiter, *The Silent Majority: Suburban Politics in the Sunbelt South* (Princeton, N.J.: Princeton University Press, 2006); Thomas J. Sugrue, *Sweet Land of Liberty: The Forgotten Struggle for Civil Rights in the North* (New York: Random House, 2008); Joseph Crespino, *In Search of Another Country: Mississippi and the Conservative Counterrevolution* (Princeton, N.J.: Princeton University Press, 2009).

7. This came to a head at the 1964 Democratic Convention, where a group of black Mississippians who had been prevented from voting in their state's primary demanded to be seated instead of the all-white delegation from the Mississippi Democratic Party; Johnson and his vice president, Hubert Humphrey, kept the white delegation in and kept the white South from bolting. See Patterson, *Grand Expectations*, 550–57; Charles M. Payne, *I've Got the Light of Freedom: The Organizing Tradition and the Mississippi Freedom Struggle* (Berkeley: University of California Press, 2007), chap. 12.

8. Richard Hofstadter, "Goldwater and Pseudo-Conservative Politics," in *The Paranoid Style in American Politics, and Other Essays* (New York: Vintage, 1965, 2008), 133. This great postwar prosperity did not treat all Americans equally, and institutionalized racial discrimination limited opportunities for many people of color. See Thomas J. Sugrue, *The Origins of the Urban Crisis: Race and Inequality in Postwar Detroit* (Princeton, N.J.: Princeton University Press, 1996); Arnold Hirsch, *Making the Second Ghetto: Race and Housing in Chicago, 1940–1960* (New York: Cambridge University Press, 1983).

9. Kim Philips-Fein, *Invisible Hands: The Making of the Conservative Movement from the New Deal to Reagan* (New York: Norton, 2009).

10. Johnson quoted in Schulman, *Lyndon B. Johnson and American Liberalism*, 88.

11. Carey McWilliams, *California: The Great Exception* (California: University of California Press, 1949, 1998), 24.

12. Quoted in Rick Perlstein, *Nixonland: The Rise of a President and the Fracturing of America* (New York: Scribner, 2008), 61.

13. Matthew Dallek, *The Right Moment: Ronald Reagan's First Victory and the Decisive Turning Point in American Politics* (New York: Free Press, 2000), 180, 187.

14. Remarks at University of Michigan, 22 May 1964, *Public Papers: Johnson, 1963–64*, 1: 704–7.

15. Quoted in "Great Society," *New York Times*, 10 January 1965, E1.

16. Schulman, *Lyndon B. Johnson and American Liberalism*, 88–98.

17. *Public Papers Johnson, 1966* (Washington, D.C.: GPO, 1967), 1: 3–12.

18. "Excerpts from Fulbright's Speech on Vietnam War," *New York Times*, 29 April 1966, 32.

19. Patterson, *Grand Expectations*, 598–99; Selective Service System, "Inductions (by year) from World War I Through the End of the Draft (1973)," www.sss.gov/induct.htm (accessed 2 July 2013).

20. "Man of the Year: The Inheritor," *Time*, 6 January 1967.

21. The disproportionate recruitment of poor minority men was in fact the result of policy intentionally designed to steer unemployed minority youth into military service. Part of the broader Great Society agenda, the "Project 100,000" program (brainchild of assistant secretary of labor Daniel P. Moynihan) lowered recruitment standards in order to "rehabilitate" 100,000 young men per year by enlisting them in the armed forces. See Myra MacPherson, *Long Time Passing: Vietnam and the Haunted Generation* (Bloomington: Indiana University Press, 2002), 559.

22. Quoted in Sam Washington, "Should We Stay in Asia?" *Chicago Defender*, 1 April 1967, 1; King quoted in Robert B. Semple, Jr., "Dr. King Scores Poverty Budget," *New York Times*, 16 December 1966, 33. Only 12 percent of the Vietnam-era military ever saw combat, but these soldiers were disproportionately poorer and less well educated; see Cynthia Gimbel and Alan Booth, "Who Fought in Vietnam?" *Social Forces* 74, 4 (June 1996): 1137–57.

23. Raymond Daniell, "U.S. Assailed on Vietnam Policy Before 17,000 at a Garden Rally," *New York Times*, 9 June 1965; John Herbers, "Vote Drive Is Set by Peace Groups; Vietnam Issue to Be Raised in Congressional Races," *New York Times*, 25 February 1966, A3.

24. A key figure in the "Dump Johnson" movement was liberal activist Allard Lowenstein; see William H. Chafe, *Never Stop Running: Allard Lowenstein and the Struggle to Save American Liberalism* (New York: Basic Books, 1993), 262–75. Lippmann quoted in Perlstein, *Nixonland*, 174.

25. Lyndon B. Johnson, Phone Conversation with Senator Richard B. Russell, 27 May 1964 (WH6405.10), Presidential Recordings Program, Miller Center, University of Virginia; Johnson quoted in Chester et al., *American Melodrama*, 26.

26. Doris Kearns, *Lyndon Johnson and the American Dream* (New York: Signet, 1976), 345–49.

27. "NUL Chief Rips Poverty Program," *Chicago Daily Defender*, 15 December 1966, 16; Sam Washington, "Residents Hit 'Ineffective' Poverty Program," *Daily Defender*, 8 December 1966, 4.

28. Brian T. Baxter, "Urban Unrest," Letter to the Editor, *New York Times*, 17 August 1966, 30.

29. U.S. Kerner Commission, *Report of the National Advisory Commission on Civil Disorders*, (Washington, D.C.: GPO, 1968); Taylor Branch, *At Canaan's Edge: America in the King Years, 1965–68* (New York: Simon and Schuster, 2006), 293–323; Gerald Horne, *Fire This Time: The Watts Uprising and the 1960s* (New York: Da Capo, 1997).

30. Stokely Carmichael, "Definitions of Black Power," Detroit, 31 July 1966, reprinted in *To Redeem a Nation: A History and Anthology of the Civil Rights Movement*, ed. Thomas R. West (New York: Brandywine Press, 1993), 245–246.

31. Chester et al., *An American Melodrama*, 68–77.

32. Ibid., 74, 76.

33. Ibid., 80.

34. "Crusade of the Ballot Children." *Time*, 22 March 1968, 31; Chester et al., *An American Melodrama*, 79–80, 98.

35. Quoted in Steven M. Gillon, *The Kennedy Assassination—24 Hours After: Lyndon B. Johnson's Pivotal First Day as President* (New York: Basic Books, 2009), 31. Regarding the 1960 convention, see Robert A. Caro, *The Passage of Power: The Years of Lyndon Johnson*, vol. 4 (New York: Vintage, 2013), 109–43. The feud was of a magnitude deserving book-length study: Jeff Shesol, *Mutual Contempt: Lyndon Johnson, Robert Kennedy, and the Feud That Defined a Decade* (New York: Norton, 1997).

36. Chester et al., *An American Melodrama*, 105–13.

37. Both quoted in "Reaction to Bobby," *Time*, 5 April 1968, 81.

38. H. Rupert Theobald and Patricia V. Robbins, eds., *The State of Wisconsin Blue Book, 1970* (Madison: Wisconsin Legislative Reference Bureau, 1970), 822–823.

39. "The New Context of '68," *Time*, 22 March 1968, 29; Chafe, *Never Stop Running*, 282–90; "Gene's Bind," *Time*, 29 March, 24.

40. James Reston, "Washington: Pray Silence for Hubert Horatio Humphrey," *New York Times*, 5 April 1968, 46; Roy Reed, "Humphrey Is Silent on Entering Race, But Support Grows," *New York Times*, 3 April 1968, 1. Also see Stewart Alsop, "Hubert Horatio Humphrey," *Saturday Evening Post*, 24 August 1968, 21–25.

41. Chester et al., *An American Melodrama*, 80.

42. Ibid., 127.

43. Thomas B. Congdon, Jr., "Kennedy Among the People," *Saturday Evening Post*, 13 July 1968, 64. Leonard J. Moore, *Citizen Klansmen: The Ku Klux Klan in Indiana*,

1921–1928 (Chapel Hill: University of North Carolina Press, 1997). Also see MacLean, *Behind the Mask of Chivalry.*

44. Quoted in Shesol, *Mutual Contempt*, 447. Also see Ray E. Boomhower, *Robert F. Kennedy and the 1968 Indiana Primary* (Bloomington: Indiana University Press, 2008).

45. David Halberstam, *The Unfinished Odyssey of Robert Kennedy* (New York: Random House, 1968); Thurston Clarke, *The Last Campaign: Robert F. Kennedy and 82 Days That Inspired America* (New York: Henry Holt, 2008).

46. "Getting Snappish," *Time*, 31 May 1968, 13; Chester et al., *An American Melodrama*, 149.

47. William A. Emerson, Jr., "From the Editor," *Saturday Evening Post*, 13 July 1968, 3.

Chapter 6. Improbable Victories

1. Quoted in Lewis Chester, Godfrey Hodgson, and Bruce Page, *An American Melodrama: The Presidential Campaign of 1968* (New York: Viking, 1969, 183.

2. Gallup Organization, Gallup Poll #736, Field Date 21–26 October 1966, http://brain.gallup.com/documents/questionnaire.aspx?STUDY = AIPO0736 (accessed 8 July 2013); Matthew D. Lassiter, *The Silent Majority: Suburban Politics in the Sunbelt South* (Princeton, N.J.: Princeton University Press, 2006), 228–29; as Lassiter observes, "demographics played a much more important role than demagoguery in the emergence of a two-party system in the American South" (228). Also see Earl Black and Merle Black, *The Vital South: How Presidents Are Elected* (Cambridge, Mass.: Harvard University Press, 1992). Cold War spending was critical to the new economic geography; see Bruce J. Schulman, *From Cotton Belt to Sunbelt: Federal Policy, Economic Development, and the Transformation of the South, 1938–1980* (Durham, N.C.: Duke University Press, 1994).

3. On Thurmond and his legacies, see Joseph Crespino, *Strom Thurmond's America* (New York: Hill and Wang, 2012). On Wallace, see Dan T. Carter, *The Politics of Rage: George Wallace, the Origins of the New Conservatism, and the Transformation of American Politics* (Baton Rouge: Louisiana State University Press, 2000) as well as the classic biography by Marshall Frady, *Wallace* (New York: World, 1968).

4. On the longer history of populism, see Michael Kazin, *The Populist Persuasion: An American History* (Ithaca, N.Y.: Cornell University Press, 1998).

5. Cathy Kunzinger Urwin, "'Noblesse Oblige' and Practical Politics: Winthrop Rockefeller and the Civil Rights Movement," *Arkansas Historical Quarterly* 54, 1 (April 1995): 30–52; "Goldwater Returns," in Black and Black, *The Vital South*, 147, cited in Lassiter, *The Silent Majority*, 229.

6. Chester et al., *An American Melodrama*, 188. For additional discussion of Kirk and the emergence of the coded racial language of homeownership, see Thomas Byrne Edsall and Mary D. Edsall, *Chain Reaction: The Impact of Race, Rights, and Taxes on American Politics* (New York: Norton, 1991). Since the New Deal, federal policies supporting home ownership had turned homes into vehicles for building personal economic security as well as potent symbols of citizenship. Yet the entire system of

residential real estate was profoundly discriminatory in terms of both race and gender, ensuring that postwar suburban neighborhoods remained, by and large, lily-white enclaves of male breadwinners and female housewives. Civil rights presented a threat to this order, and the movement of black families into these neighborhoods was seen by many homeowners as something with potentially devastating effects on home values as well as on neighborhood security. This was a nationwide phenomenon, not merely a southern one. See Thomas J. Sugrue, *The Origins of the Urban Crisis: Race and Inequality in Postwar Detroit* (Princeton N.J.: Princeton University Press, 1996); Robert Self, *American Babylon: Race and the Struggle for Postwar Oakland* (Princeton N.J.: Princeton University Press, 2003); Kevin Kruse, *White Flight?: Atlanta and the Making of Modern Conservatism* (Princeton N.J.: Princeton University Press, 2005); Sugrue, *Sweet Land of Liberty: The Forgotten Struggle for Civil Rights in the North* (New York: Random House, 2008).

7. A. F. Mahan, "Political Highway Now Beckoning to Romney," *Los Angeles Times*, 4 February 1962, F2.

8. Kennedy quoted in Rick Perlstein, *Nixonland: The Rise of a President and the Fracturing of America* (New York: Scribner, 2008), 173; Romney-Johnson polling from Theodore H. White, *The Making of the President 1968* (New York: Atheneum, 1969), 47. Also see George T. Harris, *Romney's Way: A Man and an Idea* (Englewood Cliffs, N.J.: Prentice-Hall, 1968). Among other things, Romney won 15 percent of the black vote in Michigan in 1964 (while Goldwater won a mere 2 percent), and increased his share to 30 percent in 1966 (White, *The Making of the President 1968*, 42).

9. White, *The Making of the President 1968*, 41.

10. Romney, Interview with Lou Gordon, Detroit, 31 August 1967, cited in Rick Perlstein, "What Mitt Romney Learned from His Dad," *Rolling Stone*, 17 January 2012. Also see Perlstein, *Nixonland*, 173–75; Chester et al., *An American Melodrama*, 100–102. Romney's campaign, and the attention and financial support it garnered, also foreclosed the possibilities for other moderate Republicans to get into the race; arguably, some of these men (like New York Mayor John Lindsay) might have been stronger and more resilient candidates.

11. Quoted in Chester et al., *An American Melodrama*, 236.

12. Richard M. Nixon has been chronicled, analyzed, and psychoanalyzed more than possibly any other American president. In addition to the work already cited, notable works on Nixon include Elizabeth Drew, *Richard M. Nixon* (New York: Times Books, 2007); David Greenberg, *Nixon's Shadow: The History of an Image* (New York: Norton, 2003); Melvin Small, *The Presidency of Richard Nixon* (Lawrence: University Press of Kansas, 1999).

13. Perlstein, *Nixonland*, 203. Further discussion of Nixon's comeback can be found in White, *The Making of the President 1968*, 47–70.

14. Joe McGinniss, *The Selling of the President* (New York: Trident Press, 1969), 66.

15. Chester et al., *An American Melodrama*, 256.

16. "Bailey Hits Nixon as 'Old Slasher' of '50's," *Los Angeles Times,* 10 February 1968, B10; Safire quoted in White, *The Making of the President 1968,* 58.

17. Thurmond and Reagan quoted in Perlstein, *Nixonland,* 257; also see 263. Hayes quoted in Chester et al., *An American Melodrama,* 16.

18. White, *The Making of the President 1968,* 160–61.

19. Chester et al., *An American Melodrama,* 379–401; White, *The Making of the President 1968,* 261–99.

20. Richard Nixon: "Address Accepting the Presidential Nomination at the Republican National Convention in Miami Beach, Florida," 8 August 1968, online by Gerhard Peters and John T. Woolley, The American Presidency Project, http://www.presidency .ucsb.edu/ws/?pid = 25968 (accessed 10 July 2013).

21. William Rorabaugh, *The Real Making of the President: Kennedy, Nixon, and the 1960 Election* (Lawrence: University Press of Kansas, 2009).

22. James M. Perry, *The New Politics: The Expanding Technology of Political Manipulation* (London: Weidenfeld & Nicolson, 1968).

23. Rennie Davis and Tom Hayden, Memorandum to National Mobilization Staff regarding discussion of the Democratic Convention Challenge, Hayden Exhibit No. 2, House Un-American Activities Committee, *Subversive Involvement in Disruption of 1968 Democratic Party National Convention, Part 2,* 90th Cong., 2nd Sess., December 1968 (Washington, D.C.: GPO, 1968). The Convention also has been the subject of exhaustive study; see in particular David Farber, *Chicago '68* (Chicago: University of Chicago Press, 1994). Classic analyses by participant-observers include not only White's *The Making of the President 1968* but also Norman Mailer, *Miami and the Siege of Chicago: An Informal History of the Republican and Democratic Conventions of 1968* (New York: World, 1968), chap. 2, and Todd Gitlin, *The Sixties: Years of Hope, Days of Rage* (New York: Bantam, 1987), chap. 14.

24. Quoted in Farber, *Chicago '68,* 17.

25. White, *The Making of the President 1968,* 305; Gitlin, *The Sixties,* 319.

26. Daniel Walker, *Rights in Conflict: Convention Week in Chicago, August 25–29, 1968: A Report Submitted to the National Commission on the Causes and Prevention of Violence* (New York: Dutton, 1968).

27. Chester et al., *An American Melodrama,* 523.

28. "An Unexciting Choice?" *Wall Street Journal,* 27 June 1968, 16.

29. Henry Cathcart, "Inside Washington: McCarthy Fails to Impress Blacks," *Chicago Daily Defender,* 9 May 1968, 19.

30. Paul O'Neil, "The Part Almost Came Down Around Their Ears," *Life,* 6 September 1968, 22.

31. Philips later expanded this thesis to book length in *The Emerging Republican Majority* (New York: Arlington, 1969).

32. Richard Nixon, "A New Alignment for American Unity," 16 May 1968, SR #680516, Nixon Presidential Library.

33. McGinniss, *The Selling of the President*, 103. Also see Jonathan Yardley, "Sharp Pencils Shape Elections," *Smithsonian Magazine*, November 2006.

34. "The First Civil Right," Nixon-Agnew Victory Committee, 1968, courtesy of the Nixon Presidential Library and Museum, reprinted on Museum of the Moving Image, *The Living Room Candidate: Presidential Campaign Commercials 1952–2012*, www.livingroomcandidate.org/commercials/1968/the-first-civil-right (accessed July 13, 2013).

35. George C. Wallace, *Stand Up for America* (Garden City, N.Y.: Doubleday, 1976), 121–22.

36. Wallace, Speech at Madison Square Garden, 24 October 1968.

Chapter 7. Reagan Revolutionaries and New Democrats

1. John F. Berry, "Skepticism Greets Hype Surrounding Cable News Debut," *Washington Post*, 1 June 1980, F1; Ted Turner, Welcoming Remarks, CNN, 1 June 1980.

2. "Acceptance Speech," Detroit, 17 July 1980, reprinted in *Campaign Speeches of American Presidential Candidates, 1948–1984*, ed. George Bush (New York: Frederick Ungar, 1985), 269.

3. Bruce J. Schulman, *The Seventies: The Great Shift in American Culture, Society, and Politics* (New York: Free Press, 2001).

4. Jonathan Bell and Timothy Stanley, eds., *Making Sense of American Liberalism* (Urbana: University of Illinois Press, 2012); James T. Patterson, *Restless Giant: The United States from Watergate to Bush v. Gore* (New York: Oxford University Press, 2007), 76–107.

5. *Time*, 15 November 1976, 30, quoted in Patterson, *Restless Giant*, 76.

6. John P. McIver, Table Eb309–316: "Party Identification, 1952–2000," in *Historical Statistics of the United States, Millennial Edition on Line*, ed. Susan B. Carter, Scott Sigmund Gartner, Michael R. Haines, Alan L. Olmsted, Richard Sutch, and Gavin Wright, http://hsus.cambridge.org/HSUSWeb/toc/hsusHome.do (accessed 17 July 2013). Among other moderate credentials, Carter was also a born-again Christian, and one innovation of his 1976 run was his choice to emphasize this element of his biography on the campaign trail. See Dan F. Hahn, "One's Reborn Every Minute: Carter's Religious Appeal in 1976," *Communication Quarterly* 28, 3 (Summer 1980): 56–62. Also see "The Lost Opportunity: Jimmy Carter and the Not-So-Vital Center," in E. J. Dionne, *Why Americans Hate Politics* (New York: Simon and Schuster, 1989), 116–44.

7. Leonard E. Silk, "Nixon's Program—'I Am Now a Keynesian'," *New York Times*, 10 January 1971, E1.

8. Jefferson Cowie, *Stayin' Alive: The 1970s and the Last Days of the Working Class* (New York: New Press, 2012). On the business-labor relations of the postwar period, see Jennifer Klein, *For All These Rights: Business, Labor, and the Shaping of America's Public-Private Welfare State* (Princeton, N.J.: Princeton University Press, 2003).

9. "'Welfare Queen' Becomes Issue in Reagan Campaign," *Washington Star*, 15 February 1976, 51.

10. John P. McIver, "Political Party Affiliations in Congress and the Presidency, 1789–2002," *Historical Statistics of the United States*, Table Eb296–308.

11. As James T. Patterson observes, "Whether Reagan's economy policies were good for the country was—and is—hard to judge. Most historians, however, credit his efforts to reverse the inflationary spiral that had deeply frightened Americans since the late 1970s. Reagan gave strong and undeviating support to Federal Reserve Board chairman Paul Volcker, who continued to pursue the tough monetary policies that he had initiated under Carter" (*Restless Giant*, 162).

12. "Prouder, Stronger, Better," Reagan-Bush '84, original airdate 17 September 1984, Ronald and Nancy Reagan/Ronald Reagan Presidential Library, from Museum of the Moving Image, *The Living Room Candidate: Presidential Campaign Commercials 1952–2012*, www.livingroomcandidate.org/commercials/1984/prouder-stronger-better (accessed 16 July 2013).

13. George J. Church, Sam Allis, and Hays Gorey, "Moving Toward the Middle: Sick of Caucuses, Sunbelt Democrats Form—What Else?—a Caucus," *Time*, 18 March 1985, 25.

14. Edward G. Benson and Paul Perry, "Analysis of Democratic-Republican Strength by Population Groups," *Public Opinion Quarterly* 4, 3 (1 September 1940): 464–73; Kim Phillips-Fein, *Invisible Hands: The Making of the Conservative Movement from the New Deal to Reagan* (New York: Norton, 2009); Cowie and Salvatore, "The Long Exception: Rethinking the Place of the New Deal in American History" *International Labor and Working-Class History* 74 (2010): 1–32.

15. Douglas Smith, "Into the Political Thicket: Reapportionment and the Rise of Suburban Power," in *The Myth of Southern Exceptionalism*, ed. Matthew D. Lassiter and Joseph Crespino (New York: Oxford University Press, 2010), 263–85. This was a national phenomenon as well; see Robert O. Self, *All in the Family: The Realignment of American Democracy Since the 1960s* (New York: Hill and Wang, 2012).

16. Patterson, *Restless Giant*, 59. On the New South, see David R. Goldfield, *Cotton Fields and Skyscrapers: Southern City and Region* (Baltimore: Johns Hopkins University Press, 1989); Nancy MacLean, "Neo-Confederacy Versus the New Deal: The Regional Utopia of the Modern American Right" in Lassiter and Crespino, *The Myth of Southern Exceptionalism*, 308–30. On the Sunbelt, see Carl Abbott, *The New Urban America: Metropolitan Growth and Politics in the Sunbelt Since 1940* (Chapel Hill: University of North Carolina Press, 1981); John M. Findlay, *Magic Lands: Western Cityscapes and American Culture After 1940* (Berkeley: University of California Press, 1992); Elizabeth Tandy Shermer, *Sunbelt Capitalism: Phoenix and the Transformation of American Politics* (Philadelphia: University of Pennsylvania Press, 2013).

17. Phil Gailey, "Sam Nunn's Rising Star," *New York Times*, 4 January 1987, M1.

18. Paul E. Tsongas, "Atarizing Reagan," *New York Times*, 1 March 1983, E1; "New Faces in the Senate: Atari Democrat," *Time*, 17 November 1986.

19. Margot Hornblower, "House Democrats Tackle the Issues Again—Generally," *Washington Post*, 23 September 1982, A1.

20. Phil Gailey, "Dissidents Defy Top Democrats; Council Formed," *New York Times*, 1 March 1985.

21. Charles Peters, "A Neoliberal's Manifesto," *Washington Monthly*, May 1983, reprinted in *A New Road for America: The Neoliberal Movement*, ed. Charles Peters and Phillip Keisling (Lanham, Md., Madison Books, 1985), 189–208; William V. Shannon, "A Rocky Road for Neoliberals," *Boston Globe*, 18 May 1983.

22. Kenneth S. Baer, *Reinventing Democrats: The Politics of Liberalism from Reagan to Clinton* (Lawrence: University Press of Kansas, 2000).

23. Jon F. Hale, "The Making of the New Democrats," *Political Science Quarterly* 110, no. 2 (Summer 1995), 207–32. Jackson quoted in Robin Toner, "Democrats in New York—Party Leadership: 1992 Ticket Puts Council Of Moderates to Stiff Test," *New York Times*, 15 July 1992; Arthur Schlesinger, Jr., "For Democrats, Me-Too Reaganism Will Spell Disaster" (Op-Ed), *New York Times*, 6 July 1986; Al From, "Worthy Heirs of the Democratic Legacy," (Letter), *New York Times*, 20 July 1986; Patterson, *Restless Giant*, 190.

24. Quoted in Hale, "The Making of the New Democrats," 219.

25. David Maraniss, *First in His Class: A Biography of Bill Clinton* (New York: Simon and Schuster, 1995).

26. Richard Ben Cramer, *Being Poppy: A Portrait of George Herbert Walker Bush* (New York: Simon and Schuster, 2013); Jacob Weisberg, *The Bush Tragedy* (New York: Random House, 2008); Timothy J. Naftali, *George H. W. Bush* (New York: Times Books, 2007).

27. Gil Troy, *Morning in America: How Ronald Reagan Invented the 1980s* (Princeton, N.J.: Princeton University Press, 2005); Patterson, *Restless Giant*, 193–217.

28. George Bush, "Address to the Nation Announcing Allied Military Action in the Persian Gulf," 16 January 1991. Online by Gerhard Peters and John T. Woolley, The American Presidency Project, http://www.presidency.ucsb.edu/ws/?pid = 19222 (accessed 27 June 2014).

29. Quoted in Patterson, *Restless Giant*, 238. Also see Micah L. Sifry and Christopher Cerf, eds., *The Gulf War Reader: History, Documents, Opinions* (New York: Times Books, 1991); Frank N. Schubert and Theresa L. Kraus, *The Whirlwind War: The United States Army in Operations Desert Shield and Desert Storm* (Washington, D.C.: U.S. Army Center of Military History, 1994).

30. Morton Kondracke, "Slick Willy," *New Republic* 205, 17 (21 October, 1991): 18–21; William J. Clinton: "Remarks Announcing Candidacy for the Democratic Presidential Nomination," 3 October 1991, Peters and Woolley, American Presidency Project.

Chapter 8. The CNN President

Quoted in Joe Klein, "Bill Clinton: Who Is This Guy?" *New York Times*, 20 January 1992.

1. Keith Herndon, "CNN Turns a Corner: The Rising Fortunes of the Fourth Network," *Washington Journalism Review* 7, 12 (December 1985): 28–30; Desmond Smith, "Is the Sun Setting on Network Nightly News?" *Washington Journalism Review* 8, 1 (January 1986): 30–33.

2. Lynn E. Gutstadt, "Taking the Pulse of the CNN Audience: A Case Study of the Gulf War," *Political Communication* 10, 4 (October 1993): 389–409.

3. CNN audience research from A.C. Nielsen micronode data, cited in Gutstatdt, "Taking the Pulse," fig. 1.

4. T. Carroll Morganthau, "The Wild Card," *Newsweek*, 27 April 1992, 20.

5. Mary Matalin in Mary Matalin, James Carville, and Peter Knobler, *All's Fair: Love, War, and Running for President* (New York: Random House, 1994), 148.

6. Robert Fitch, "Welfare Billionaire." *Nation* 254, 23 (15 June 1992): 815–16; Morganthau, "The Wild Card." Also see Gerald Posner, *Citizen Perot: His Life and Times* (New York: Random House, 1996).

7. For example: H. Ross Perot, *My Life and the Principles for Success* (Arlington, Tex.: Summit, 1996).

8. Peter Elkind, "Perot and Con," *Washington Monthly* 22, 10 (November 1990): 51.

9. "Ross Perot," *Larry King Live*, CNN, 20 February 1992, quoted in Peter Elkind, "The Ross Perot You Don't Know," *Washington Monthly* 24, 5 (May 1992): 14; Jeffrey Schmalz, "The 1992 Campaign: Voters; Perot Petition Embraces as Manifesto of Change," *New York Times*, 31 May 1992, 20.

10. Gallup Organization, "Ross Perot Poll," sponsored by CNN/*USA Today*, 3/31/1992-4/01/1992, http://brain.gallup.com/documents/questionnaire.aspx?STUDY = cn n222048 (accessed 18 July 2013). Also see Jack W. Germond and Jules Witcover, *Mad as Hell: Revolt at the Ballot Box, 1992* (New York: Warner, 1993); Peter Goldman, Thomas M. DeFrank, Mark Miller, Andrew Murr, and Tom Matthews, *Quest for the Presidency 1992* (College Station: Texas A&M University Press, 1994).

11. Catherine Crier, "Ross Perot—White Knight?" CNN, 1 June 1992; "Guests Discuss Ross Perot's Effect on Presidential Race," CNN, 4 June 1992.

12. John H. Summers, "What Happened to Sex Scandals? Politics and Peccadilloes, Jefferson to Kennedy," *Journal of American History* 87, 3 (1 December 2000): 825–54.

13. Schulman, *The Seventies*, 144–58.

14. Kevin M. Kruse, "The Real Loser: Truth," *New York Times*, 5 November 2012, Opinion; Stefano DellaVigna and Ethan Kaplan, "The Fox News Effect: Media Bias and Voting," *Quarterly Journal of Economics* 122, 3 (August 1, 2007): 1187–1234.

15. Mandy Grunwald, quoted in Matalin et al., *All's Fair*, 169.

16. "Mario Cuomo, Hamlet on the Hudson," *The Economist*, 28 September 1991, A34; Gallup Organization, "October Wave 3," 17–20 October 1991, http://brain.gallup .com/documents/questionnaire.aspx?STUDY = GNS222020 (accessed 18 July 2013).

17. "Mario Cuomo: Keeping the Faith," Interview with Craig Horowitz, New York, 6 April 1998.

18. George Stephanopoulos, *All Too Human: A Political Education* (Boston: Little, Brown, 1999), 51–52; Evans and Novak, "Cuomo Departure Elevated Clinton," *Omaha World-Herald*, 4 January 1992. Shelby switched to the Republican Party in 1994.

19. Longtime Clinton aide Betsey Wright coined the term "bimbo eruption," which she repeated (to her fellow staffers' horror) to Michael Isikoff, "Clinton Team Works to Deflect Allegations on Nominee's Private Life," *Washington Post*, 26 July 1992, A18.

20. Kevin Merida, "It's Come to This: A Nickname That's Proven Hard to Slip," *Washington Post*, 20 December 1998, F1.

21. Gwen Ifill, "The 1992 Campaign: New Hampshire; Clinton Thanked Colonel in '69 for 'Saving Me from the Draft,' " *New York Times*, 13 February 1992, A1; Stephanopoulos, *All Too Human*, 69–80.

22. Stephanopoulos, *All Too Human*, 82.

23. Robin Toner, "The 1992 Campaign: Primaries; Clinton Is Victor In New York with 41 percent of Democratic Vote; Tsongas Edges Brown For 2d" *New York Times*, 8 April 1992; Goldman et al., *Quest for the Presidency 1992*, 156.

24. Goldman et al., *Quest for the Presidency 1992*, 206.

25. Ibid., 283.

26. Ibid.; Dan Balz and David Broder, "Party Cements Case for Change," *Washington Post*, 16 July 1992, A1.

27. Matalin et al., *All's Fair*, 173, 172.

28. Richard Cohen, "In a Muddle," *Washington Post*, 17 January 1992, A21; Timothy Stanley, *The Crusader: The Life and Tumultuous Times of Pat Buchanan* (New York: Thomas Dunne, 2012), 142.

29. Matalin et al., *All's Fair*, 53–57; Stanley, *The Crusader*, 139–152.

30. Buchanan, "1992 Republican National Convention Speech," Houston, 17 August 1992, http://buchanan.org/blog/1992-republican-national-convention-speech -148 (accessed 19 July 2013).

31. Catherine Crier and Bernard Shaw, "Republicans Are Nervous About Bush Campaign," CNN, 23 July 1992.

32. Gary Wills, "George Bush, Prisoner of the Crazies," *New York Times*, 16 August 1992, 17.

33. Dan Balz and Ann Devroy, "How Perot's Presence Is Altering Campaign," *Washington Post*, 27 May 1992, A1.

34. Larry King, "Bill Moyers and William Safire on Convention Eve," CNN, 10 July 1992.

35. "Guests Discuss Ross Perot's Effect on Presidential Race," CNN, 4 June 1992.

36. Matalin et al., *All's Fair*; Goldman et al., *Quest for the Presidency 1992*, 413–82.

37. Goldman et al., *Quest for the Presidency 1992*, 467; Michael Isikoff, "Rollins, Top Aides Leave Troubled Perot Campaign," *Washington Post*, 16 July 1992.

38. Goldman et al., *Quest for the Presidency 1992*, 446–48, 453.

39. Ken Moritsugu and Ron Thompson, "Perot Supporters Express Shock, Anger," *St. Petersburg Times*, 17 July 1992, C1; "Perot Goes Poof," Editorial, *St. Petersburg Times*, 17 July 1992, 12A.

40. Quoted in Joel Achenbach, "Little Rock, Where Spin Meets Homespun," *Washington Post*, 2 October 1992, C1. Details of the 1992 Clinton-Gore campaign are also informed by personal recollections of the author, who worked at the Little Rock headquarters from July to October 1992, in the Michigan field office in October 1992, and on the transition team from November 1992 to January 1993.

41. Achenbach, "In Little Rock."

42. Goldman et al., *Quest for the Presidency 1992*, 549.

43. Ibid., 552.

44. George H. W. Bush, Debate with Bill Clinton and Ross Perot (11 October 1992), American President: A Reference Resource, Miller Center for Public Affairs, University of Virginia, http://millercenter.org/president/speeches/detail/5532 (accessed 22 July 2013).

45. Kathleen H. Jamieson and David S. Birdsell, *Presidential Debates: The Challenge of Creating an Informed Electorate* (New York: Oxford University Press, 1990), 84–193; William L. Benoit and William T. Wells, *Candidates in Conflict: Persuasive Attack and Defense in the 1992 Presidential Debates* (Tuscaloosa: University of Alabama Press, 1996).

46. Goldman et al., *Quest for the Presidency 1992*, 580.

47. Bush to Marlin Fitzwater, quoted in Goldman et al., *Quest for the Presidency 1992*, 596.

48. Leslie Gelb, "George, Bill, and Millie," *New York Times*, 1 November 1992; B. Drummond Ayres, "Bush Eases Hammering of the Press—New York Times," *New York Times*, 28 October 1992.

49. George Bush: "Remarks in Houston on the Results of the Presidential Election," 3 November 1992, Gerhard Peters and John T. Woolley, American Presidency Project, http://www.presidency.ucsb.edu/ws/?pid = 21734 (accessed 22 July 2013).

50. "1992 Presidential Election: Clinton Victory Speech from Little Rock," CNN, 3 November 1992.

Conclusion. Hope and Change

1. Gallup Organization cited in Scott Neuman, "Just How Independent Are Independent Voters?" NPR, 27 March 2012.

2. "Bush Closes Race, Assailing Gore on His Home Turf; Confident Aides Are Planning Celebration," *St. Louis Post-Dispatch*, 7 November 2000.

3. Dana Milbank, "The Greens Refuse to Sing Dem Blues." *Washington Post*, 8 November 2000, C8.

4. Ibid.

5. "TV Goof About Florida Contest Put Anchors Back to Square One," *New York Daily News*, 8 November 2000, A1.

6. Kevin Sack and Frank Bruni, "Changing Circumstances: How Gore Stopped Short on His Way to Concede," *New York Times*, 9 November 2000, A1.

7. Democratic National Convention, Boston, 27 July 2004.

8. For discussion of the "post-racial" society of the Obama era, see Thomas J. Sugrue, *Not Even Past: Barack Obama and the Burden of Race* (Princeton, N.J.: Princeton University Press, 2010).

9. The burgeoning field of the history of conservatism has made important insights into the long history of the movement and its New Deal roots. In particular, see Kim Phillips-Fein, *Invisible Hands: The Businessmen's Crusade Against the New Deal* (New York: Norton, 2008).

INDEX

*

ACKNOWLEDGMENTS

*

Just like a successful presidential campaign, this book would not have been possible without the support and encouragement of many people. I first thank my colleagues at the University of Washington Department of History, where this book got its start as the department's annual public lecture series in the autumn of 2012. Thank you to John Findlay, for suggesting the idea in the first place, and to Lynn Thomas, who provided further resources and stellar leadership. Thanks also to Matt Erickson, Stefanie Starkovich, Bryce Barrick, as well as John Haslam and the crew from UWTV; their hard work made my job a lot easier. Randy Hodgins provided the sponsorship that allowed the lectures to be televised and, more generally, has helped make my job at the UW one of the best academic gigs around.

Additional people provided important support as the manuscript developed. John Findlay and William Rorabaugh provided helpful comments on early chapter drafts. Conversations with Brian Balogh, David M. Kennedy, Sid Milkis, and Julian Zelizer helped sharpen and frame my arguments. Kayla Schott-Bresler not only provided impeccable research assistance, but also provided insightful comments that made this book better. Many thanks go to the two readers from the University of Pennsylvania Press for their incisive reports and truly helpful suggestions. Last but not least, I must express my deep appreciation to my editor, Robert Lockhart. Bob's sure hand guided this project from start to finish, from early conceptual conversations to spot-on final edits, providing consistent inspiration and encouragement. An author could not wish for a better experience than I have had with Bob and his colleagues at Penn Press.

Friends and family have supported me in countless other ways. My Arkansas family, including my parents Joel and Caroline Pugh and my uncle Bob Pugh, gave me a deep understanding of the politics of that state and region as well as teaching me the art of historical thinking. My parents-in-law, Frank and Marge O'Mara, have always cheered me on and made sure this working parent had the village she needed to get work done. I finished this book in the beautiful and peaceful setting of Harpswell, Maine, at the house of my fabulous sister-in-law Erin O'Mara. Thanks, Erin, for the hospitality and generosity this year and every year. The chief inspiration for this book came from my favorite former Congressional press secretary, Jeff O'Mara. Incisive critic, editor, and all-around idea man, Jeff persuaded me to continue on this excellent adventure, and I am so grateful he did. As always, his love and support makes everything possible, and everything better.

Pivotal Tuesdays is dedicated to my amazing daughters, Molly and Abigail O'Mara, who provide daily inspiration and exhilaration. Throughout this process, they've faithfully been asking, "Mama, is your book done yet?" Yes, girls, it now is done, and I hope you like it.